War in Syria

This edition is dedicated to Dermot McMahon,
remembering our days in Riyadh.

War in Syria

R.M.P. Preston's
The Desert Mounted Corps

Edited and introduced by
Paul Rich

WESTPHALIA PRESS
An imprint of Policy Studies Organization

War in Syria
R.M.P. Preston's *The Desert Mounted Corps*

SYRIA AT WAR:
PREFACE TO THE NEW EDITION

This book is authoritative on the capture of Damascus and conquest of Syria during World War I. It is introduced by Lieutenant-General Harry Chauvel, commander of the Desert Corps during World War I and a staunch defender of the role of cavalry in the Middle East campaigns of the conflict.

The account begins with the assault on Beersheba. The HarperCollins blogger Ben Thompson remarks, "Of the 800 cavalrymen who participated in this unbelievable charge, the Australians suffered just 31 troopers killed and 36 wounded. They captured 750 Turks, 9 artillery pieces, 3 machine guns, and tons of other munitions and supplies. Even more importantly, they seized 17 of the 19 wells intact, recovering 90,000 gallons of fresh, drinkable water from the town. In addition to giving the army a chance to stave off death by dehydration, victory at Beersheba turned the Ottoman flank, allowing the British Army to eventually roll up the enemy forces and defeat them once and for all. Jerusalem fell two months later, and all of Palestine crumbled soon afterwards. The defeat in Palestine caused the Ottoman Empire to drop out of the war, and ultimately caused the destabilization and collapse of a 500 year-old Empire dating back to the days of Hayreddin Barbarossa. With the stalemate still holding strong in the West, this was a major moral victory for the Allies as well

E

as a military one. The Great War would be over within a year."

He continues, "Nowadays there is some debate as to whether launching the balls-out cavalry charge at Beersheba was the most tactically brilliant move the Allies could have undertaken during the Palestine Campaign. Many revisionist military historians with too much time on their hands complain that this insane charge was a lot of wasted effort (historians just love to argue about hypothetical nonsense), and that this crazy suicide attack could have just as easily have blown up in everybody's faces. Sure, while galloping full-speed towards a half-dozen machine guns might not have been the smartest idea anyone ever came up with, nobody in their right minds could ever doubt the bravery or toughness of the men of the Australian Light Horse – these guys were stone-cold hardasses who took a seemingly-foolhardy suicide attack and turned it into the last great cavalry charge in history."

The Desert Corps included not only Australians but French and the Indian Cavalry Division, and helped drive the Turks from the Suez Canal prior to the Palestinian and Syrian campaigns. The operations in Syria were crucial for retaining hard won Jerusalem. At a time when Syria is again engulfed by war, and written by a veteran of that historic campaign, the book gives some idea of the long past and complicated political history that underlies Syria's problems.

Paul Rich

F

The original text of *The Desert Mounted Corps* contains two large fold-out maps. These cannot be scanned into this edition in their original size, but are shown here in miniature.

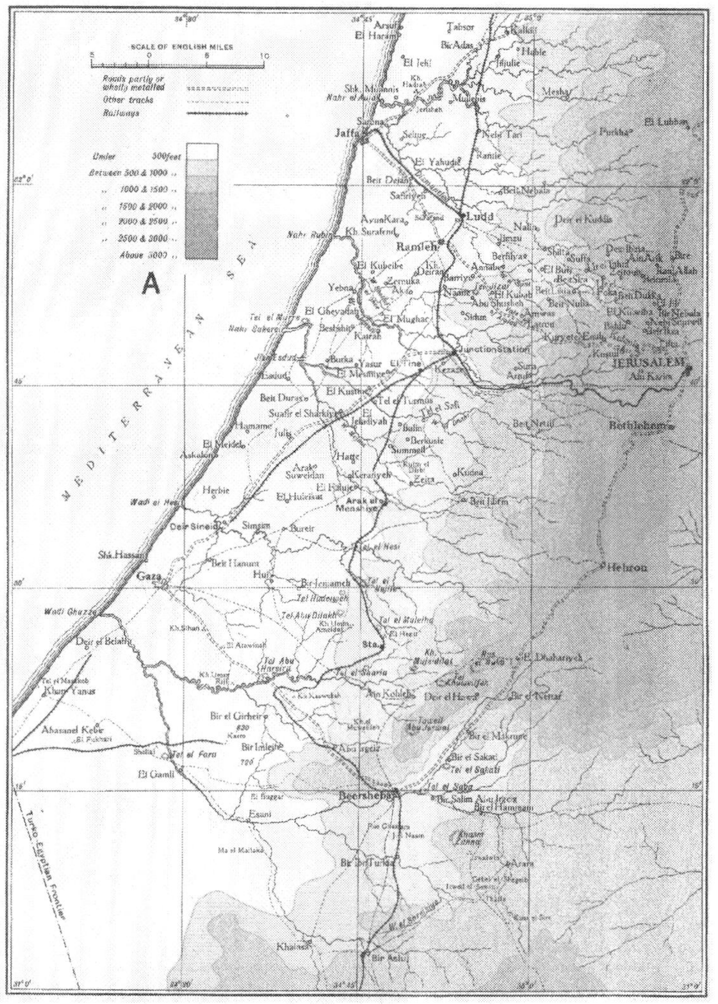

Originally placed between pages 122 & 123.

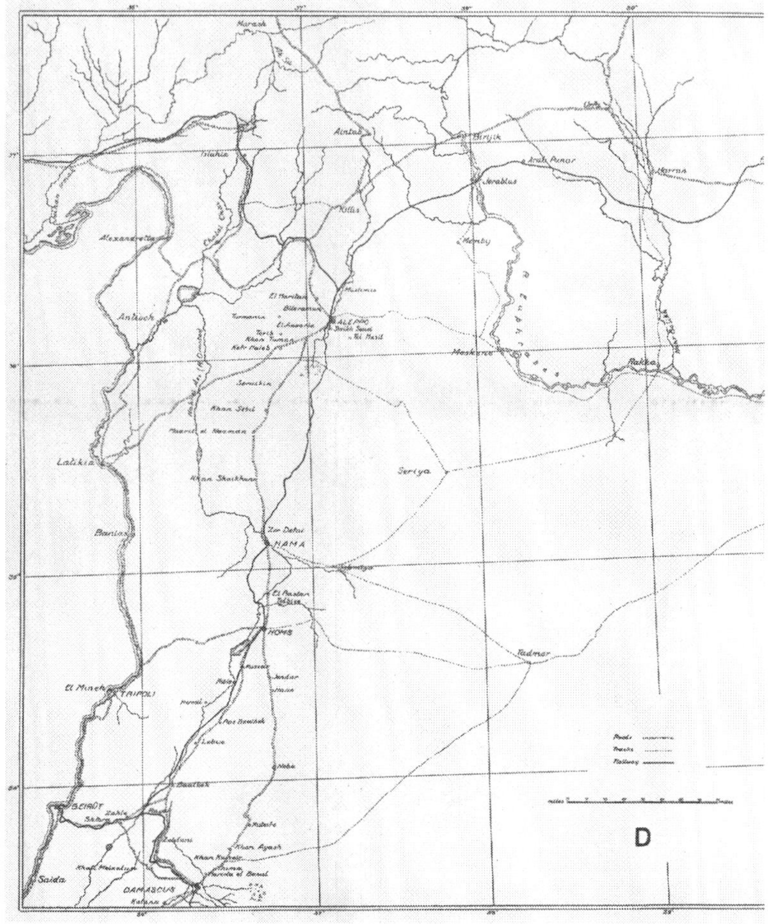

Originally placed between pages 294 & 295.

To see color scans of the original maps in full size, visit the Westphalia Press website through the Policy Studies Organization: http://www.ipsonet.org.

H

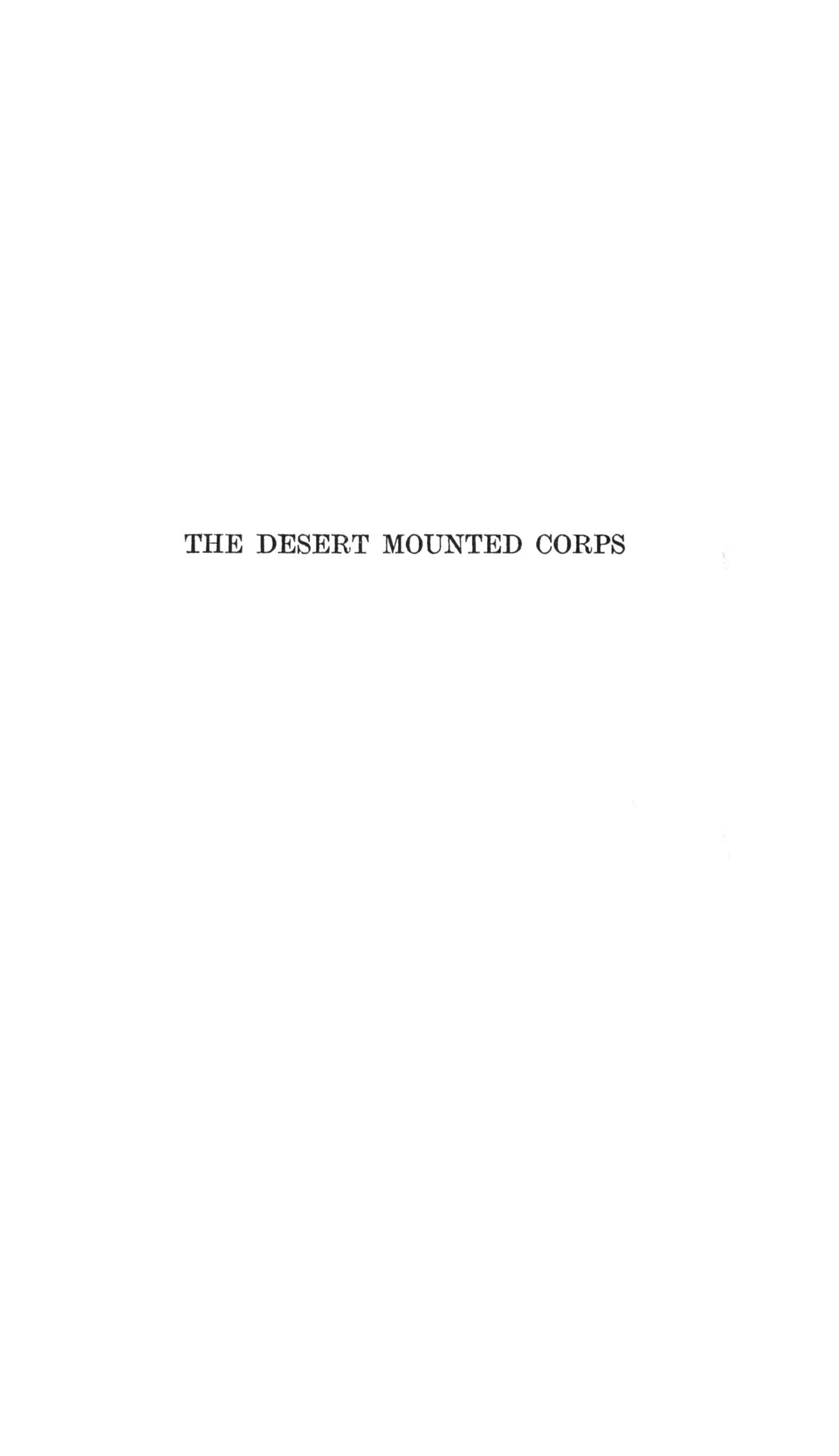

THE DESERT MOUNTED CORPS

LIEUTENANT-GENERAL SIR H. G. CHAUVEL, K.C.B., K.C.M.G.
Commanding the Desert Mounted Corps.

THE
DESERT MOUNTED CORPS

AN ACCOUNT OF THE CAVALRY OPERATIONS
IN PALESTINE AND SYRIA
1917-1918

BY

LIEUT.-COLONEL

THE HON. R. M. P. PRESTON, D.S.O.

With an Introduction by

LIEUT.-GENERAL

SIR H. G. CHAUVEL, K.C.B., K.C.M.G.

LONDON

CONSTABLE AND COMPANY LTD.

1921

TO

B

DEAR LOYAL FRIEND AND PERFECT COMRADE

WITHOUT WHOSE ENCOURAGEMENT AND HELP

THIS BOOK WOULD NEVER HAVE

BEEN WRITTEN

INTRODUCTION

It gives me great pleasure to write a few words of introduction to Lieut.-Col. Preston's *History of the Desert Mounted Corps*, which I had the honour to command. In writing this History Lieut.-Col. Preston has done a service to his country which I am sure will be fully appreciated, particularly, perhaps, by those who served in the Corps, and who feel that the part they played in the Great War is but little known to the general public. As a work on Cavalry Tactics, I trust it will be of some value to the student of Military History, and, if it does nothing else, it must demonstrate to the world that the horse-soldier is just as valuable in modern warfare as he ever has been in the past. Indeed, the whole of the operations in Palestine and Syria, under General Allenby, were text-book illustrations of the perfect combination of all arms, both in attack and defence, and the last operations in this theatre, which led to the total destruction of the Turkish Arms and the elimination of Germany's Allies from the War, could not have been undertaken without large masses of Cavalry.

Lieut.-Col. Preston is well qualified to undertake the work. First of all in command of one of my finest Horse Batteries, and subsequently as C.R.A. of the Australian Mounted Division, he was often in touch with my Staff, being constantly employed on reconnaissance duties, in which he was peculiarly expert. He served throughout the whole of the operations of which he writes, and had considerable previous experience in the Sinai Campaign, in which the Horse Artillery of the Desert Column played so conspicuous a part.

This History commences with the re-organisation of the British Troops in the Egyptian theatre of the War, on Sir Edmund Allenby taking over command in June 1917. The troops operating East of the Suez Canal had hitherto been known as the ' Eastern Force,' which had been successively commanded by Sir Herbert Lawrence, Sir Charles Dobell and Sir Philip Chetwode, who were again directly under the orders of the Commander-in-Chief in Cairo.

The advanced troops of ' Eastern Force,' viz., all the available Cavalry, Horse Artillery and Camel Corps, with from one to two Divisions of Infantry, had been organised into what was called ' The Desert Column.' Sir Edmund Allenby decided to take command of the troops in the Eastern Field himself. The available Infantry was formed into two Army Corps, and the Cavalry of the Desert Column was formed into a Cavalry Corps of three Divisions (subsequently increased to four on the arrival of the Indian Cavalry from France early in 1918). The name of the original Desert Column was preserved as far as possible in the title of the new Cavalry Corps, as most of the troops composing it had fought throughout the Sinai Campaign, and by them much had already been accomplished. The Turk had been driven from the vicinity of the Suez Canal, across the Sinai Desert to the Palestine Border and beyond, and several hard-won battles had been fought. Also, covered by these operations, a railway and pipe line had been constructed, without which, under modern conditions, the further invasion of Palestine could not have been attempted.

The Desert Mounted Corps was composed of Australians, New Zealanders, British Yeomanry, and Territorial Horse Artillery and Indian Cavalry, with French Cavalry added for the last operations; and it says much for the loyalty of all, and the mutual confidence in each other, that the whole worked so harmoniously and efficiently to one end. It will be readily understood, too, that operations of the nature Colonel Preston describes could not have been carried out successfully without a highly efficient staff. I was peculiarly fortunate in the *personnel* of my staff and also in my Divisional Commanders, two of whom were Indian Cavalry Officers, one a British Cavalry Officer, and the fourth an Officer of the New Zealand Staff Corps.

To a leader or a student of military history the campaign was intensely interesting, but at the same time there were many hardships—intense heat in the summer, with dust and insect pests inconceivable to those who did not go through the campaign, and cold and heavy rains in the winter. The fortitude and endurance of the troops was beyond all praise, but the summer of 1918 spent by the Corps in the Jordan Valley, at about 1200 feet below sea-level, with a temperature varying from 110 to 125 degrees, will not be forgotten by them.

The occupation of this area was essential to the success of General Allenby's final operations; and everything possible was done to alleviate the conditions—with considerable success, as, though our wastage from malaria and other diseases was heavy, the greater bulk of the cases of malaria were contracted after leaving the areas which had been treated under the supervision of our Medical Staff. Our most serious losses occurred after reaching Damascus, and, on the farther advance to Aleppo, one division was brought to a complete standstill by the ravages of this disease.

Though drawn from such widely different quarters of the Empire, the *personnel* of the Corps was well fitted for the class of warfare it was called upon to undertake. The horsemen of Australia and New Zealand were accustomed to wide spaces and long days in the saddle, and were full of initiative, self-reliance and determination to overcome every obstacle in their way. The Yeomanry, though not so accustomed to hardships, had behind them the glorious traditions of the British Cavalry, in the annals of which their charges at Huj and El Mughar will live for all time. The Horse Artillery too, drawn from the Counties of England and Scotland and the City of London, lived through the whole of the campaigns in Sinai and Palestine with their comrades from overseas, and showed themselves no whit behind-hand in the matter of endurance. The value of their work is best shown by the esteem in which they were held by the other troops. The long apprentice-ship of the Indian Cavalry to the trench warfare of the Western Front had robbed them of none of their dash and brilliancy in the open warfare to which they were so eminently fitted. The *personnel* of the Signal Service, Engineers, Army Service Corps, Army Ordnance Corps, Army Medical Corps, and Army Veterinary Corps came from the same sources as the other troops—units often being composed of mixed *personnel*—and to the efficiency of these the successes attained by the Corps were very largely due.

HARRY CHAUVEL,
Lieut.-General,
late Commanding the Desert Mounted Corps.

COMMONWEALTH OF AUSTRALIA,
DEPARTMENT OF DEFENCE,
OFFICE OF THE INSPECTOR-GENERAL,
3rd September 1920.

AUTHOR'S NOTE

As regards both the numbers engaged and the results achieved, the campaign in Palestine and Syria ranks as the most important ever undertaken by cavalry. In the first series of operations our troops made a direct advance of seventy miles into enemy territory, and captured some 17,000 prisoners and about 120 guns. The final operations resulted in an advance of 450 miles, the complete destruction of three Turkish Armies, with a loss of about 90,000 prisoners and 400 guns, and the overwhelming defeat of what had hitherto been considered one of the first-class Military Powers.

These remarks must not be taken, in any way, as underrating the value of the work of our infantry, who, as always, bore the brunt of the fighting, while denied much of the interest and excitement of the long pursuits that fell to the lot of the cavalry. In both the main series of operations, the infantry prepared the way for the cavalry, and enabled them to complete the victory won, in the first instance, by the bayonets.

General Allenby's campaign divides itself naturally into three phases. First, the Beersheba-Gaza battle and the subsequent pursuit over the Philistine Plain, culminating in the capture of Jerusalem; secondly, the operations in the Jordan Valley, and east of the river Jordan; and thirdly, the final series, resulting in the destruction of the Turkish Armies, and the capture of Damascus, Aleppo, etc., followed by the capitulation of the Turkish Empire.

Though the Turks at their best are not to be compared in fighting value with the troops of the first-class fighting nations of Europe, such as the British, French, and Germans, they generally fought well against our infantry, attacking with vigour, and defending their entrenched positions most stubbornly. They were well supplied with all the appurtenances of modern warfare, and, in the first part of the campaign, were generally well led.

At the commencement of the operations, the Turkish soldiers were of good *morale* on the whole, their physique was excellent, and their health satisfactory. There was a large proportion of seasoned soldiers among them, many with the Gallipoli medal. In the latter part of the campaign, however, their *morale* had deteriorated considerably, their physique was greatly undermined by disease, and there were few old soldiers left, nearly all having been killed or captured, or died of disease. Many units were full of untrained troops, ill-disciplined and demoralised. After the first day's fighting, there was little resistance by the enemy, except when stiffened by a large proportion of German troops, as at Semakh and Jisr Benat Yakub.

There were doubtless many causes for this deterioration of *morale* among the Turkish troops, but, unquestionably, one of the chief was the constant friction that existed between Turkish and German officers, which spread downwards to the ranks of both nations. The hectoring stupidity of the Prussian was nowhere better exemplified than in his treatment of his Turkish Allies. German officers openly and constantly expressed their contempt for the Turks, whom they compared to niggers, and numerous instances came to our knowledge of German N.C.O.'s and privates beating and kicking Turkish officers.

The three things which the Turks feared most were a threat to their communications, a charge of cavalry, and a heavy aerial attack. As regards the first, there was, I believe, no instance in the campaign when they fought on to the end after being surrounded, though, on several occasions, Turkish units continued to attack till annihilated.

The losses of the Turks were much heavier than ours in every action of the campaign, even when they were successful, or partially so, as in the two trans-Jordan raids.[1] This fact was largely due to their bad rifle shooting. While our troops were good enough shots to pick off Turkish soldiers showing their heads above rocks and trenches, the Turks, as a rule, could only hit our men when standing up during an advance. When the enemy made his great effort to re-take Jerusalem, on the 26th of December 1917, the number of dead Turks found on the position after the battle was greater than our total casualties.

As a set-off to their bad rifle shooting, the enemy troops were supplied with a far larger proportion of machine guns than we were. Their machine-gun companies, which were largely staffed by Germans, were generally effective, and caused us the major part of our casualties during the war.

Their field artillery work in general was slow and inaccurate, but the heavy artillery, manned by Germans or Austrians, was almost invariably good.

The above remarks as to *morale* should be borne in mind in estimating the tactics of General Allenby.

---

[1] Except in the two first battles of Gaza, April and May 1917, when our losses, in comparison with the numbers engaged, were as severe as in some of the hardest fought battles on the Western Front.

It will be noticed that he took greater risks in the latter part of the campaign than he had done at the beginning. These risks were fully justified by the very complete knowledge of the reduced state of the enemy's *morale* which had been acquired by our Intelligence Staff.

In spite of the indifferent *morale* of the enemy troops, the campaign is of great value to the student of cavalry tactics, being, as it is, the only instance in modern war of cavalry operating on a large scale. It demonstrated once more the soundness of the principles laid down in our training manuals, which appear to be immutable, in spite of aircraft and other devilish inventions of present day warfare.

The value of aeroplanes and armoured cars acting in conjunction with cavalry was very clearly brought out, notably in the final series of operations.

My thanks are due to Lieutenant-Colonel R. H. Osborne, D.S.O., M.C., 20th Hussars, cavalry instructor at the Staff College Camberley, for very kindly reading the manuscript, and for many valuable suggestions and corrections. Also to Major A. F. Becke, R.A., in charge of the Historical Section, W.D., for much help in studying war diaries and maps.

My thanks are also due to the many officers, too numerous to mention individually, who have very kindly lent me their private diaries, or given me information about obscure points. I have taken every care to make the narrative as accurate as possible, but, if any who read it notice inaccuracies, I shall be very grateful if they will point them out to me. I have also to thank those who have allowed me to use photographs taken by them as illustrations. A number of the photographs taken on the enemy side were obtained from Mr. C. Raad, photographer, of Jerusalem, who had secured the original negatives, and by whose permission they are reproduced in the book.

Lastly, I desire to thank Lieutenant-General Sir H. G. Chauvel, K.C.B., K.C.M.G., Commander of the Desert Mounted Corps throughout the campaign, for his help and encouragement, and for having very kindly written the preface to the book.

CONTENTS

CHAPTER I

ILLUSTRATIONS

LIST OF MAPS AND DIAGRAMS.

THE DESERT MOUNTED CORPS

AN ACCOUNT OF THE CAVALRY OPERATIONS
IN PALESTINE AND SYRIA, 1917-1918

CHAPTER I

THE COUNTRY AND THE OPPOSING FORCES

WHEN General Allenby arrived in Egypt in June 1917, and assumed command of the Egyptian Expeditionary Force, British prestige in the East was at a very low ebb. The evacuation of Gallipoli in December 1915, followed by the fall of Kut el Amara four months later, and by our two unsuccessful attacks on Gaza in the spring of the following year, had invested the Turkish arms with a legend of invincibility which was spreading rapidly in all Moslem countries. For the first time in seven centuries, sang the journalistic bards of Stamboul, the followers of Islam had triumphed over the Infidel; Allah was leading the Faithful to victory; the Empire of the Moslems was at hand.

The fall of Baghdad in March 1917 somewhat dashed these high hopes, it is true. But the Germans, to whom the city was, at the moment, of no more importance than any other dirty Eastern village, had little difficulty in persuading the Turks that its loss was a mere incident in the world war, which would be more than made good in the final, and glorious, peace terms. Nevertheless, the Turks insisted on making an effort to recapture the place, and for this purpose a special, picked force, known as the *Yilderim,*

A

or Lightning, Army Group, was in process of formation in northern Syria at this time. The command of this group had been entrusted to the redoubtable von Falkenhayn, who was at Aleppo, directing the training and organisation of the troops.

Comforted by highly coloured accounts of the efficiency and fighting value of this force, the Turks rapidly recovered from the effects of the loss of Baghdad. Bombastic articles, inspired by Potsdam, began to make their appearance in the Turkish press, chronicling the doings of the ' Lightning ' armies. They were to recapture Baghdad, drive the British into the Persian Gulf, and then march to the ' relief ' of India. Afterwards the presumptuous little force that had dared to oppose the Turks' advance into their own province of Egypt would be dealt with in a suitable manner ; Egypt would be delivered ; and the Suez Canal, ' the jugular vein of the British Empire,' would be severed.

Aided by such writings, and supported by German money, Pan-Islamic emissaries were busily engaged in every Moslem or partly Moslem country, stirring up the Faithful to sedition and revolt. India, Afghanistan, Persia, and Egypt were all in a state of suppressed excitement and unrest, and it is probable that one more British reverse in the East would have been sufficient to set all these countries in a blaze. The least imaginative can form some idea of the tremendous consequences that such an upheaval would have had upon the war in general. Yet the newspapers of that time show clearly that there was a considerable, and vociferous, body of public opinion, both in England and in France, that regarded the Syrian and Mesopotamian campaigns as useless and extravagant ' side-shows,' and clamoured insistently for the recall of the troops engaged in them.

Thus, both for the purpose of re-establishing our waning prestige in the East, and of silencing the mischievous agitation at home, it was imperative that a signal defeat should be inflicted on the Turks as soon as possible. The capture of Jerusalem, which city ranks only after Mecca and Stamboul among the holy places of Islam, would set a fitting seal upon such a defeat, and would be certain to create a profound impression upon Moslems the world over.

Jerusalem, therefore, became the political objective of the new British Commander-in-Chief. The strategical objective will be discussed later.

The situation in Palestine in the summer of 1917 was not, however, at first sight, very encouraging. Our two abortive attempts on Gaza had shown the German commanders the weak points in the Turkish defences, and they had set to work, with characteristic energy and thoroughness, to strengthen them. ' Gaza itself had been made into a strong, modern fortress, heavily entrenched and wired, and offering every facility for protracted defence. The remainder of the enemy's line consisted of a series of strong localities, viz. : the Sihan group of works, the Atawineh group, the Abu el Hareira-Abu el Teaha trench system (near Sharia), and, finally, the works covering Beersheba. These groups of works were generally from 1500 to 2000 yards apart, except that the distance from the Hareira group to Beersheba was about four and a half miles. . . . By the end of October these strong localities had been joined up so as to form a practically continuous line from the sea to a point south of Sharia. The defensive works round Beersheba remained a detached system, but had been improved and extended.' [1]

---

[1] General Allenby's despatch, dated 16th December 1917.

The Turkish forces were thus on a wide front, the distance from Gaza to Beersheba being about thirty miles, but a well-graded, metalled road, which they had made just behind their line, connecting these two places, afforded good lateral communication, and any threatened point of their front could be very quickly reinforced.

From July onwards continual reinforcements of men, guns, and stores had arrived on the enemy's front, and he had formed several large supply and ammunition depots at different places behind his lines.   He had also laid two lines of railway from the so-called Junction Station on the Jerusalem-Jaffa line, one to Deir Sineid, just north of Gaza, and the other to Beersheba, and beyond it to the village of El Auja,[1] on the Turko-Egyptian frontier, some twenty-five miles south-west of Beersheba.   It was evident that the Turks intended to hold on to the Gaza-Beersheba line at all costs, in order to cover the concentration and despatch of the Yilderim Force to Mesopotamia.

This Junction Station was to be the strategical objective of our operations.   From the junction a railway ran northwards, through Tul Keram, Messudieh, Jenin and Afule, to Deraa on the Hedjaz Railway, whence the latter line continued to Damascus, Aleppo, and the Baghdad Railway.   With the junction in our hands, any enemy force in the Judæan hills, protecting Jerusalem, would be cut off from all railway communication to the north, and would be compelled to rely for its supplies on the difficult mountain road between Messudieh and Jerusalem, or on the longer and still more difficult road from

---

[1] The portion of the line between Beersheba and El Auja was raided by our cavalry in May 1917, and about thirty miles of the track destroyed, in order to prevent any attempted raid on our communications *via* the latter place.

Amman station on the Hedjaz Railway, thirty miles east of the Jordan, *via* Jericho to Jerusalem.

Our own position extended from the sea at Gaza to a point on the Wadi Ghuzze near El Gamli, some fourteen miles south-west of Sharia and eighteen miles west of Beersheba. The opposing lines thus formed a rough ' V,' with its apex at Gaza, where the lines were, in some places, only a couple of hundred yards apart. From here they diverged to El Gamli, which was about nine miles from the nearest part of the Turkish positions. The intervening space was watched by our cavalry.

The right flank of our line being thus ' in the air ' out in the desert, it was a comparatively easy matter for enemy spies, disguised as peaceful natives, to pass round it under cover of darkness, and approach our positions from the rear in daylight. Native hawkers, other than those with passes from the Intelligence Staff, were forbidden to approach our lines, but it was impossible to control all the natives in such a scattered area, and much can be seen, with the aid of a pair of field-glasses, from the top of a hill a mile away. There were also at least two very daring Germans, who several times penetrated our lines disguised as British officers. They were both exceedingly bold and resourceful men, and it is probable that they obtained a good deal of useful information, before they met the almost inevitable fate of spies.

Before the end of our time of preparation, however, methods were evolved to deal with this nuisance, and the enemy was kept in ignorance of our movements and intentions with that success which always attended the efforts of General Allenby in this direction. An enemy staff document, subsequently captured by us, and dated just prior to the commencement of the operations, stated that: ' An outflanking attack on Beersheba with about one infantry and one cavalry division is indicated, but the main attack, as before, must be expected on the Gaza front.' How far wrong was this appreciation of the situation will be apparent later on. The same document also stated that we had six infantry divisions in the Gaza sector, whereas at the time there were only three.

The Royal Air Force was an important factor in denying information to the enemy during the latter part of our time of preparation. One of the first things the Commander-in-Chief had done on his arrival at the front, was to re-equip the force completely. Hitherto the German Flying Corps had done what it liked in the air over our lines. For several months on end our troops had been bombed, almost with impunity, every day. Our own pilots, starved alike of aeroplanes and of materials for repairs, gingerly manœuvring their antiquated and rickety machines, fought gallantly but hopelessly against the fast Taubes and Fokkers of the German airmen, and day by day the pitiful list of casualties that might have been so easily avoided grew longer.

In four months all this had changed. Our pilots, equipped with new, up-to-date and fast machines, met the Germans on level terms, and quickly began to obtain supremacy in the air. By the end of October this supremacy was definitely established, and the few enemy pilots who crossed our lines at that time flew warily, ever on the look-out for one of our fighting machines.

The country occupied by the opposing armies varied considerably in character. The district near the coast consisted of a series of high dunes of loose, shifting sand, impassable for wheeled traffic. Farther east the ground became harder, but it was still sandy and heavy going for transport. Eastwards again, towards Beersheba, the country changed to a wilderness of bare, rocky hills, intersected by innumerable wadis (dry river beds). These wadis were, for the most part, enclosed between limestone cliffs, sometimes 100 feet or more in height, and impassable except where the few native tracks crossed them. The whole of this part of the country was waterless, except for three very deep wells at Khalasa and one at Asluj (all of which had been destroyed by the Turks), and some fairly good pools in the Wadi Ghuzze at Esani and Shellal. In Beersheba itself there were seven good wells.

Northwards of the enemy's positions, between the Judæan mountains and the sea, stretched the great plain of Philistia, a strip of rolling downland fifteen to twenty miles wide, admirably suited for the employment of mounted troops.

The appointment of General Allenby, himself a cavalryman, to the command of the Egyptian Expeditionary Force, presaged the employment of cavalry on a much larger scale than had hitherto been attempted. From his first study of the problem before him, the new Commander-in-Chief realised the predominant part that cavalry would play in the operations, and devoted himself, with his customary energy, to organising a force suitable for the work in prospect.

For the advance across the Sinai Desert from the Suez Canal, a special force had been organised, under the command of Sir Philip Chetwode. This force, which was known as the Desert Column, consisted of the Australian and New Zealand Mounted Division (which then included the 1st, 2nd, and 3rd Australian Light Horse Brigades and the New Zealand Mounted Brigade), the 5th Mounted Brigade (Yeomanry), and the 42nd and 52nd Infantry Divisions.

The 2nd Mounted (Yeomanry) Division, which had arrived in Egypt in April 1915, had been sent to Gallipoli dismounted. After the evacuation of the peninsula, part of this division had been re-mounted. The 5th Mounted Brigade had taken part in the advance across Sinai, and other units of the division had been employed in the campaign against the Senussi, and in the Fayoum and other parts of Egypt. Most of these scattered units had been collected prior to the first battle of Gaza, and organised into two divisions of four brigades each, including a new brigade of Australian Light Horse (the 4th) which had been formed, partly out of Light Horsemen who had returned from Gallipoli, and partly out of reinforcements from Australia. General Allenby now remounted the remainder of the Yeomanry in Egypt, and formed out of them two new brigades. The ten brigades thus available were organised as a corps of three divisions: the Australian and New Zealand (1st and 2nd A.L.H. Brigades and the New Zealand Brigade), generally known as the Anzac Mounted Division; the Australian Mounted Division (3rd and 4th A.L.H. and 5th Mounted Brigades); and the Yeomanry Division (6th, 8th, and 22nd Mounted Brigades). The corps reserve consisted of the 7th Mounted Brigade, and the Imperial Camel Corps Brigade, while the (Indian) Imperial Service Cavalry Brigade [1] formed part of the Army troops. Only the Yeomanry Division and the 7th Mounted and Imperial Service Cavalry Brigades were at this time armed with swords.

It was originally intended to call this force the 2nd Cavalry Corps, but General Chauvel, who was appointed to command it, asked that the name of the Desert Column might be perpetuated in that

[1] Raised and equipped by some of the ruling princes of India.

of the new force. It was accordingly named the Desert Mounted Corps.[1]

The infantry of the Expeditionary Force, largely augmented by troops in Egypt, was formed into two corps of three divisions each, the 20th under Sir Philip Chetwode, and the 21st commanded by Lieutenant-General Bulfin, with one other infantry division. The 20th Corps (10th, 53rd, and 74th Divisions, with the 60th Division attached) was in the eastern sector of our line, while the 21st Corps (53rd, 54th, and 75th Divisions) held the trenches opposite Gaza.[2]

The Imperial Service Cavalry Brigade was attached to the 21st Corps during the operations. This brigade had not yet seen any serious service, and its fighting qualities were rather an unknown factor. Later on in the campaign, however, all three regiments distinguished themselves greatly, and established a fine reputation for dash.

Our total forces numbered some 76,000 fighting men, of whom about 20,000 were mounted, with 550 guns. The enemy troops opposed to us consisted of nine Turkish divisions, organised in two armies, the VIIth and VIIIth, and one cavalry division, a total of about 49,000 fighting men, 3000 of whom were mounted, with 360 guns.[3] Our superiority in numbers, though considerable, thus fell short of the Napoleonic minimum for the attack of entrenched positions, but our large preponderance of cavalry promised great results, if we could succeed in driving the Turks out of their fortifications.

---

[1] See Appendix I. *a.*   [2] See Appendix I. *b.*

[3] The VIIth Army was commanded by the German General Kress von Kressenstein, and the VIIIth by Fevzi Pasha. The general staff of all the enemy formations was in the hands of the Germans. All ranks of the flying corps, heavy artillery and motor transport corps, and the officers of the engineer and supply services and of the railway administration were also Germans. There were a few German and Austrian infantry battalions.

CHAPTER II

THE PLAN OF OPERATIONS

THE Commander-in-Chief's plan was bold and simple, and promised great results. It depended for its success largely on the resolution and vigour with which the first part of the plan, the attack of Beersheba, was carried out. Owing to the waterless nature of the country, this place had to be in our hands within twenty-four hours from the commencement of the operations. If it were not, the troops would have to be withdrawn, owing to lack of water, the attack abandoned, and the operations commenced anew at some later date, against an enemy forewarned of our plans, and with the prospect of the winter rains putting a stop to our advance before it had well begun.

The operations as a whole divided themselves naturally into three main parts, in each of which the fighting would be of a totally different character. First, the attack and capture of the enemy's entrenched positions from Beersheba to the sea. This was primarily an infantry operation. Secondly, the pursuit of the enemy over the plain of Philistia, culminating in the capture of Junction Station, and the consequent isolation of any enemy force endeavouring to cover Jerusalem. This was to be the cavalry's opportunity. And lastly, the advance through the Judæan hills, and the capture of the Holy City.

For obvious reasons only the first part of these

operations could be thought out in detail beforehand. The plan for this phase was as follows :—

1. To seize Beersheba and the high ground to the north and north-west of it, by a combined attack of cavalry and infantry, thus throwing open the left flank of the main enemy position at Hareira and Sharia. After the fall of Beersheba the cavalry would thus all be concentrated on the right flank of our forces, ready to pursue the enemy when driven from the remainder of his positions. The possession of Beersheba would, it was hoped, give us the necessary water to enable us to maintain our cavalry on this flank till the conclusion of the second phase of the attack.

2. To deliver the main infantry attack against the enemy's open left flank at Hareira, and endeavour to roll up his line from east to west.

3. In order to deceive the enemy up to the last moment as to the real point of our main attack, to pin him to his positions, and to draw reinforcements away from his left flank, an attack, preceded by a week's bombardment, was to be launched on the Gaza defences twenty-four to forty-eight hours previous to 2.

As the attack on Beersheba necessitated a march of some seventy miles on the part of the cavalry, who were to attack from the east, and of about twenty for the infantry, over unknown country, a great deal of preliminary work was required. The water supply had to be developed, tracks and the crossing places of wadis improved and marked on the maps, and the enemy positions south and west of Beersheba most carefully reconnoitred. It was also very desirable that all commanders should gain some knowledge of the country over which they were to lead their troops.

To these ends our line was organised as follows :—

A permanent position, strongly entrenched and wired, was constructed from the sea at Gaza to Shellal on the Wadi Ghuzze, and held by infantry. From Shellal a lightly entrenched line extended to El Gamli, and this was held by one cavalry division, which also supplied the outposts and patrols in the wide ' no man's land ' at this end of the line. A second cavalry division was held in support in the neighbourhood of Abasan el Kebir, and the third was in reserve, resting, on the seashore near Tel el Marrakeb. These divisions relieved one another every month.

The cavalry divisions in the line and at Abasan lived in bivouacs made of light, wooden hurdles, covered with grass mats, and erected over rectangular pits dug in the ground. These bivouac shelters gave fair cover from the sun, and the pits afforded some protection from enemy bombs. The division on the seashore was accommodated in tents.

The two former divisions had to be ready at all times to move out to battle at half an hour's notice, and much of the training was directed towards cutting down the time taken to turn out in ' marching order.' The division in the line had plenty of work to do, with daily outposts, extended patrol work, and the long reconnaissances undertaken every fortnight, so that the training was confined to the periods spent at Abasan.

As the operations were to take place in the late summer, and, it was hoped, would be concluded before the winter rains set in, no great provision against cold and wet was called for. Blankets and greatcoats were, therefore, not to be carried. Each man was provided with a pair of officers' pattern saddle-wallets, in which he carried three days' rations (including the iron ration) of bully beef, biscuit, and groceries, besides the few articles of clothing he was allowed to take. Two nose-bags on each saddle carried 19 lb. of grain (two days' forage on the marching scale). A third day's forage was carried in limbered G.S. wagons, three to each regiment. The divisions were, therefore, self-supporting for three days, without recourse to their divisional trains. The latter, during the subsequent operations, did not accompany their divisions, but acted as carriers between them and the advanced ration dumps established by the corps' lorry column each day. One other L.G.S. wagon was allowed per regiment for technical stores, cooking utensils, etc. All entrenching tools were carried on pack animals.

In order to test the mobility of the troops, it was the custom for each divisional commander, during the period when his division was in the Abasan area, to issue from time to time a surprise order for the troops to turn out ready for operations, and rendezvous by brigades or regiments in stated places, where they were carefully inspected. These orders were generally issued in the early morning, and, as no hint of them was ever given beforehand, even to the Staff, they constituted a real test of mobility. The time taken by each unit to turn out was noted by Staff officers, and the keenest rivalry sprang up between the divisions and the different units of each division to make the best showing. Ration and store wagons were packed each night, nose-bags filled after the last feed and tied on the saddles, and all harness and saddlery laid out in order behind the horses. The men's wallets were kept packed permanently, the rations in them being renewed from time to time, when the old ones were consumed. The record ultimately went to one of the Horse Artillery

batteries, which turned out complete in full marching
order, with all its ammunition, rations, and stores
correct, in eleven minutes from the receipt of the
order.

About once a fortnight the cavalry division that
was in the line made a reconnaissance towards
Beersheba, the other two divisions closing up to
Shellal and Abasan respectively. Moving out in the
afternoon, the division would march all night, and
occupy a line of posts on the high ground west of
Beersheba by dawn next morning. Behind this
line of protecting posts the infantry corps and
divisional commanders, and innumerable lesser fry,
disported themselves in motor cars and on horseback.
The senior corps commander and his staff used to be
irreverently referred to as the ' Royal Party,' a
flippant term which may be excused by the tedium
and discomfort of the operations.

After seeing the last of the infantry commanders
safely away, the cavalry used to withdraw, and
march back to Shellal during the night. The reconnaissances thus entailed two nights and a day of
almost continual movement and watchfulness, without any sleep or rest, during which time it was not
uncommon for regiments to cover seventy miles or
more. Apart from the fatigue occasioned by thirty-
six hours of constant anxiety and hard work, the
absence of water caused severe hardship to the
horses and no little discomfort to their riders. No
water for horses was available from the afternoon
of the day on which the division moved out till the
evening of the following day, when, as a rule, they
got a drink at Esani on the way back to Shellal.
The men started with full bottles, and got one refill
from the regimental water-carts.

The day was made up of a series of petty annoyances. The scattered squadrons were invariably bombed by the enemy, generally with effect, and the Turks' light guns, brought out to concealed positions, from which they had previously registered all the high ground, wadi crossings, etc., added to the general discomfort by their continual, galling shell fire. Many of the crossings in this part of the country consisted of a narrow, stony cleft in the rock sides of the wadi, down which troops could only move in very narrow formation, often only in single file. When, as sometimes happened, a whole brigade of cavalry had to cross by one of these narrow drifts, while the bed of the wadi was being swept by shrapnel and high explosive shell the whole time, tempers were apt to get short. We on our side could rarely spare an aeroplane to observe for one of our own batteries, and so were seldom able to locate the hostile guns. The inability to reply effectively increased the exasperation caused by their fire. Many of the surrounding natives had been armed by the Turks and stirred up against us, and, though they never succeeded in causing us any casualties, their hostility added to the general insecurity, and increased the need for watchfulness.

For the rest, the country was a desert of blistering rocks and stones, the temperature ranged up to 110 degrees in the shade (of which there was none save that cast by the bodies of men and horses), and the flies were innumerable and persistent. It was with a sigh of heartfelt relief that the troops saw the last of the motor cars of the ' Royal Parties ' disappear in a cloud of dust to the north-west, and received the welcome order to withdraw and march back to Shellal through the cool night.

There was, however, one never-failing amusement to be got out of these reconnaissances. This came on the following day, when we intercepted the Turkish wireless *communiqué* on its way to the Berlin press. These *communiqués* never varied in their description of the operations. ' The enemy made a determined attack on Beersheba with about seventy squadrons supported by artillery.' This was the invariable formula. ' After heavy fighting, the hostile forces were defeated and driven right back to their original positions, having suffered important losses ! ' One imagines that even the simple Berliner must have become, at last, somewhat sceptical of these regular, fortnightly victories.

The result of this series of reconnaissances to the west and south-west of Beersheba was that every general officer who was to lead troops over this area gained a very thorough knowledge of the country, which was of the highest value in the subsequent operations. The sappers attached to the cavalry divisions also took advantage of the reconnaissances to reconnoitre for water at Khalasa and Asluj, where they subsequently repaired the wells that had been destroyed by the Turks, and to develop the supply at Esani in the Wadi Ghuzze. They also improved and marked many of the wadi crossings, and made route surveys of the whole area.

Our line of communications, at this time, consisted of a broad-gauge railway, which had been laid by the Royal Engineers across the 130 miles of desert from Kantara on the Suez Canal to Deir el Belah, about eight miles south of Gaza. The railhead of this line had followed close behind the Desert Column during its advance across Sinai. After the occupation of El Arish, the doubling of the railway track had been taken in hand, and, by the end of September 1917, the double track extended as far as Deir el Belah. During September and October a branch line was laid from this place to Shellal, where it was carried over the Wadi Ghuzze, here some 800 yards wide and sixty feet deep, on a fine trestle bridge built by British and Australian Sappers. Work was then continued towards Karm, whence a narrow-gauge line was to be run out to Beersheba, as soon as that place was in our hands.

In order to relieve the railway of some of its heavy traffic, to enable it to bring up stores for the ' Big Push,' a sea-borne supply line from Port Said to Deir el Belah was organised by the Royal Navy during September. All the supplies for the 21st Corps, which held the coastal sector of our line, were then carried by sea, and landed in surf boats on the coast. The shipping, convoying, and landing of stores were admirably carried out by the Navy, under great difficulties.

Towards the end of October these long and careful preparations were completed, and the troops began to move unobtrusively to their concentration areas, leaving their old camps standing, in order to deceive enemy aircraft. So well were these large troop movements concealed, that, up to the moment when our attack was launched, the enemy believed that we had six infantry divisions still in the Gaza sector and only one in the eastern sector. This apparent disposition of our troops confirmed him in his mistaken opinion that our main attack would be delivered against Gaza, and caused him to concentrate most of his available reserves behind the western portion of his line, a fact which contributed materially to our success in the subsequent operations.

CHAPTER III

THE FIRST ROUND

OCTOBER the 31st was the date fixed for the capture of Beersheba, which was to be the first phase of the operations. The plan of attack was as follows :—

The 60th and 74th Divisions were to attack the outer defences on the west and south-west, immediately after dawn, and, having captured them, were to hold the high ground west of the town. The 53rd Division and the Camel Corps Brigade were directed to protect the left flank of these operations.

Meanwhile the Anzac and the Australian Mounted Divisions, starting respectively from Asluj and Khalasa, were to march during the night, south of Beersheba, right round the enemy flank, and attack the town from the east, where the defences were known to be less formidable. These two divisions thus had night marches of twenty-five and thirty-five miles respectively before reaching their first objectives. The 7th Mounted Brigade, marching direct from Esani, had the task of masking the strongly entrenched hill of Ras Ghannam, which formed the southern end of the enemy's outer defences, and of linking up the Australian Mounted Division and the 20th Corps. To the cavalry thus fell the task of seizing the town of Beersheba itself.

It will be seen that, during the attack on Beersheba, there would be a gap of some seventeen miles between the 20th Corps on the right and the 21st Corps in the coastal sector. Our railway ran right

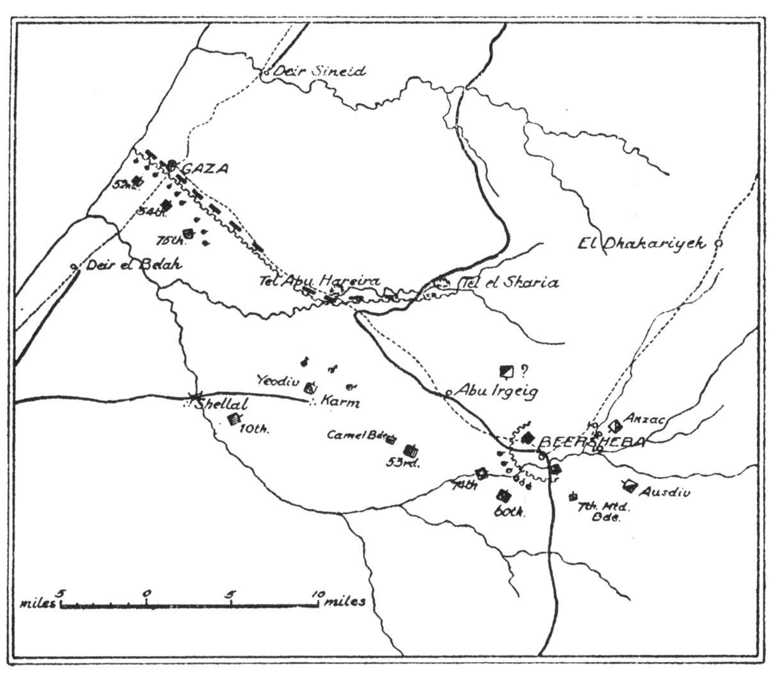

Diagram illustrating the position of troops on the 31st. of Oct. 1917.

up into this gap, the railhead at Karm being actually in front of our line, and within eight miles of the main enemy positions about Hareira.

To cover this gap, and to deal with any attempted counter-attack against our railhead, the Yeomanry Division was to concentrate at, and east of, Karm, with the 10th Division in support about Shellal. The action of the Commander-in-Chief in thus trusting the guarding of this wide gap to so small a force is of particular interest as indicating his readiness to accept a considerable risk in order to achieve victory. It also demonstrates his complete confidence in the success of his efforts to deceive the enemy as to our real intentions.

The fortifications of Beersheba consisted of two lines of defensive positions. The outer line, heavily entrenched and wired, ran in a semicircle along the high ground north-west, west, and south-west of the town, from the Gaza-Beersheba road to Ras Ghannam, at an average distance of 7000 yards from the town. On the north-east, east, and south-east the outer defences were not continuous, but consisted of a series of strong posts, chief of which were Tel el Sakaty, Tel el Saba, and two stone block-houses on the north bank of the Wadi Saba. The inner line ran completely round the town itself, and on its outskirts, crossing the Wadi Saba just south of the railway bridge. It was believed, but not with any great degree of certainty, that the portion of this line on the east of the town was not protected by wire.

Beersheba is situated on the east bank of the wadi, at the north-western end of a flat, treeless plain, about four miles long and three miles wide, completely surrounded by ranges of tumbled, rocky hills. To the north-east these hills rise gradually to join the main Judæan range, along the backbone of which

Australian engineers developing the water supply at Esani.

Cavalry country! Near Beersheba.

runs the road to Jerusalem, through El Dhahariyeh, Hebron, and Bethlehem.

On the evening of the 26th of October all preliminary arrangements for the attack were complete, and the 20th Corps was concentrating about Shellal. The Australian Mounted Division was in the line from Shellal to Gamli, and held a line of outposts covering the railway construction at Karm, from El Buggar, through points 720 and 630, nearly to the Wadi Sharia, a distance of about fourteen miles. This outpost line was manned by the 8th Mounted Brigade, which had been lent for the purpose by the Yeomanry Division, and which came under the orders of the 53rd Division at midnight on the 26th. The Yeomanry Division was concentrated in the neighbourhood of Hiseia and Shellal, the Anzac Division was at Abasan el Kebir, and the Camel Brigade at Shellal.

At dawn on the 27th, the centre of the thinly held cavalry outpost line was suddenly attacked by an enemy force of all arms, between 3000 and 4000 strong. The post on point 630 was driven in, but the squadron of the Middlesex Yeomanry that formed the garrison withdrew to a cruciform trench just below the top of the hill, which had been cleverly sited by the general staff of the Australian Mounted Division. In this trench, though surrounded by the enemy and repeatedly attacked, the little garrison held out all day with the greatest gallantry, till relieved by a brigade of the 53rd Division at half-past four in the afternoon.

As soon as news of the enemy attack was received, General Hodgson, realising that it was impossible for the infantry to reach the outpost line in time to save the situation, despatched the 3rd A.L.H. Brigade and the Notts Battery R.H.A. to the aid of the

Yeomanry. Before they arrived on the scene, however, the small garrison on point 720 had been subjected to a concentrated shell fire, and overwhelmed by a combined mounted and dismounted attack. This was the first and last time that the Turkish cavalry screwed themselves up to the point of a charge. One of the only three survivors of the garrison estimated that about seventy saddles were emptied, but the Turks rode on like men, and galloped right over the post.

The reserve regiment of the 8th Brigade held the line till the arrival of the Australians, and frustrated the enemy's attempt to break through the gap between points 630 and 720. The enemy withdrew at dusk, and our troops reoccupied the position.

From the large force employed by the Turks in this operation, it appears probable that they had intended to hold the 630-720 ridge permanently, if they succeeded in capturing it. The ridge commanded a full view of all the country lying between it and the Wadi Ghuzze, and, at the same time, concealed this bit of country from direct observation from the Turkish positions farther east.

The Anzac Mounted Division moved out from Abasan el Kebir on the evening of the 27th, and reached Khalasa early next morning, where it remained during the day.

The bombardment of Gaza commenced on this day, and continued with gradually growing intensity till the morning of the 2nd of November, when the outer defences of the town were captured by the 21st Corps.

On the 28th of October the 53rd Division relieved the Australian Mounted Division on the El Buggar outpost line, the 8th Mounted Brigade rejoined the Yeomanry Division, and the Australian Mounted

Division moved out at dusk and marched to Khalasa, arriving early on the morning of the 29th. The Anzac Division marched the same night from Khalasa to Asluj. The two divisions rested at these places during the 29th and 30th, in preparation for the strenuous work ahead of them. During these two days the 60th Division marched from the Shellal area to Bir el Esani, the advanced brigade pushing on to a point near Ma el Mallaka. One brigade of the 74th Division moved forward to fill the gap between the 53rd and 60th Divisions, and the 10th Division concentrated near Shellal.

Soon after dark on the night of the 30th the troops left their bivouacs, and commenced to move silently on the unconscious enemy. The Anzac Mounted Division, in the lead, was to send one brigade, *via* Bir el Arara, against Bir el Hammam and Bir Salim Abu Irgeig, the first objectives, the remainder of the division marching *via* the Wadi el Shreikiye, Gebel el Shegeib, and Iswaiwin to attack Tel el Sakaty and Tel el Saba, and then close in on Beersheba.

The Australian Mounted Division, following the Anzac Division along the Wadi el Shreikiye, was to halt at a point a little north of Iswaiwin, and be prepared to act either northwards, in support of the Anzac Division, or westwards towards Beersheba, as might be required. The 7th Mounted Brigade was ordered to march from Esani, *via* Itweil el Semin, against Ras Ghannam.

The leading of the troops, never an easy matter at night, was rendered more troublesome by the fact that the country beyond Asluj was quite unknown to us, and was, besides, of a most difficult and intricate nature. Maps, though accurate in the main, were lacking in detail, and the employment of native guides was too risky an experiment to be contemplated.

However, favoured by a bright moon, which rose soon after dark, the marches were accomplished without mishap, and the Anzac Mounted Division secured its first objectives without serious opposition about eight o'clock. The 2nd A.L.H. Brigade was now directed on Tel el Sakaty, and the New Zealanders on Tel el Saba, the 1st A.L.H. Brigade following in reserve.

The Headquarters of the Australian Mounted Division reached the high hill of Khashim Zanna about ten o'clock, and looked down upon the plain of Beersheba and the picturesque little town, which had to be in our hands by nightfall at all costs. Shells from the guns of the 60th Division were bursting all along the ridge beyond the town, and, away to the right, the rattle of machine-gun fire told where the Anzac Mounted Division was engaged at Tel el Sakaty. Patrols from the Australian Mounted Division were pushed out to the west to reconnoitre the approaches to Beersheba, south of the Wadi Saba.

Meanwhile the 7th Mounted Brigade dismounted, and, scrambling up the rocky steeps of Ras Ghannam, was meeting with strong opposition from the well-entrenched Turks on the top of the hill.

The enemy resistance soon began to increase considerably, and the Anzac Division made but slow progress across the bare open plain. The entrenched hill of Tel el Sakaty was captured by the 2nd A.L.H. Brigade about one o'clock, after a stiff fight, and half an hour later this brigade got across the Jerusalem road.

Shortly before this, a patrol of the Australian Mounted Division had smartly rounded up and captured a Turkish officer with a small escort. He turned out to be the personal aide-de-camp of Ismet Bey, the commander of the Beersheba garrison.

It appeared that Ismet had been sitting in his battle headquarters, on a hill west of the town, since early morning, watching with complete equanimity the attack of our infantry, which he believed to consist of only one division. About eleven o'clock, happening to turn his head, he received a distinct shock on seeing the plain behind him covered with cavalry. He at once sent his staff officer off *ventre à terre* to find out if the cavalry intended to attack, or were only making a demonstration. The officer received full information on this point, but, as he was not in a position to take it back to his chief, the latter became uneasy, and shortly afterwards appears to have lost his head completely, for he proceeded to fling all his reserves into the fight on the west, before the battle was well begun.

By half-past one our infantry had captured all their objectives west of the town, and commenced to consolidate on the positions won. From the Cavalry Corps headquarters the enemy troops could be seen retiring in an orderly manner into Beersheba.

The headquarters of the two cavalry divisions were at this time with corps headquarters, on Khashim Zanna, which was the highest hill for miles around. After a light but satisfactory lunch, the three headquarters Staffs sat down in a long line on the very top of the hill, with maps and field-glasses, to watch the ' manœuvres ' in the plain below. Observing the irresistible target thus presented to the enemy artillery, the gunnery staffs of the two divisions, moved by a common impulse, faded silently into the comparative safety of the open plain. Immediately afterwards a salvo of high-velocity shells landed right on top of the hill, scattering maps, field-glasses, and staff officers like chaff before the wind ! Fortunately, no one was hurt, but for the rest of the day the staff treated the enemy gunners, always good, with the respect due to them.

Meanwhile the advance of the cavalry across the plain dragged slowly on. The country was flat and open, and there were no trees or scrub to afford cover even to dismounted men. The whole plain was swept by the fire of numerous machine guns and field guns concealed in the town of Beersheba, along the banks of the Wadi Saba, in the two block-houses on the north bank of the wadi, and on the strongly entrenched hill of Tel el Saba. From the last-named position any advance across the plain was enfiladed, and it was clear that this hill would have to be taken before any further progress could be made.

The New Zealand Brigade had worked along the dry bed of the Wadi Saba for some distance, and then, leaving the horses under cover, advanced to attack the position on foot. The hill is steep and rugged, and overlooks the bed of the wadi for some 400 yards to the east, where it makes a sharp bend. The New Zealanders got as far as this bend, but could make no farther progress, as every part of the confined river bed in front of them was swept by rifle and machine-gun fire. One regiment got out of the wadi on the north side, and made a detour to try and take the hill in rear, but could make little headway over the exposed ground, in face of the heavy enemy fire. About the same time the 3rd A.L.H. Brigade and two batteries from the Australian Mounted Division were pushed in to assist the attack from the south.

The day was now far gone, and the advance seemed to be at a standstill. General Chaytor then put in his reserve brigade (the 1st), to co-operate in the attack on Tel el Saba from the south.   General Cox, commanding the brigade, directed the 2nd A.L.H. Regiment on the two block-houses, and the 3rd on Tel el Saba.   From the shelter of a small wadi, some three miles south of the hill, the two regimental commanders scrutinised the open plain in front of them in an effort to find some covered way of approach.   None could be found, so the two commanders determined to make a dash for it mounted, and get as near as possible before dismounting to continue the attack on foot.

Deploying from the wadi, the two regiments swung out into line of troop columns at wide interval, and galloped forward over the open plain in full view of the enemy.   Several Turkish batteries at once opened fire on them, but they were advancing so fast that the enemy gunners seemed to be unable to get the range, and but little damage was caused by their fire.   It was not, indeed, till the regiments came under machine-gun fire that casualties began to occur, and, even then, our loss was slight, probably owing to the comparatively steep angle of descent of machine-gun bullets at long ranges, and to the difficulty of finding and keeping the range.   At 1500 yards from the position, they rode into a convenient depression, and here they dismounted and continued the advance on foot.

There was no cover of any sort, and their approach from this point was necessarily slow, in face of the heavy fire which they encountered.   Now that they were on foot, and moving slowly, they began to suffer severely, whereas they had advanced mounted for over two miles with scarcely any casualties.   An intense fire fight developed, as the two brigades closed gradually in on the enemy. Our little thirteen-pounder Horse Artillery guns, though pushed up boldly to close range, could make little impression on the well-built enemy trenches and machine-gun emplacements on Tel el Saba, and none at all on the thick stone walls of the block-houses. They did good service, however, in keeping down the hostile fire.

About two o'clock, the 2nd A.L.H. Regiment reached and stormed the block-houses, and, from the captured positions, poured a heavy fire into the flank of Tel el Saba. This caused some slackening of the enemy's fire, of which the New Zealanders took prompt advantage. With a sudden, tremendous rush, they charged down the bed of the wadi, up the steep sides of the hill, and into the position, almost before the Turks were aware of the attack. A few minutes' sharp bayonet fighting completed the capture of the hill, with about 120 prisoners and a large number of machine guns. This success removed the last obstacle to our advance on Beersheba, but the town itself still held out, and there was a wide space of open ground still to be crossed before it could be assaulted.

Orders were issued at once for the whole of the two divisions, less the 5th Mounted Brigade, to advance mounted, and endeavour to get close enough to the town to make a dismounted attack before darkness fell. This order reached the 4th A.L.H. Brigade, which had not yet been in action, at half-past four. It was then waiting at the south-eastern edge of the plain, fully three miles from Beersheba, and, as sunset was due at five o'clock, there was no time to be lost.

Making up his mind instantly, General Grant, commanding the brigade, collected the two regiments he had with him, the third being engaged in reconnaissance work, and moved rapidly forward to the shelter of some dead ground about 3000 yards from the enemy trenches south-east of the town.   Having sent a message to the two nearest batteries of the division, ' A ' Battery H.A.C. and the Notts Battery R.H.A., to be ready to support his attack, he ordered a charge.   The two batteries at once limbered up, and, moving rapidly forward, galloped into action in the open, at a range of about 2500 yards, and opened a heavy fire on the Turkish trenches and field guns in front, and on a nest of machine guns to the left front.

As soon as the batteries were in action, General Grant's two regiments swept out into the open, in column of squadrons in line, and galloped straight at the Turkish trenches.

Seen from the rising ground on which our guns were in action, it was a most inspiriting sight.   It was growing dark, and the enemy trenches were outlined in fire by the flashes of their rifles.   Beyond, and a little above them, blazed the bigger, deeper flashes of their field guns, and our own shells burst like a row of red stars over the Turkish positions.   In front the long lines of cavalry swept forward at racing speed, half obscured in clouds of reddish dust.   Amid the deafening noise all around, they seemed to move silently, like some splendid, swift machine.   Over the Turks they went, leaping the two lines of deep trenches, and, dismounting on the farther side, flung themselves into the trenches with the bayonet.[1] The whole position was in our hands in ten minutes, and was consolidated immediately.

It was now quite dark, so General Grant collected his squadrons together, attended to casualties, and rounded up his prisoners.   Then, leaving a guard

---

[1] They had charged with bayonets drawn and extended in front of them like swords.

with the prisoners, and remounting the remainder of his men, he sent them at a gallop into the town itself. Through the streets they raced in the darkness, riding down all opposition, and so hustling the Turks that they never had a chance to rally. Before six o'clock the town, with 1200 prisoners and 14 guns, was in our hands. Ismet Bey escaped in a motor-car ten minutes before the final charge.

In the interval between the capture of the trenches and the charge into the town, the enemy had begun to blow up the wells and ammunition depots. Huge, mushroom-shaped columns of violet flame and smoke shot up here and there, accompanied by sullen, heavy explosions. Shortly afterwards, the main store and some of the railway station buildings were set on fire, and the flames from these burning buildings lighted up the whole town, and, as it happened, materially assisted our troops in their task of handling the prisoners. These proved surly and rather truculent, and two incidents which occurred during the early part of the night warned us that it would be well to get them away as soon as possible. As a body of prisoners was being marched out of the town to a piece of open ground on the east side, where they were being collected and counted, some of them suddenly halted and fired several Verey lights into the air, evidently with the intention of signalling to their comrades in the north. Shortly afterwards another party of them made a sudden and determined rush for one of the captured guns, and several had to be shot down before the rush was stopped. The attitude of these prisoners was in marked contrast to that of most of the Turks whom we captured, who generally accepted their fate stoically, if not with satisfaction. They seemed to resent the charge extremely, and there is no doubt that they were expecting to be able to retire quietly along the Gaza-Beersheba road during the night, when the sudden dash of the Australians surprised them.

Including those taken by our infantry, about 2000 prisoners were captured at Beersheba, and over 500 Turkish corpses were buried on the battle-field. The casualties in the two regiments of the 4th Brigade, 32 killed and 32 wounded, may be considered remarkably light, in view of the strength of the enemy.

General Grant's action forms a notable landmark in the history of cavalry, in that it initiated that spirit of dash which thereafter dominated the whole campaign. When he received the orders for the attack, he had to consider that the enemy was known to be in strength, well posted in trenches, and adequately supplied with guns and machine guns. In order to reach the town itself, it would be necessary to cross the Wadi Saba, of unknown depth, and, possibly, with precipitous banks. The character of the intervening country was known only in so far as it had been revealed by field-glasses. It was not even certain that there was no wire in front of the enemy's position. On the other hand, the town had to be in our hands before nightfall, or the whole plan failed.

He weighed the chances, and made up his mind instantly to risk all in a charge, and the success he achieved surprised even the most ardent votaries of the white arm.

The remainder of the Australian Mounted Division moved into Beersheba during the night, leaving the 3rd Brigade to assist the Anzac Division in holding an outpost line north and north-east of the town, from Bir el Hammam to the Gaza-Beersheba road. The 7th Mounted Brigade, which had had a day of desultory fighting, joined the division in the town early next morning.

With the capture of Beersheba, the first phase of the operations had ended satisfactorily, and, as the earlier reports from the town as to the water supply were favourable, it was decided to commence phase two, the attack on Gaza, on the night of the 1st of November. The attack was launched at 11 P.M., and stubborn fighting continued all night. By half-past six on the morning of the 2nd, the whole of the front line and support trenches, from ' Umbrella ' Hill, about the middle of the system, to Sheikh Hassan on the sea coast, were in our hands. Sheikh Hassan was some distance behind the enemy's front line, and its capture therefore threatened his right flank. The positions won were consolidated, and no further advance was attempted, as it was considered that the object of the attack, which was to deceive the enemy and to retain his reserves in the coastal sector, had been fully secured.

Preparations were at once commenced for phase three, the main attack on the enemy's exposed left flank about Sharia and Hareira. For this purpose the 53rd Division made a long march on the 1st, and occupied a line from Toweil Abu Jerwal to Khurbet el Muweileh, with the Camel Brigade on its right. The Anzac Mounted Division, prolonging this line from Abu Jerwal to the Hebron road about Bir el Makruneh, met with more opposition than had been expected, the reason for which was to become apparent in the course of the next few days. The division captured about 200 prisoners and a number of machine guns during the day.

Reports sent back from this area indicated such a lack of water that it was clear that no more than one cavalry division could be maintained there. Accordingly the Australian Mounted Division was ordered to remain in Beersheba, in general reserve, and was directed to endeavour to improve the water supply there. There were a few surface pools in the Wadi Saba, the result of a thunderstorm that had broken a few days previously, but these were already rapidly drying up. Of the seven good wells in the town, five had been blown up by the Turks on the night of the 31st, and the remaining two had been prepared for demolition, but the charges had not been fired. Our sappers were left in splendid isolation, as they gingerly probed the *débris* round these wells, and eventually located the charges and safely removed them.

The enemy had evidently intended, in the event of his having to abandon Beersheba, to leave nothing but ruins behind him, for the whole place was a nest of explosive charges, ' booby traps ' and trip wires. By a fortunate chance the German engineer who was responsible for the destruction of the town was away on leave in Jerusalem at the time of its capture. Consequently most of these trip wires were not yet attached to their detonators. A few, however, had been connected up before the town was taken. The writer came across one such, while making a rapid artillery reconnaissance round the town at daybreak on the 1st of November. Luckily it was noticed before the party rode over it, and, on being cut and followed to its source, was found to be connected to a detonator concealed in twenty cases of gelignite in the railway station,—enough to have laid the whole town in ruins.

Large numbers of hand grenades had been concealed in stores of grain and food in different parts of the town, and there were one or two accidents at first among parties of too eager explorers. Sir Philip Chetwode, commander of the 20th Corps, moved his headquarters into Beersheba a day or two later, and occupied the house of the enemy commander. On examining the building before he moved in, our sappers found it packed from cellar to garret with cases of explosives, all connected to trip wires.

This house was one of the fine stone buildings, of which there were a number, surrounding a large public garden, and which had been built by the Germans during the war. The whole of this modern portion of the town appeared to have been built for propaganda purposes, or like the cities of lath and plaster which are run up in a few days for cinematograph productions. From time to time articles on the war in the East appeared in the German papers, generally synchronising with some reverse on the Western Front. In these articles, which were lavishly illustrated, Beersheba figured under headings such as ' the Queen City of the Prairies.' Apparently, in order to supply the necessary pictures, the Germans had laid out a large public garden, and built around it a series of imposing public buildings, including a Governor's house, Government offices, hospital, barracks, mosque, and even an hotel. The surrounding country abounds in a species of hard white limestone admirably suited for building, and all the houses were built of this and roofed with red tiles. They were ranged round the square, like four rows of stiff white soldiers with red helmets, and were so sited that any number of photographs could be taken from various positions, each showing a different view, and each hiding the real town behind the brand new German architecture. But once behind these houses, a shocking contrast met the eye. Here was the real Beersheba, a miserable collection of filthy mud hovels, huddled shrinkingly together as though trying to hide their shabbiness from their gorgeous neighbours. The *place* in the centre was conspicuously labelled ' Bier Garten,' and was laid out with a number of little paths in an exact, geometrical pattern. The flower-beds supported a few dusty shrubs and a quantity of those hideous ' everlastings ' so dear to the Teuton heart. All the buildings were laid out exactly facing the four points of the compass, except the mosque, which, in deference to Moslem prejudices, had been built with its *mihrab* turned towards Mecca, and consequently was lamentably askew. The Huns had taken their revenge, however, by garnishing the windows with German stained glass of an ugliness so startling that the Australians vowed their horses shied at it !

The railway, built by the German engineer, Meissner Pasha, of Baghdad Railway fame, was an admirable piece of work, metalled throughout, and carried over the numerous wadis on fine, arched bridges of dressed stone. The bridge over the Wadi Saba was upwards of 400 yards long. One wonders who paid for all the work.

While we were in occupation of Beersheba, some one in the Intelligence Branch of the staff conceived the brilliant idea of trying to impress the local Arabs, some of whom were hostile to us, with the majesty and power of the British Empire. Accordingly, after a good deal of trouble, a few of the neighbouring sheikhs were induced to come into the town, and were escorted round by an officer who spoke Arabic. They were shown first a regiment of cavalry, which left them cold, as the horses appeared clumsy to them in comparison with their own little Arabs. Then lines of marching infantry were pointed out to them, and field guns, and more cavalry, and motor lorries. All to no purpose.

An occasional grunt and a half concealed yawn were all the response the perspiring officer received. When a sixty-pounder gun, drawn by a ' caterpillar ' motor tractor, hove in sight, they showed some signs of uneasiness, and eyed this new form of devil carriage with profound distrust. But when they found that it could only move at a walking pace, they became reassured and lost all interest in it. The hard-working staff officer was in despair, when, towards evening, the first ration convoy of camels arrived. We had at that time about 30,000 camels in the force, and they were in magnificent condition—big, strong beasts, covered with muscle, and free from the blemishes which so disfigure the desert Arabs' animals.

Here was something the sheikhs could understand. They watched the camels winding into the town, line after line, hundred after hundred, and their eyes grew round with wonder. The first eager talk died away to an astonished silence. When all the convoy, about 1000 strong, was in, and *barracked* in an open space, the natives turned to the officer with a volley of questions. Seeing the impression made, he told them, in an off-hand manner, that the British had more than twenty times that number with their army. The sheikhs' looks politely conveyed the message that they considered him a liar. Determined to strike while the iron was hot, he bundled them all into a couple of motor cars, after some signs of panic on their part, and ran them across to Shellal, where in truth they saw more camels than they had ever dreamed of. They spent all the afternoon visiting the camps of the Camel Transport Corps, and watching the departure of laden convoys and the return of empty ones. In the evening they mounted their horses

Beersheba. From an enemy photograph taken before the completion
of the new German buildings.

Arrival of the first enemy train in Beersheba. Meissner Pasha in white helmet
and gaiters. The inscription on the coach means "Stamboul to Cairo."
(From an enemy photograph)

again, and rode off into the darkness to rejoin their own people. But before they left, the chief among them, acting as spokesman for all, told our staff officer that they were now quite convinced that the *Ingilizi* were certainly the greatest tribe in the world, and that they would advise their young men to keep on friendly terms with us and help us in every way. They were as good as their word, and we had no more trouble from hostile Arabs.

CHAPTER IV

THE DECISIVE BATTLE

THE next five days were occupied in securing the necessary concentration of troops for the main attack on Sharia and Hareira, and in developing the scanty water supply, and organising water convoys to enable these troops to subsist in the barren country in which they were to operate.

The Anzac Division, pushing northwards on the 2nd, astride the Hebron road and on the right of the 53rd Division, encountered increasing resistance, and made but slow progress. Very hard fighting continued during the 3rd, 4th, and 5th, in the course of which it became clear that the enemy had concentrated practically the whole of his available reserves in this area. The 19th Turkish Division, the remains of the 27th (the late garrison of Beersheba), and part of the 16th Division, together with the whole of the 3rd Cavalry Division, were identified in this fighting round Ain Kohleh and Tel Khuweilfeh.

In thus throwing the whole of their available reserves against our extreme right flank, the Turks were committed to a bold but dangerous course. It was evident that they hoped to compel the British Commander-in-Chief to detach part of his force to meet this counter-attack. Had they succeeded in involving any considerable portion of our army in the difficult, waterless country around Tel Khuweilfeh, it is probable that our main force would have been so weakened as to be unable to attack the Sharia and Hareira positions with any chance of success. Such a failure might well have brought the whole of our offensive to a standstill, and enabled the Turks to establish themselves on a new line from Sharia to the Hebron road.

On the other hand, should we succeed in holding the enemy's counterstroke without having to weaken our main striking force, he ran the risk of finding his reserves immobilised at the critical moment, and thus prevented from rendering any assistance to the garrisons of Sharia and Hareira when those places were attacked. This, in fact, was exactly what happened. General Allenby refused to be drawn to the east, and, relying on the Anzac and 53rd Divisions to hold the enemy in check at Tel Khuweilfeh, proceeded resolutely with his preparations for the assault on the left flank of the main Turkish position.

On the 2nd of November the 3rd A.L.H. Brigade, less one regiment, rejoined the Australian Mounted Division, and the 5th and 7th Mounted Brigades were attached to the Anzac Division. The 5th Brigade remained in Beersheba, but the 7th joined the Anzac Division, and had a stiff day's fighting, culminating in the seizing of the hill of Ras el Nukb, near Tel Khuweilfeh, to which the enemy attached great importance, and which he defended most stubbornly. The brigade withdrew from Ras el Nukb at nightfall, as it was too much in advance of our general line to be held during the night. The Anzac Division occupied a line from about Bir el Nettar to Deir el Hawa, and thence south-west to Khurbet el Likiye, whence the Camel Corps Brigade carried on the line to the right of the 53rd Division near Toweil Abu Jerwal.

Next day the 53rd Division attacked the heights of Tel Khuweilfeh, but met with strong resistance from the enemy, and by evening had gained only a precarious footing on the south-western spur of the hill.   The cavalry were engaged throughout the day on the right of the 53rd, towards Dhahariyeh and east of Tel Khuweilfeh.

The fighting continued day and night during the 4th and 5th.   As the time passed, and our preparations for the main attack neared completion, the enemy, who must by this time have realised our intention, flung his reserves more and more recklessly against our weak right flank, in a desperate endeavour to drive it in.   He completely failed in his effort, and our troops, after three days and nights of incessant fighting, short of food and water, and, at one time, perilously short of ammunition, not only held their own, but drove back the Turks inch by inch, and at last, on the morning of November 6th, the 53rd Division captured the ridge of Tel Khuweilfeh.   One magnificent counter-attack the enemy made, which drove our men off the ridge again, but it was a last despairing effort.   His exhausted troops were quickly dislodged from the position, and the ridge remained in our hands.

The fine fighting and grim endurance of the 53rd and the Anzac Mounted Divisions during these three days played a vital part in the success of the subsequent operations, by engaging the enemy's principal reserves and defeating his counterstroke, thus permitting our concentration for the main attack to proceed unhindered.   The cavalry had an especially hard time.   The country was quite unsuited for mounted work, and so all their fighting was done on foot.   But it was necessary to keep their horses always near them in order to be in a position to pursue the enemy at once, should he give way and endeavour to withdraw. Water was very scarce, and the few known wells were quite inadequate for the requirements of the division.

When our troops had first entered this region there were a number of pools in the wadis, left by the thunderstorm which had broken a few days before the operations began, but these rapidly dried up, and, by the morning of the 5th of November, had finally given out. The horses then had to be sent back to Beersheba to water. From the Dhahariyeh area to Beersheba and back again is twenty-eight miles, and a record of the movements between these two places from the 3rd to the 6th of November will give some idea of the extra work entailed on horses and men by the lack of water.

On the 3rd of November the 1st Brigade was relieved by the 5th, and marched back to Beersheba to water, their horses having then been thirty hours without a drink. On the 4th the New Zealanders relieved the 5th Brigade at Ras el Nukb for the same purpose. This brigade had also been thirty hours without water. On the 5th the New Zealanders remained at Ras el Nukb, since there was no brigade available to relieve them, but sent all their horses back to Beersheba during the night. They had then been unwatered for forty-eight hours. On the 6th it was the turn of the 2nd Brigade to make the weary pilgrimage to Abraham's Well.

Thus the horses of each of these brigades had only one really good drink during the four days they were in this area. Some of them, it is true, picked up a little water here and there, generally at night. Indeed many units of the division spent every night in a search for water that too often proved fruitless, and only added to the fatigue of men and horses.

The 7th Brigade found enough water on the east of the line to eke out a bare existence for its horses.

During all this period the cavalry were continually engaged with the enemy, and some of the fighting was severe. The Turks assaulted Ras el Nukb repeatedly on the 3rd, 4th, and 5th of November. This hill was held in turn by the 7th Brigade, which had captured it in the first instance, the 1st, 5th and New Zealand Brigades, and each of these had to withstand one or more attacks.

By the evening of the 5th of November the 20th Corps was in readiness for the assault on the Sharia-Hareira positions, which was to complete the defeat of the Turks.

The situation was now slightly different from what had been expected. The action of the enemy in counter-attacking against our right flank had resulted in prolonging his line to the east. The coming operations, therefore, consisted in an attempt to pierce his line at Sharia, instead of an attack against his left flank, as had been anticipated. In order to secure the troops engaged in this attempt from molestation by the considerable body of enemy about El Dhahariyeh, a force, known as Barrow's Detachment,[1] was formed to protect our right flank. This force consisted of the 53rd Division, the New Zealand Mounted Brigade, and the Camel Corps Brigade, with the Yeomanry Division, which crossed over to the right of our line on the night of the 4th to join the detachment. All the horses of this division had to be sent back to Beersheba, fifteen miles away, to water. The Australian Mounted Division had left Beersheba on the 4th, having nearly exhausted all the water there, and moved to

---

[1] From its commander, Major-General Sir G. de S. Barrow, G.O.C. of the Yeomanry Division.

Karm, taking up a line of observation from the Wadi Hanafish to Hiseia.

There was now a gap some twelve miles wide between the 21st Corps at Gaza and the 20th Corps opposite Sharia, and it was possible, though not very probable, that the enemy might attempt to throw his cavalry through this gap in an endeavour to raid our communications. It was part of the task of the Australian Mounted Division to frustrate any such attempt.

At dawn on the 6th November the 10th, 60th, and 74th Divisions attacked the south-eastern portion of the Hareira defences, known as the Kauwukah and Rushdi systems. The 74th, after some of the hardest fighting of a day of hard fighting, succeeded in capturing all its objectives by half-past one. The 10th and 60th Divisions, which were attacking on the left of the 74th, had farther to go, and the heavy wire of the main Kauwukah position had to be methodically cut before the attack could be launched. To reach its objectives, the 10th (Irish) Division had to cross a perfectly flat, open plain, two miles wide, which was swept from end to end by the fire of enemy guns of all calibres, and by machine guns and rifles. The advance of this grand division, marching across the fire-swept plain as steadily as though on parade, was a sight that will never be forgotten by those who were privileged to see it.

By half-past two in the afternoon both the 10th and the 60th Divisions had penetrated the enemy lines, and captured the whole of the Kauwukah and Rushdi systems. The 60th Division reached Sharia station, but was unable to cross the Wadi Sharia to capture the hill of Tel el Sharia that night. This hill, together with the main redoubts of Hareira, remained, therefore, for the next day's task.

During the night the Australian Mounted Division marched to a concealed position three miles south-west of Sharia, in readiness for the expected break-through. The 5th Mounted Brigade rejoined the division here, and the 7th went into Corps Reserve.

The rôle of the cavalry during the next few days was to sweep across the plain to the north-west, in order to cut off or pursue the retiring enemy troops, after they had been driven out of their positions from Sharia to the sea. In pursuance of this rôle, the Anzac and Australian Mounted Divisions were ordered to push forward, as soon as the way was clear, the Anzac Division, on the right of the movement, being directed to keep well in advance, so as to outflank any enemy opposition. The 60th Division was to move in support of the cavalry on the left flank, and the Australian Mounted Division, in the centre, was to maintain touch with the Anzacs and the 60th. The Yeomanry Division would remain, at first, with the 53rd Division, to carry out a special task.

Water for the cavalry horses was an essential preliminary to the pursuit of the enemy. The country north of Sharia was sparsely populated, and the few wells to be found there were of great depth and poor supply. The only water sources on our front which were believed to be capable of supplying the large number of horses we had were at Bir Jemameh, where there was reported to be a good well with a steam pumping plant, and at Tel el Nejile and Huj. The Anzac Division was accordingly directed on the two first-named places, and the Australian Division on Huj. The former division had only two brigades with it, having left the New Zealand Brigade in the Jurat el Mikreh, under the orders of the 53rd Division.

The attack of our infantry was resumed early on the 7th, and the 10th Division stormed the Hareira positions in the morning. The 60th Division secured the hill of Tel el Sharia in the early afternoon, but the enemy succeeded in withdrawing in good order to a long ridge on the north side of and overlooking the Wadi Sharia, where he held out all the afternoon. The approach to this ridge was up a long, bare slope, devoid of cover, and the enemy made full use of his many machine guns and of his heavy artillery.[1]

At four o'clock in the afternoon, the 4th A.L.H. Brigade, supported by two batteries of the Australian Mounted Division, was sent across the Wadi Sharia dismounted, in order to cover the concentration of the 60th Division for a final assault. When the position was carried, just before dark, it took some time to disengage this brigade, and the division was consequently unable to move farther that night. The 3rd A.L.H. and the 5th Mounted Brigades, however, were sent round the right flank of the 60th Division, to endeavour to make a mounted attack on the retreating enemy. They had to ride two miles to the east, before a possible crossing place over the wadi was found, and it was then too late to do anything more. Two regiments of the 5th Brigade did indeed draw swords, and canter out into the open north of the wadi, but darkness fell before they were able to close with the enemy.

The Anzac Mounted Division, more fortunate, had been able to push through the gap formed in the enemy's line, by the driving in of his inner left flank, and advanced on its first objective, the station of

---

[1] On one occasion, the Huns, with characteristic ferocity, deliberately turned their heavy artillery on to a convoy of ambulance camels bearing wounded out of the fight, and utterly destroyed it.

Umm el Ameidat on the Junction Station–Beer-sheba line, where the enemy had a large supply and ammunition depot. The 1st Brigade, in the lead, moved forward in open formation over the plain, being severely shelled by enemy guns from the west and north-west.

About 11 A.M. the advanced troops were fired at on approaching the station. The vanguard regiment at once closed up and charged, capturing the place after a sharp fight, with about 400 prisoners and a great quantity of ammunition and stores. Reconnaissances pushed out at once to the north and east located a strong enemy rearguard in position on the hill of Tel Abu Dilakh. The 2nd Brigade was despatched to the assistance of the 1st, and the two brigades attacked the hill dismounted. The position was taken just before dark, after severe fighting, but our troops were then heavily shelled on the hill, and the Turkish rearguard only retired a short distance to the ridges north of the position. The division held a battle outpost line for the night from Abu Dilakh to a point about two miles east of the railway.

Scouts of the 3rd A.L.H. Brigade succeeded in gaining touch with the Anzac Division about Abu Dilakh late at night. No water was obtainable for the horses of either division.

There had been an extraordinary instance in the morning of ' counting chickens before they are hatched.' After the attack on Beersheba, the heavy wagon échelons of the cavalry ammunition columns had been withdrawn from their divisions, brigaded together, and placed under the direct command of the Corps. The intention was to direct this Corps column each day on a pre-arranged place, and notify its location to the divisional ammunition columns,

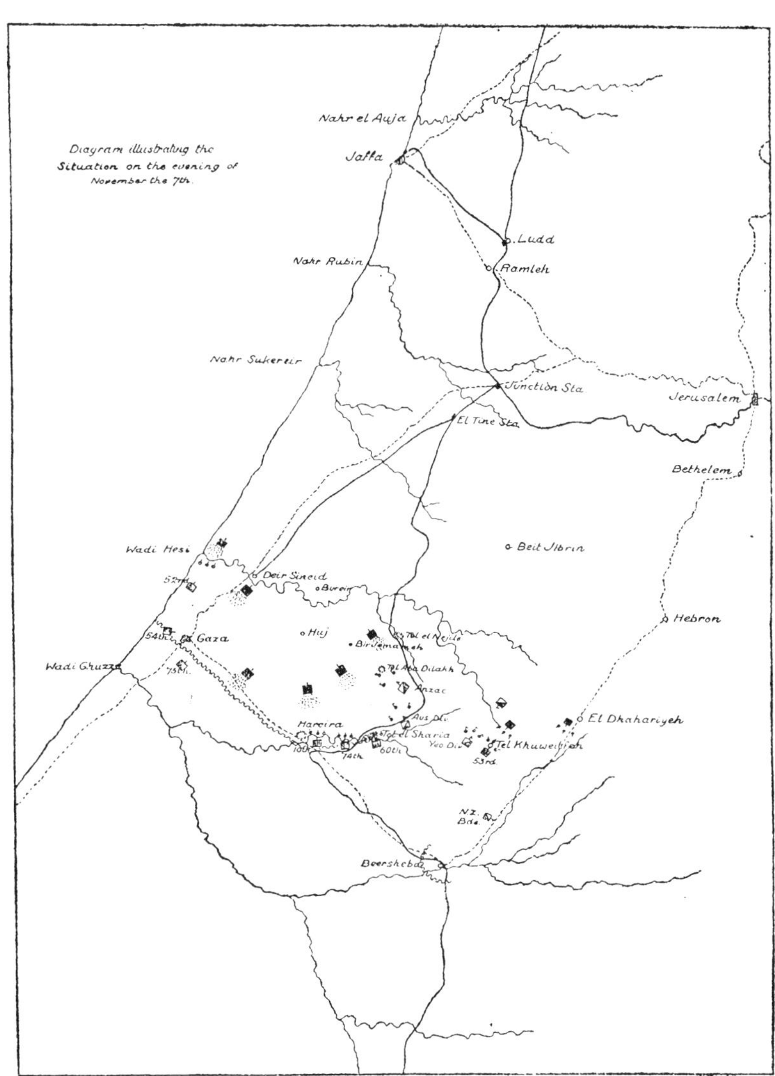

Diagram illustrating the Situation on the evening of November the 7th.
Nahr el Auja
Jaffa
Ludd
Ramleh
Nahr Rubin
Nahr Sukereir
Junction Sta
Jerusalem
El Tine Sta
Bethelem
Wadi Hesi
Beit Jibrin
Deir Sineid
52nd
Burein
Hebron
Huj
Tel el Nejile
54th
Gaza
Bir Ismain
Wadi Ghuzze
75th
Tel Abu Dilakh
Anzac
Hareira
Aus Dl.
El Dhahariyeh
Tel Sharia
Tel Khuweilfeh
100th
74th
60th
Yeo Div
53rd
N.Z. Bde.
Beersheba

which could then send their light, limbered wagons to that place to refill. The spot chosen for the 7th of November was Tel el Sharia, and the column was directed to report there at 11 A.M. The order was actually issued on the morning of the 6th, the staff officer who gave it believing that the place would be in our hands that night, whereas it was not taken till the following afternoon. Accordingly, about nine o'clock on the morning of the 7th, the ammunition column was seen marching steadily towards the enemy, to the admiration of the spectators, and the no small consternation of the staff officer who had given the order !

Fortunately the commander of the column noticed, as he explained afterwards, that ' there seemed to be *something wrong* at Tel el Sharia, so he thought he had better go to ground with the column till he could find out who the beggars on the hill really were.'

While the 20th Corps was thus occupied driving in the enemy's left flank, the 21st Corps, in the coastal area, was administering the *coup de grâce* to Gaza. The bombardment had been resumed on the 3rd, and had continued for the following three days with growing intensity. On the 5th and 6th the Navy joined in the fight, and plastered the town with shells of heavy calibre. During the night of the 6th a series of attacks carried out by our infantry on the enemy positions met with only half-hearted resistance, and, when a general advance was made on the morning of the 7th, it was found that the Turks had retired during the night.

The Imperial Service Cavalry Brigade at once went forward, riding through the ruins of Gaza, and reached Beit Hanun, just south of the Wadi Hesi, early in the afternoon. At the same time two brigades of the 52nd Division made their way along

Turkish Cavalry near Sharia.
(From an enemy photograph.)

A Turkish cavalry machine-gun battery in action near Sharia.
(From an enemy photograph.)

the seashore under cover of the cliffs, and seized the high ground north of the Wadi Hesi, in the face of strong resistance from the enemy.

This rapid move of the 52nd Division was of the greatest value to us. The Turks had constructed a strong, defensive line just north of the wadi, and had evidently hoped, in the event of being driven out of Gaza, to be able to rally on this line, and hold up our farther advance. Some of our cavalry subsequently took prisoner the engineer officer who had superintended the making of this line. He expressed keen disappointment that the Turks had been driven out of it before they had had time to settle down, and declared that, had they got there a few hours sooner, all our operations would have come to a standstill. No doubt he was biassed in favour of his own handiwork, but there is little doubt that the Turks would, at the least, have been able to organise their retreat, had they succeeded in holding this line even for a short time. Now, however, driven out of their last entrenched position, and with their forces disorganised and split into two widely separated groups, they were compelled to retreat over open country, pursued by a vigorous and successful enemy.

CHAPTER V

THE PURSUIT

ON the morning of the 8th of November the pursuit began. The enemy had made the best use of the night to put such a distance between his troops and ours that his rearguards were able to entrench lightly, and thus offered a sturdy resistance to our advance all day. He well knew that, if he could keep our cavalry away from water for another 48 hours, they would have to be withdrawn. Once free from the harassing menace of the mounted troops, the Turks, who could always outmarch our infantry, would have experienced little difficulty in retiring rapidly to the north, aided by their two railways, and would have had time to select and entrench a strong position in the Judæan foothills, on which to bar our farther advance.

The cavalry, supported by the 60th Division, were ordered to continue their advance to the north-west, and to push on with the utmost vigour, so as to intercept the retirement of the Gaza garrison. The Anzac Division was directed on Bureir, some twelve miles north-east of Gaza, with the Australian Mounted and 60th Divisions on the left, in échelon to the rear. The country was open, rolling down-land, devoid of trees or scrub, and dotted with prominent hills or ' tels.' The ground surface was hard, and the whole terrain was admirably suited for cavalry work.

The Anzac Division moved off at dawn, with the 1st and 2nd Brigades in line covering a front of some six miles, with centre about Abu Dilakh, and in touch with the Australian Mounted Division on the left. The 7th Mounted Brigade, which had joined the division from Corps Reserve early in the morning, marched in support.

From the commencement of the advance, the Turks resisted strongly. Having been retiring during the two previous nights, and pressed by our cavalry on the intervening day, they had not had any opportunity of organising a definite line of resistance, but bodies of them, varying from a company to several regiments, occupied every tel or other commanding ground along the line of our advance, and held on tenaciously.

About nine o'clock, in order to expedite the advance, General Chaytor pushed up the 7th Brigade between the other two, which were encountering strong resistance. At eleven o'clock the enemy counter-attacked strongly against the 2nd Brigade, which was on the right of our line, near Tel el Nejile, and held up its advance. The 7th Brigade, in the centre, continued to push on, and had nearly reached Bir el Jemameh, about one o'clock, when it was heavily attacked by a large force of the enemy covering the water supply there. The brigade was forced back, and its left flank was endangered, when the 1st Brigade came up on the west, and drove back the Turks. Following up their advantage, the leading troops of this brigade fought their way into Bir el Jemameh shortly after three o'clock, capturing the steam pumping plant intact and complete, even to the engineer in charge. This individual had been left behind to blow up the plant, but instead remained to work it for us with great docility.

A regiment of the 1st Brigade pushed out to the north, and secured the high ground overlooking Bir el Jemameh, and, under cover of this regiment, the

7th Brigade and the rest of the 1st were able to water all their horses. The enemy fell back after dark, and the 2nd Brigade occupied Tel el Nejile. Some water was found here in the Wadi el Hesi, but it was not possible to water the horses of the outpost troops. The division established a night outpost line, protecting Nejile and Jemameh.

Meanwhile the Australian Mounted Division, on the left of the Anzacs, and with the 60th Division in its rear and a little farther west, pushed slowly after the retreating enemy, engaged in continuous, isolated troop actions throughout the day, in the course of which a number of enemy guns, particularly heavy howitzers, were captured. The 3rd A.L.H. Brigade especially distinguished itself in this form of warfare. Troops of the brigade repeatedly stalked enemy guns during the day, and then charged them suddenly from the rear, killing the gun crews and capturing the guns. It became a commonplace to find an enemy 5·9-inch howitzer in a hollow in the ground, with the detachment dead around it, and the words ' captured by the 3rd A.L.H. Brigade ' scrawled in chalk on the chase of the gun.

Early in the afternoon, a regiment of the 4th A.L.H. Brigade was ordered to try and gain touch with the right of the 21st Corps, which was out of communication with our troops in the centre. All the afternoon, the regiment rode hard over the plain to the north-west, avoiding the enemy troops where possible, brushing them aside when encountered, and succeeded in linking up with the Imperial Service Cavalry Brigade about Beit Hanun before nightfall. It rejoined the division at Huj next day.

About 3 P.M., as the right flank of the 60th Division was approaching Huj, it came suddenly under a devastating fire at close range from several concealed batteries of enemy artillery, which, with two battalions of infantry, were covering the withdrawal of the VIIIth Army headquarters. The country was rather like Salisbury Plain, rolling down-land without any cover, and our troops suffered severely from the murderous fire. Major-General Shea, commanding the division, finding Colonel Gray-Cheape of the Warwick Yeomanry close by him, requested him to charge the enemy guns at once. Colonel Cheape collected a few troops of his own regiment that he had with him, and some of the Worcester Yeomanry, and led them away to the right front. Taking advantage of a slight rise in the ground to the east of the enemy position, he succeeded in leading his troops to within 800 yards of the Turkish guns unseen. He then gave the order to charge, and the ten troops galloped over the rise, and raced down upon the flank of the enemy guns. The Turks had in position a battery of field and one of mountain guns, with four machine guns on a low hill between the two batteries, and three heavy howitzers behind.

As our cavalry appeared, thundering over the rise, the Turks sprang to their guns and swung them round, firing point-blank into the charging horsemen. The infantry, leaping on the limbers, blazed away with their rifles till they were cut down. There was no thought of surrender; every man stuck to his gun or rifle to the last. The leading troops of the cavalry dashed into the first enemy battery. The following troops, swinging to the right, took the three heavy howitzers almost in their stride, leaving the guns silent, the gun crews dead or dying, and galloped round the hill, to fall upon the mountain battery from the rear, and cut the Turkish gunners to pieces in a few minutes. The third wave, passing the first battery, where a fierce sabre *v.* bayonet fight was going on between our cavalry and the enemy, raced up the slope at the machine guns. Many saddles were emptied in that few yards, but the charge was irresistible. In a few minutes the enemy guns were silenced, their crews killed, and the whole position was in our hands.

Most of the Turkish infantry escaped, as our small force of cavalry was too scattered and cut up by the charge to be able to pursue them, but few of the enemy gunners lived to fight again. About seventy of them were killed outright, and a very large number were wounded.

This was the first time that our troops had 'got home' properly with the modern, cavalry thrusting sword, and an examination of the enemy dead afterwards proved what a fine weapon it is. Our losses were heavy. Of the 170 odd who took part in the charge, seventy-five were killed and wounded, and all within a space of ten minutes. In this charge, as in all others during the campaign, it was noticeable how many more horses were killed than men. Apart from the fact that a horse presents a much bigger target than a man, it is probably that infantry, and especially machine gunners, when suddenly charged by cavalry, have a tendency to fire ' into the brown,' where the target looks thickest, which is about the middle of the horses' bodies, thus dropping many horses but failing to kill their riders. A man whose horse is brought down is, however, by no means done with, as the Turks learnt to their cost. In this, as in subsequent charges, many a man whose horse had been shot under him, extricated himself from his fallen mount, and, seizing rifle and bayonet, rushed on into the fight.

It is sad to have to relate that the gallant officer who led this great charge, met his death subsequently, not on the field of battle as he would have wished, but in the Mediterranean, when the transport that was taking him and his regiment to France for the final act of the war, was torpedoed and sunk by an enemy submarine.[1]

The action was of interest as an indication of what may be accomplished, under suitable conditions, by even a very small force of cavalry when resolutely led. The charge was made on the spur of the moment, with little preliminary reconnaissance of the ground, without fire support, and with the equivalent of little more than one squadron of cavalry. It resulted in the capture of eleven guns and four machine guns, and the complete destruction of a strong point of enemy resistance, at a cost of seventy-five casualties.

There was considerable divergence of opinion in the cavalry as to the best method to be employed in a mounted attack. As there were no reliable precedents in modern warfare, with its machine guns and quick-firing artillery, brigadiers had been given a free hand to develop the tactics they favoured, subject to the principle that fire support should always be provided if available, and that the line of fire and the direction of the mounted attack should be as nearly as possible at right angles to one another.

Prior to the operations the 5th Mounted Brigade had been practising the following method for the attack of lightly entrenched troops. A regiment charged in column of squadrons in line, with a distance of 150 to 200 yards between squadrons. The leading squadron charged with the sword, and, having passed over the enemy position, galloped straight on to attack any supports that might be coming up. The remainder of the regiment charged

---

[1] The charge formed the subject of a brilliant picture by Lady Butler painted from notes made by an eye-witness of the action.

without swords. The second squadron galloped over the trench while the enemy troops were still in a state of confusion, dismounted on the farther side, and attacked from the rear with the bayonet. The third squadron dismounted before reaching the trench, and went in with the bayonet from the front. Two machine guns accompanied this last squadron, and came into action on one or both flanks, as the situation demanded, to deal with any counter-attack that might develop. If more than one regiment took part in the attack, the machine guns, of course, moved on the outer flanks of the regiments.

Unfortunately this brigade never had an opportunity of putting this method to the test, but the 4th A.L.H. Brigade used it in a modified form at Beersheba, with excellent results.

The wisdom of accompanying a mounted attack by one or two machine guns was generally recognised, and in most cases where a charge was made deliberately and after due preparation, and the guns were available, this method of support was employed.

Where a mounted attack had to cover a considerable distance of open ground before reaching charging distance, the most usual formation was in column of squadrons in line of troop columns. Our own gunners were of opinion that this formation offered the most difficult target to artillery, provided the interval between troops was not less than 25 yards, and the distance between squadrons not less than 100 yards. The experience of the campaign seemed to point to the fact that cavalry also suffered less from machine-gun fire in this formation than in any other, at any rate at ranges beyond 1000 yards.

The Turks had their main ammunition depot at Huj. A squadron of the Worcester Yeomanry came upon this depot just after the charge, and found a party of enemy cavalry engaged in setting fire to it. The squadron commander of the Worcesters at once decided to charge the fire instead of the enemy, and his prompt action was the means of putting out the fire and saving the ammunition. Later on in the campaign we made considerable use of captured enemy guns, especially those of heavy calibre, and this vast store of shells was of the greatest value to us.

General Kress von Kressenstein and his staff, who were still at Huj when our cavalry made this charge, narrowly escaped capture, and had to leave everything behind them in their hurried flight, even to their wireless code book. The Turks had, of course, abandoned all their telephone and telegraph wires, when they were driven off their positions from Gaza to Beersheba. During the retreat over the plain of Philistia their units were so scattered and disorganised that they had to rely almost entirely on gallopers for all orders and messages. Once in the Judæan hills, however, they re-established their wireless service, and thereafter all orders were sent by wireless, until the arrival of fresh telephone and telegraph equipment in January 1918. Armed with their code book, we were able to decode all their messages, and were thus always in possession of enemy orders as soon as they were issued. This piece of luck stood us in good stead later on, more particularly at the time when the Turks made their big effort to recover Jerusalem at the end of December.

As soon as it had arrived at Huj the Australian Mounted Division set about watering horses from the two wells there. These wells were each about 150 feet deep, and, as the Turks had destroyed the winding apparatus, water could only be obtained by the laborious process of letting down and hauling up by hand a few small canvas buckets attached to a length of field telephone wire. Most of the horses had been without any water since the afternoon of the 6th, and the poor brutes were raging with thirst, and drank inordinately. In some cases a single troop took over an hour to water. All night long and all the next day the weary work went on, but, on the evening of the 9th, when the advance was resumed, the horses of the divisional ammunition column had not yet been watered.

The task of the Yeomanry Division on the 8th of November was to attack the eastern group of the enemy forces on its right flank, so as to drive it across the front of the 53rd Division and the Camel Corps Brigade about Tel Khuweilfeh. The Turkish flank was located in a strong position on the high and broken ground at Khurbet el Mujeidilat. The 8th Mounted Brigade attacked this position, but was unable to dislodge the enemy, and, before a further attack could be organised, orders were received to break off the action and march to Sharia to water, preparatory to taking part in the more important task of pursuing the enemy forces over the coastal plain. The 53rd Division and the Camel Corps remained in observation of the enemy. The Yeomanry watered at Sharia that evening, and marched to Huj on the following day.

It was now clear that the attempt to cut off the whole of the enemy forces had failed. Most of the rearguards left by the troops who had been driven out of the Sharia-Hareira positions had been disposed of by the Anzac and Australian Mounted Divisions during the past two days, but the sturdy resistance offered by these rearguards, coupled with the delay caused to our cavalry by the scarcity of water, had afforded time for the Gaza garrison and some of the enemy troops east of Gaza to make good their escape.

The rôle of the cavalry thus changed to a direct pursuit of the enemy. Accordingly the Anzac Division, which had got some water on the evening of the 8th, and was ready to move, was ordered to push across the plain towards the coast, with Bureir as the first objective and El Mejdel as the second. The Australian Mounted Division, on completing the watering of horses at Huj, was to move to the north on Arak el Menshiye and El Faluje, thus coming up on the right of the Anzac Division. The Yeomanry, when they had reached Huj, were to push on and come into line on the right of the Australian Division. The Corps would then be in line across the plain, from the foothills to the sea, and ready for the further pursuit of the enemy.

The Anzac Division started soon after daylight on the 9th, with the 1st and 2nd Brigades in line, each being responsible for the protection of its own front and outer flank, and the 7th Brigade in support. The 1st Brigade, on the left, entered Bureir about half-past eight, after encountering some opposition. About an hour later, the 2nd Brigade, nearing El Huleikat, located a body of the enemy occupying some high ground north-west of the village. The brigade attacked dismounted, and drove off the Turks, capturing about 600 prisoners. There was no water available at either place.

About mid-day the 1st Brigade reached El Mejdel, which was seized with little difficulty, the small force of Turks there making but a feeble stand. One hundred and seventy prisoners were taken. There was a good well with a steam pump here, and the brigade was able to get water for all the horses.

A message now arrived from the Corps to the effect that the 21st Corps was marching on El Mejdel and Julis, and that the Anzac Division was to push on to the neighbourhood of Beit Duras. The division accordingly wheeled to the right, and the line of advance became north-east. The troops pressed on as fast as their jaded horses could carry them, and, towards evening, the 1st Brigade reached Esdud, and the 2nd entered the villages of Suafir el Sharkiye and Arak Suweidan. On the way the latter brigade had captured a Turkish convoy, with its escort of about 350 men. While these prisoners were being sent to the rear, some enemy guns farther north opened fire and shelled captors and captives with a fine impartiality. This shelling of their own men when taken prisoner was of such frequent occurrence that it is impossible not to suspect German inspiration.

Just before dark the 2nd Brigade rounded up another 200 Turks. The division occupied a battle outpost line along the high ground south of the Wadi Mejma, from near Esdud to Arak Suweidan. Just at dusk a small body of Turks advanced with fixed bayonets to attack the outposts of the 2nd Brigade. When they were close up to our line, an officer in the brigade, who had evidently been studying the *Handbook of Turkish Military Terms*, shouted in Turkish a peremptory command to surrender. The weary Turks, thinking that the order had been given by one of their own officers, and being only too glad to comply with it, obediently laid down their arms, and were added to the bag !

The enemy troops encountered during the day, and especially towards evening, were utterly disorganised, and offered little resistance to our advance. They were quite worn out by their exertions of the past three days. Many of them had dysentery, and all were suffering severely from thirst.

The advanced troops of the 52nd Division, 21st Corps, reached El Mejdel in the evening.

CHAPTER VI

OVER THE PHILISTINE PLAIN

ON the evening of the 9th of November, as the Anzac Mounted Division was ' in the air,' it was necessary for the other two divisions of the Desert Mounted Corps to press on and join it as soon as possible. The Australian Mounted Division, therefore, left Huj on the evening of the 9th, although all its horses were not yet watered, and marched to the north-east, the first objective being Tel el Hesi, and the second Arak el Menshiye and El Faluje. This was the only night march made by the cavalry in enemy country during the pursuit. The 3rd Brigade, with a battery attached, acted as advance guard, being followed by the 5th and 4th. The advance guard dropped pickets along the route every quarter of a mile, which were picked up by the 5th Brigade. This brigade, in turn, dropped pickets to be picked up by the rearguard. Signallers with lamps were sent by the two leading brigades on to every prominent hill top during the march, to flash the letters of the divisional signal call intermittently in a south-westerly direction. These arrangements worked well, and the division arrived at Tel el Hesi at half-past four in the morning, and halted there till daylight.

There were several large pools of good water in the Wadi Hesi, and the rest of the horses got their fill at last, having been without water for *three days and four nights.*

The division pushed on at once, and came up on the right of the Anzac Division at Faluje and Arak el Menshiye Station about eight o'clock. It was joined, some few hours later, by the Yeomanry Division, which had left Huj early in the morning, after having spent all the previous night trying to water horses. This division took over Arak el Menshiye, and extended a little farther east. Thus, on the afternoon of the 10th, the whole of the Corps, with the exception of the New Zealand Mounted Brigade, was in line from a point a little east of Arak el Menshiye to the sea, and ready for the further pursuit of the enemy.

The cavalry were now some thirty-five miles in advance of railhead at Deir el Belah, and the problem of supply became pressing. No help could be obtained from the two enemy railways, as the Turks had blown up bridges and culverts, and destroyed portions of the line during their retreat. Our only means of supply was, therefore, by motor lorries and camels along the single, narrow, ill-metalled road from Gaza to Junction Station. Between Gaza and Beit Hanun the road was unmetalled and deep in sand, and lorries had great difficulty in getting over this part, even with the light load of one ton, which was the maximum allowed to be carried. The marching ration of our horses was only $9\frac{1}{2}$ lbs. of grain a day, without any hay or other bulk food, but even this small ration, when multiplied by 25,000 (approximately the number of horses in the Corps), worked out at over 100 tons of forage a day. In addition to this there were the rations for the men of the Corps, and the food and forage for the infantry.

In order to enable the pursuit to continue, it was clear that the greater part of the infantry would have to be left behind. Accordingly, on the 9th, the whole of the 20th Corps, with the exception of the 53rd Division, which was still watching the right group of the enemy forces, withdrew to railhead at Karm. Of the 21st Corps, only the 52nd and 75th Divisions continued the advance. The 54th, which had remained at Gaza, gave up all its transport to assist the other two divisions. All the available motor lorries and camels were organised in convoys along the Gaza-Junction Station road, from Deir el Belah to El Mejdel, whence the supplies were distributed to divisions by the horse-drawn wagons of the divisional trains. These trains had heavier work than any other part of the force. Even on the rare occasions when the cavalry got some rest at night, there was none for them, as they were distributing supplies from nightfall till dawn. Men and horses got into the habit of sleeping as they marched, and, as long as one or two men kept awake to lead the way, the wagons always reached their destination safely. The Divisional Ammunition Columns were in little better case, and the *Sharki*, or hot wind from the east, that commenced to blow on the 10th, added to the sufferings of the unfortunate horses.

The whole Corps was suffering from lack of water, but the Australian Mounted Division, which was advancing through the almost waterless country along the edge of the Judæan range, was in an almost desperate condition. The Anzac Division, although operating in the better watered coastal area, had moved farther and faster and had more fighting than the other two, and was also in a bad way. Moreover, owing to the rapid advance of the last two days, forage and rations had failed to reach this division. There was absolutely no grazing to be found, and what little grain the Turks had left in the villages was securely hidden.   The 2nd A.L.H. and 7th Mounted Brigades, some of the horses of which had not had a drink for eighty-four hours, carried on all through the night of the 9th, trying to water with buckets from two or three deep wells, but got little satisfaction.   The depth of the shallowest of these wells was 150 feet, and of the deepest nearly 250 feet.   It was quite clear that these two divisions could make no further substantial move forward till all their horses had been watered and fed.

Had water been available in abundance throughout the advance, there is little doubt that our cavalry would have been able to overwhelm the retreating Turkish armies, and the capture of Jerusalem might then have been accomplished by a rapid raid of mounted troops.   As it was, each night was spent by a large part of the cavalry in a heart-breaking search for water, that too often proved fruitless, while the enemy, moving in his own country, utilised the hours of darkness to put such a distance between his troops and their pursuers as enabled him generally to entrench lightly before our cavalry came up with him in the morning.   The marching powers of the Turks are phenomenal.   Time after time, after fighting all day, they would retire when darkness fell, and march all night, and repeat this performance of fighting all day and marching all night for several days in succession.   During their retreat they systematically destroyed the water-lifting apparatus of all the wells they passed, thus incidentally depriving the native inhabitants of water.

The inevitable delay caused by the necessity of resting our cavalry now gave the enemy the opportunity to collect his scattered forces and organise some sort of line of resistance. Already, on the 10th of November, his troops could be seen digging in along the high ground on the right bank of the Nahr Sukereir, and aeroplane reports indicated that he was preparing a second line farther north.

The 1st A.L.H. Brigade, reconnoitring northwards on the 10th, located the Turks in position from the hill of Tel el Murre near the sea, along the high ground on the right bank of the Nahr Sukereir, through Burka to Kustine. Finding a small force of Turks holding the bridge at Jisr Esdud, the 1st A.L.H. Regiment attacked, and drove them off. General Cox at once ordered a bridgehead to be established on the north bank, and entrenched. The possession of this bridge was of great value to us during the next few days. The Nahr Sukereir, in its lower course, runs between high, precipitous banks, and forms a barrier to movement north and south very difficult to pass except by this one bridge. The enemy was well aware of this, and squandered some of his best and freshest troops in a desperate attack on our bridgehead, supported by heavy artillery, but the 1st Brigade stood fast, and beat off the attack.

The 2nd A.L.H. Brigade continued the weary business of watering from two very deep wells at Suafir el Sharkiye, but there were 800 prisoners here clamouring for water, and the local inhabitants, who had been driven from the wells by the retiring Turks, had had none for twenty-four hours. In the middle of the pandemonium created by this fight for water, some enemy guns opened fire on the village, causing a number of casualties among the Arabs and Turks. The Arabs fled to the shelter of their houses, and the prisoners were sent back out of the way. Later on in the morning, some troops of the brigade returned to the village to continue watering. No sooner had they entered the place, than the enemy guns opened fire again. A thorough search of the houses now revealed two Turks concealed in one of them, directing the fire of the enemy guns by telephone. They were promptly shot, and the firing at once ceased. A more callous action than this of directing gun-fire on to a village full of their own captured comrades and harmless natives could hardly be imagined. It again suggests German influence, as the Turks did not, as a rule, do such things on their own initiative.

In the evening part of the 52nd and 74th Divisions arrived at Esdud and Suafir el Sharkiye, and the weary 2nd A.L.H. and 7th Mounted Brigades were withdrawn to water and rest near Hamame. The 1st A.L.H. Brigade held an outpost line during the night from the sea west of Jisr Esdud to a point on the Wadi Mejma just north of Beit Duras, in touch with the infantry on the right.

Meanwhile the Australian Mounted Division and the Yeomanry Division, on the east, pushing their tired horses slowly after the retreating Turks, advanced a few miles, and located the left half of the enemy's line running from Kustine, roughly through Balin and Berkusie, to the neighbourhood of Beit Jibrin.

The headquarters of the Australian Division was at El Faluje on the 10th and 11th. Shortly after its arrival there, the headman of the village, which is the seat of a *Nahie*,[1] came to pay his respects to the British General. After a few polite compliments, he asked anxiously if we had any men from his village

---

[1] Turkish provinces are divided into a number of Sanjaks, each under a Mutasserif; these in turn are divided into Kazas, each under a Kaimakam; and each Kaza into several Nahies under Mudirs or headmen of villages.

among our prisoners. We, of course, could not tell, as all prisoners were sent back as soon as possible after being taken. The old man remarked sadly that he had not had much hope of finding any of them, as he believed they had all gone to the Caucasus. About two years ago, he said, a Turkish battalion had suddenly arrived at the village one morning, and carried off 500 of his young men to be pressed into the Army, and from that day no word had been heard from any of them.

All through the campaign we heard similar accounts of Turkish recruiting methods. The Turks always sent their conscripts to fight in a theatre of war as far removed from their native country as possible, in order to discourage desertion. In spite of this, their soldiers were constantly deserting, either to find a ready hiding-place in some neighbouring town or village, or to give themselves up to us. So serious had the question become in the Turkish Army that there was a standing reward of £5 Turkish offered to all natives for delivering a deserter to the Army authorities. An organised propaganda was also carried on by the officers, by means of lectures to their men, the chief feature of which was a description of the tortures and hideous deaths inflicted on their prisoners by British soldiers. These lectures were illustrated by pictures supplied by Berlin. Our reply to this propaganda was to scatter from our aeroplanes hundreds of handbills over the Turkish lines. These sheets showed, on one side, the signed photograph of a fat and smiling Turk, one of our prisoners, with an autograph letter from him, inviting his friends to join him, and, on the other side, a bill of fare of the prisoners' camps that must have made the hungry Turkish soldiers positively slobber !

The strange fact was that, in spite of these constant

desertions, the Turks, when brought to bay, nearly always fought splendidly, and that not alone in defence, but in attack also. Indeed, some of their counter-attacks were simply heroic. Out-numbered, out-gunned, out-manœuvred, doomed to defeat before even the attack was launched, they yet advanced with the most reckless courage, shouting their war cry, 'Allah! Allah! Allah!' The explanation must probably be sought in their religious hatred of the infidel. The Turks opposed to us in Palestine at this time were mostly Anatolians, of fine physique, and sturdy fighters.

The Commander-in-Chief determined to continue the advance on the 12th, devoting the preceding day to preparations for the attack on the enemy positions. The delay would afford time for the 52nd and 74th Divisions to close up and move forward to their preliminary positions.

He decided to attack the right centre of the Turkish line with his infantry, and turn the right flank with his cavalry. The Anzac Division had now, however, only one brigade (the 1st) in a fit state to continue the operations. Accordingly the Yeomanry Division was ordered to march on the 11th right across from east to west, behind our line, and relieve the 2nd and 7th Brigades on the coast. The Australian Mounted Division was directed to extend to the east, to a point south-west of Zeita, so as to cover the country vacated by the Yeomanry. Its rôle was to protect the right flank of our forces during the operations, and to attract the enemy's attention to this flank. All patrol work was to be made as conspicuous as possible, and reconnaissances were to be pushed forward vigorously. This work was excellently carried out throughout the day, along a front extending from near Zeita nearly to Suafir el Sharkiye.

The Yeomanry Division marched *via* Tel el Hesi, in order to get water for its horses, and arrived at El Mejdel in the evening. At the same time the New Zealand Brigade and the Camel Corps were ordered up from the Beersheba area, to join the cavalry force on the left of our line. These two brigades started on their forty-mile march on the morning of the 11th, and reached El Mejdel late on the following afternoon.

In order to facilitate the crossing of the Nahr Sukereir, the 1st A.L.H. Brigade was directed to enlarge the bridgehead at Jisr Esdud. This was found to be impossible as long as the enemy held the hill of Tel el Murre, which commanded the country north of the bridge. There were no troops available to assist the 1st Brigade, but General Cox obtained permission to attempt the capture of the hill. The 2nd A.L.H. Regiment, which was selected for the task, reconnoitred the river west of the bridge during the day, but found no crossing place. Undeterred by this, the regiment concentrated in the evening under cover of the hill of Nebi Yunus, which concealed it from the Turks, and the Australians swam their horses across the river, which was here some fifty yards wide and ten feet deep. Moving forward dismounted in the darkness, they completely surprised the Turks, who had fancied themselves protected on that side by the river, and captured the hill after a sharp bayonet fight. Now, with Tel el Murre and the Esdud bridge in our hands, we had a strong hold on the north bank of the river.

There was a good landing-place on the coast here, and, a few days later, when our troops had pushed farther north, the navy reopened the sea-borne supply line, with the mouth of the Nahr Sukereir as its terminus. The reopening of the sea route greatly eased the supply situation, and enabled two more infantry divisions to be brought up to the front.

During the past two days, the 10th and 11th, there had been a noticeable stiffening of the enemy resistance all along the line, and this fact, coupled with the capture of prisoners from almost every unit of the Turkish army, showed that the enemy rearguards had been driven in on his main body, and that we were now opposed by the whole of the remainder of his force. It was soon apparent that he intended to rally on a line north of the Nahr Rubin, and make a supreme effort to hold us off the vital Junction Station till he had been able to steady his forces and organise his retreat.

During the past few days several new units, portions of the much vaunted Yilderim group, had arrived from the north. Assisted by these fresh troops, and favoured by the delay to our cavalry caused by lack of water, the enemy had prepared, and partly entrenched, a defensive line, which was located by the Royal Air Force on the 11th, running from Kubeibe, three miles north-east of Yebnah, through Zernuka, El Mughar, Katrah and Tel el Turmus, to about Beit Jibrin. Each of these localities had been prepared for defence, and was held by a considerable force of Turks. The intervening spaces were covered by machine-gun fire from the defended posts. The forward positions already located by our cavalry north of the Nahr Sukereir had evidently been established to delay our advance long enough to enable the main line to be entrenched and consolidated.

Thus, though he had been retiring to the north, the enemy's line now ran nearly north and south. This position was forced on him, partly by the pressure of our advance, and partly by the lie of the ground. The line ran parallel to, and about five miles to the west of, the railway he wished to defend. The right flank rested on a high, steep ridge connecting the villages of El Mughar and Zernuka, and extending north-westwards to Kubeibe. The southern extremity of this ridge commanded the flat country to the west and south-west for a distance of two miles or more.

The attack on this formidable line, originally planned for the 12th of November, was now put off till the next day, owing to the necessity of first driving the enemy from his advanced positions along the north bank of the Nahr Sukereir. The hot east wind had continued to blow throughout the 10th and 11th, raising clouds of suffocating dust over all the country, and adding to the discomforts caused by the lack of water.

In order to clear the enemy from his advanced positions, a brigade of the 52nd Division crossed the Esdud bridge on the morning of the 12th, and advanced against Burka, supported on the left by the 1st A.L.H. Brigade, and on the right by part of the 75th Division. The Turks were well posted, and fought stubbornly, and the village was only taken after an hour and a half of strenuous fighting. After its capture, our infantry advanced a short distance without further opposition, and established an outpost line a few miles north of the Nahr Sukereir.

The Yeomanry Division came up in the afternoon on the left of the infantry, and the 1st A.L.H. Brigade withdrew to bivouac south of Esdud. The 8th Mounted Brigade had arrived in time to take part in the capture of Burka. The New Zealand Brigade rejoined the Anzac Division in the evening, and the Camel Corps Brigade, on arrival, was attached to the Yeomanry.

On the right of our line the Australian Mounted Division continued its task of making a big noise, and carried it out so effectively as to attract rather more attention from the enemy than was altogether pleasant.

The 5th Mounted Brigade was ordered to push into Balin, and then make a vigorous reconnaissance as far north as the Wadi Dhahr, from Tel el Safi to the Beersheba Railway. The 3rd A.L.H. Brigade, concentrated in a concealed position at Summeil, sent a squadron into Berkusie, and pushed out strong, fighting patrols to the east and south-east. The 4th A.L.H. Brigade was directed to send a squadron to the high ground near the Deir Sineid Railway line, about a mile south-west of Tel el Turmus, watch the country between that point and Balin, and force the enemy to disclose his positions.

About one o'clock the enemy suddenly flung a force of about 5000 men against the 5th Brigade in Balin. This was by far the heaviest counter-attack we had experienced since the break-through at Sharia on the 7th, and there is reason to believe that it was directed by Marshal von Falkenhayn in person. The attack was made by two columns, one of which had come down the track from Junction Station to Tel el Safi, and the other by rail to El Tine Station. Just after the attack was launched two large motors came tearing down the road to Tel el Safi. From one of these several officers got out, and climbed a little way up the hill to watch the development of the attack. One of them, from his great height, was believed to be the Marshal, but unfortunately the party was out of range of our thirteen-pounders in Balin.

The enemy attack was pressed with the greatest

vigour, and the 5th Brigade was almost surrounded. At one time it appeared likely that the guns of ' B ' Battery H.A.C., attached to the brigade, would be lost, as the country was a mass of rocks, and it was impossible to move them quickly. Assisted by the magnificent fighting of the Brigade Machine Gun Squadron, however, the battery was able to withdraw slowly by sections, firing at point-blank range most of the time.

The 3rd Brigade was sent up at a canter from Summeil, followed by the remaining two batteries of the division, and the leading regiment came up on the right of the 5th Brigade just as the latter had cleared Balin. Almost immediately afterwards the enemy turned his attention to Berkusie, now occupied by a regiment of the 3rd Brigade. Supported by a heavy fire from several batteries, the Turks attacked this village, and forced the regiment to retire.

All the available troops of the division were now engaged, and, as the enemy still pressed on, the situation became somewhat anxious. The 4th Brigade was strung out to the west as far as the Deir Sineid line, and could render no effective aid to the other two brigades. General Hodgson, therefore, ordered the division to withdraw slowly to the line Bir Summeil-Khurbet Jeladiyeh. Hardly had the order been given when an enemy train appeared, coming south along the Beersheba line. It stopped west of Balin, and disgorged a fresh force of Turks, which deployed rapidly, and advanced against the left of the 5th Brigade. Our other two batteries were now, however, in action on the high ground north-west of Summeil, and they at once engaged this force. The Turks were moving over an open plain, in full view of our gunners, who took full advantage of the excellent target offered by the enemy, and made such good practice that the attack was broken. The enemy troops fell back a little on this flank, and commenced to dig themselves in.

Fighting steadily and skilfully, the two brigades withdrew till they reached the edge of Summeil village. Here, favoured by the protection afforded by the houses and walls of the village, and by the rocky ground on either side of it, they were able to make a stand, and the enemy's attack was finally held.

The Turks did not attempt to renew their attack, which was just as well, as no troops could have been spared to assist the Australian Division. Our losses had been somewhat severe, especially in the 5th Brigade Machine Gun Squadron, whose fine fighting was the chief factor in extricating the brigade from Balin. Towards the end of the fighting there, the Turks had got to within a few hundred yards of our troops on three sides. A few of them even succeeded in getting across our line of withdrawal, and several of the battery drivers were shot from the rear while getting the guns away. The division occupied a battle outpost line for the night from near Arak el Menshiye, through Summeil and along the high ground north of the Wadi Mejma, to Khurbet Jeladiyeh, in touch with the 75th Division on the left.

The employment of the artillery in this action deserves notice. In some of the cavalry divisions it had been the custom to attach a battery of Horse Artillery permanently to each brigade. General Hodgson, however, elected to keep his artillery together, and under his immediate command, only attaching a battery to a brigade when on some special mission, as in this case, when the 5th Brigade, with ' B ' Battery H.A.C. attached, was sent forward into Balin, acting as a sort of advance guard to the division, which was écheloned to the rear or either side of it.

Though there may be something to be said in favour of the principle of attaching each battery to a brigade when, as was generally the case in these operations, a division is moving on a very wide front, there is little doubt that it is the sounder plan for the divisional commander to keep at least a part of his artillery in his own hands.

In this action General Hodgson, having his other two batteries in hand, and well up behind the centre of the front covered by his division, was able to throw them at once into the fight at the critical moment, and there is no doubt that their fire materially assisted in the final defeat of the enemy thrust. Had these two batteries been attached to the 3rd and 4th Brigades, one of them would probably have been far to the south towards Zeita, and the other possibly nearly as far west as the Deir Sineid Railway. Both would almost certainly have been unavailable at the moment when their services were most urgently needed. This subject is dealt with more fully in Chapter XXIV.

The attempt of the enemy to arrest our pursuit by using his reserves in a bold attack against our weak right flank deserved better success than it achieved. It was a repetition, on a smaller scale, of his tactics at Tel Khuweilfeh, after the battle of Beersheba. In both instances, had his troops been as bold in attack as they were tenacious in defence, the campaign might well have taken a different turn.

One of General Allenby's most marked character-istics was his capacity for gauging the fighting qualities of his enemy. He rarely underestimated the Turks' strength or *morale*, but he seemed to know, as by instinct, the minimum force necessary to hold any counter-thrust that might possibly be made. In this case aeroplane and cavalry reconnaissances had established the fact that there was a considerable force of the enemy on our right, but the Commander-in-Chief left the task of dealing with it, with complete equanimity, to one cavalry division.

Huj. After the charge.

British Horse Artillery and Australian Cavalry advancing
over the Philistine Plain.

CHAPTER VII

NEARING THE HILLS

EARLY on the morning of the 13th the attack on the enemy positions began.

The Yeomanry Division and the Camel Corps Brigade advanced on the left of our line, with the 52nd Division on their right. Then came the 75th Division and the Australian Mounted Division, the latter covering a front of about eight miles. The orders to this division were to watch the right flank of our line, and attract the enemy's attention, as on the previous two days. In view of the large area of country to be covered, the 2nd A.L.H. Brigade, now Corps Reserve, was stationed at Khurbet Jeladiyeh. The 7th Mounted Brigade relieved the 5th, the horses of which were exhausted. The 2nd and 7th Brigades had only been withdrawn from the line late on the evening of the 11th, and had thus had but one day's complete rest. One of the chief difficulties of the Corps Commander at this time, and one which increased daily, lay in the fact that one or another of his brigades was always on the verge of coming to a standstill owing to the exhaustion of its horses. This fact compelled the continual movement of brigades from one part of the line to another, to relieve others unable to carry on the pursuit, thus increasing the fatigue and distress of the horses.

The country in which our troops were now operating is an undulating, treeless plain, rising here and there into isolated, rocky hills, similar in character to the country farther south. It is, however, much more populous than southern Palestine, and is extensively cultivated, though at this time of year the crops had all been gathered, and the land was as bare as a village common. Partly, no doubt, for purposes of defence, and partly to avoid wasting the fertile plain land, most of the villages are built on the tops of the hills, where the rock, outcropping over large areas, renders the land unsuitable for cultivation. Many of these villages are surrounded by trees and small enclosed gardens, and some are encircled by stout mud walls. All of them command the surrounding country for a wide space, and, with their walls and cactus hedges, form admirable strong points, very difficult to reduce without the aid of heavy artillery. The village of El Mughar, on its high and rocky ridge, is one of the most prominent of these hill strongholds, and forms a notable landmark from the flat country to the west and south of it.

The 8th Mounted Brigade, leading the Yeomanry Division, approached Yebnah about eight in the morning, and two troops were sent forward to gallop into the village from either side. This was the usual method adopted by our cavalry, when approaching villages during a rapid advance, unless they were definitely known to be strongly held by the enemy. If there proved to be few Turks in the village, or none at all, these troops would signal back to their regiment or brigade to advance. If, however, the village proved to be strongly held, the few men in the exploring troops, moving in extended order and at a very fast pace, seldom sustained many casualties, while they nearly always succeeded in gaining a fairly accurate idea of the numbers of the enemy, the location of his machine guns, etc.

In the present case Yebnah was found very lightly held, and the 8th Brigade at once pushed through it, and advanced to the attack of the villages of Zernuka and Kubeibe, on which rested the extreme right flank of the enemy's line. The Turks were found in force in these two places, and the brigade was unable to make any substantial progress, in the face of very heavy machine-gun fire.

The 6th Mounted Brigade remained in divisional reserve at Yebnah, and the 22nd was ordered to try and push between Zernuka and El Mughar, and seize the village of Akir, behind the enemy's line. Intense machine-gun fire from Zernuka, however, on the flank of the line of advance, prohibited the brigade from moving forward till this place had been taken.

A brigade of the 52nd Division attacked the village of Katrah from the south about nine o'clock, and captured it by a fine bayonet charge, taking 600 prisoners and a large number of machine guns. The brigade then advanced on El Mughar, and succeeded in reaching the Wadi Jamus, about half a mile farther north. From the wadi to El Mughar the ground sloped gently upwards, devoid of any cover, and traversed by no depression capable of concealing troops. The infantry extended along the wadi, and attempted to advance up the slope towards El Mughar, but were checked by a tremendous fire from machine guns and riflemen concealed in the gardens of the village, and from field guns in action farther north. It was soon apparent that they could not hope to cross the wide stretch of open ground, and they were withdrawn into the shelter of the wadi. The 52nd Division then sent a message to the Yeomanry, asking the latter to co-operate by attacking El Mughar from the east.

General Barrow ordered the 6th Mounted Brigade, which was now extended from Yebnah to El Gheyadah, about a mile north of Beshshit, to carry out the attack.

From his position at El Gheyadah, General Godwin had observed that the infantry advance on El Mughar had been held up, and was anticipating an order to co-operate with his brigade. He had accordingly already got one of his regiments, the Bucks Yeomanry, into the Wadi Jamus, at a point about a mile south-east of Yebnah, and had sent officers' patrols forward to reconnoitre a line of approach. The reports of these patrols confirmed the General's own impression that the enemy position could only be reached by a mounted charge. The country west of El Mughar was just as bare and open as that to the south, over which our infantry had found themselves unable to advance. On the other hand, the absence of obstacles favoured a galloping attack, and, though the distance to be traversed in the open (over two miles) was considerable, there appeared to be a good prospect of the enterprise succeeding, provided it was adequately supported by the R.H.A. and machine gunners.

Having decided on a mounted attack, General Godwin brought up the Dorset Yeomanry, and galloped them across the open in small parties, into the shelter of the Wadi Jamus. This regiment was directed on the left, or northern, end of the enemy position, and the Bucks on a portion of the ridge to the right of the Dorsets' objective, and immediately north of the village itself. The Berks Yeomanry was held in reserve, west of the wadi and near the south end of Yebnah. The Berks Battery R.H.A., which was at Beshshit, and the Machine Gun Squadron were ordered to provide covering fire from the south.

Diagram illustrating the action of El Mughar

The 8th Mounted Brigade, which was attacking Zernuka, would afford protection to the left flank of the 6th during the action.

The Berks Battery was soon in action among some trees north of El Beshshit, registering the village of El Mughar, and the ridge to the north of it. The machine gunners, taking advantage of some broken ground south-east of Yebnah, got into the Wadi Shellal el Ghor, and worked their way along it to a position about 1000 yards south-west of El Mughar village.

As soon as the steady bursts of fire from the wadi apprised General Godwin that his machine guns were in action, he gave the order to advance, and the two regiments scrambled up the steep sides of the Wadi Jamus into the open, and trotted forward over the plain in extended order, the squadrons of each regiment following one another at a distance of about 200 yards. Two machine guns on pack horses accompanied each regiment, moving on the outer flanks.

The appearance of the cavalry was the signal for a tremendous fire on both sides. Every weapon the enemy had in action was turned on the advancing lines of cavalry, while the Berks Battery and the 6th Brigade Machine Gun Squadron poured an intense fire on the ridge of Mughar, sweeping it from end to end.

The regiments trotted quietly across the open till they were some half a mile from the enemy position, when they shook out into a fast canter, and swung up the rocky slope at the Turks. A hundred yards from the top the order to charge was given, and the men sat down and rode.

The leading squadron of the Bucks went through the Turks with the sword in ten seconds, killing many of them, and galloped right over the ridge before they could pull up. Ere the enemy troops had time to rally, the second and third squadrons dashed into them, completing the rout. In a few minutes from the time when the order to charge was given, the Bucks Yeomanry had secured their objective, and commenced to consolidate on the position.

The Dorset Yeomanry, on the left, encountered more broken ground, and the leading squadron dismounted and attacked with the bayonet. The other two squadrons, however, stuck to their horses, and reached the top first. There was not much momentum left in the charge by the time the cavalry met the enemy, but the long swords do not need much pace behind them to do their work properly, and the issue of the fight was never in doubt. Before the dismounted squadron had gained the summit of the ridge, the other two had cleared the position, and the surviving Turks were in flight or had surrendered. Incidentally it may be remarked that the squadron on foot lost more heavily, both in men and horses, than the two that had gone in with the sword.

While the position was being cleared and consolidated, a number of the enemy in the village opened fire on our troops with machine guns, inflicting some loss, and interfering with the work. Two squadrons of the Berks were sent up at a gallop, and fought their way into the village on foot, clearing the Turks out of it, and taking about 400 prisoners.

About 600 enemy dead were counted on the position afterwards, and many more were killed, as they were trying to escape, by the fire of the machine guns which had accompanied each regiment in the charge. 'In addition to those taken in Mughar village, 1100 prisoners fell into our hands, with three guns and a large number of machine guns. The enemy's right was completely broken. His troops evacuated Kubeibe and Zernuka after dark, and fell back in considerable confusion.

Our casualties in the two regiments were 129 officers and men and 265 horses killed and wounded, not an unduly heavy bill when compared to the number of enemy dead, and, still more, to the great results obtained.

The 22nd Mounted Brigade rode forward to attack Akir, as soon as Mughar had been taken, but was held up till nightfall by unexpectedly strong enemy opposition. The Brigade rounded up seventy prisoners and a few machine guns retiring from El Mughar, and occupied Akir next morning, the enemy having retired during the night.

Meanwhile, in the centre, the 75th Division had captured Mesmiye with the bayonet, taking 200 prisoners, and reached a point on the Deir Sineid line about two miles west of Junction Station in the evening. The Turks attacked in considerable force during the night, but were driven off, and the division entered Junction Station early next morning.

The Australian Mounted Division advanced a few miles, covering the right flank of the 75th Division, and seized Tel el Turmus without encountering serious opposition. During the day the headquarters of this division, at the village of El Jeladiyeh, three miles east of El Suafir el Sharkiye, got into touch by helio with the 53rd Division twenty miles away to the east, and exchanged news. This was the first and last communication between the two parts of our force, from the day of the battle of Sharia, till the 7th of December, when the 10th A.L.H. Regiment gained touch with the 53rd Division in the hills ten miles south of Jerusalem, two days before the city fell.

Next day, as soon as it was light enough to see, our line was on the move in pursuit of the enemy.

Early in the morning a couple of armoured cars, sent forward to reconnoitre, entered Junction Station, and drove suddenly into a crowd of some 400 Turks employed in setting fire to the buildings, and doing a little private looting on their own account. The commander of the leading car summoned these men to surrender, and was answered by a scattering volley from their rifles. Whereupon he shut the armoured doors of his car, and charged down upon them, with his machine gun going full blast. The discomfited Turks turned and fled, pursued for two miles by the cars. Over 200 of them were killed or wounded; the remainder escaped into the hills.

The 75th Division entered Junction Station shortly afterwards, and collected 100 prisoners, a number of guns, and a quantity of rolling stock.

The Australian Mounted Division pushed on to the north-east, the 4th Brigade seizing El Tine Station, on the Beersheba line, early in the morning, where large quantities of ammunition and stores were found intact. Continuing their move, units of the division penetrated through the enemy front, which was now broken at Junction Station, and reached the railway two miles east of the station.

The Yeomanry Division, moving in advance of the 52nd, pushed through Akir to Naane. The two brigades which occupied the latter place were heavily shelled by the enemy from about Abu Shusheh, some three miles farther east, but no other opposition was met with.

The rapidity with which the Mughar-Kutrah line

had been captured on the previous day had resulted in the Turkish army being again broken into two separate parts. The thrust of the Yeomanry to Naane had now driven a wedge between these two parts, and the operations of the next two days were directed towards widening the gap. The larger portion of the enemy force entered the hills to the east, and commenced to retire along the main road towards Jerusalem, shepherded by the Yeomanry and Australian Mounted Divisions. The smaller portion retired northwards over the plain, followed by the Anzac Division. The 1st A.L.H. and New Zealand Brigades made good Kubeibe and Zernuka early in the morning, and then advanced on Ramleh and Khurbet Surafend respectively, with the Camel Corps Brigade patrolling the sand dune country on their left. The New Zealanders encountered a force of Turks on the high hill of Ayun Kara (Richon-le-Zion) about two in the afternoon, and drove them off without much difficulty. Half an hour later the Turks emerged from the shelter of the large fruit orchards and vineyards which surround Ayun Kara, and launched an unexpected counter-attack on the New Zealand Brigade. They were well supplied with bombs, and pushed their attack fiercely right up to our line. The New Zealanders then went in with the bayonet, and drove them back to the bottom of the hill, inflicting heavy losses on them. Two squadrons from the 1st Brigade and a company of the Camel Corps reinforced the New Zealand Brigade, which had suffered somewhat severely, but the enemy had had enough, and made no further attack. This was the only serious fighting of the day.

The two brigades held an outpost line for the night from the sea coast, through Ayun Kara to Khurbet Deiran, in touch with the Yeomanry on their right.

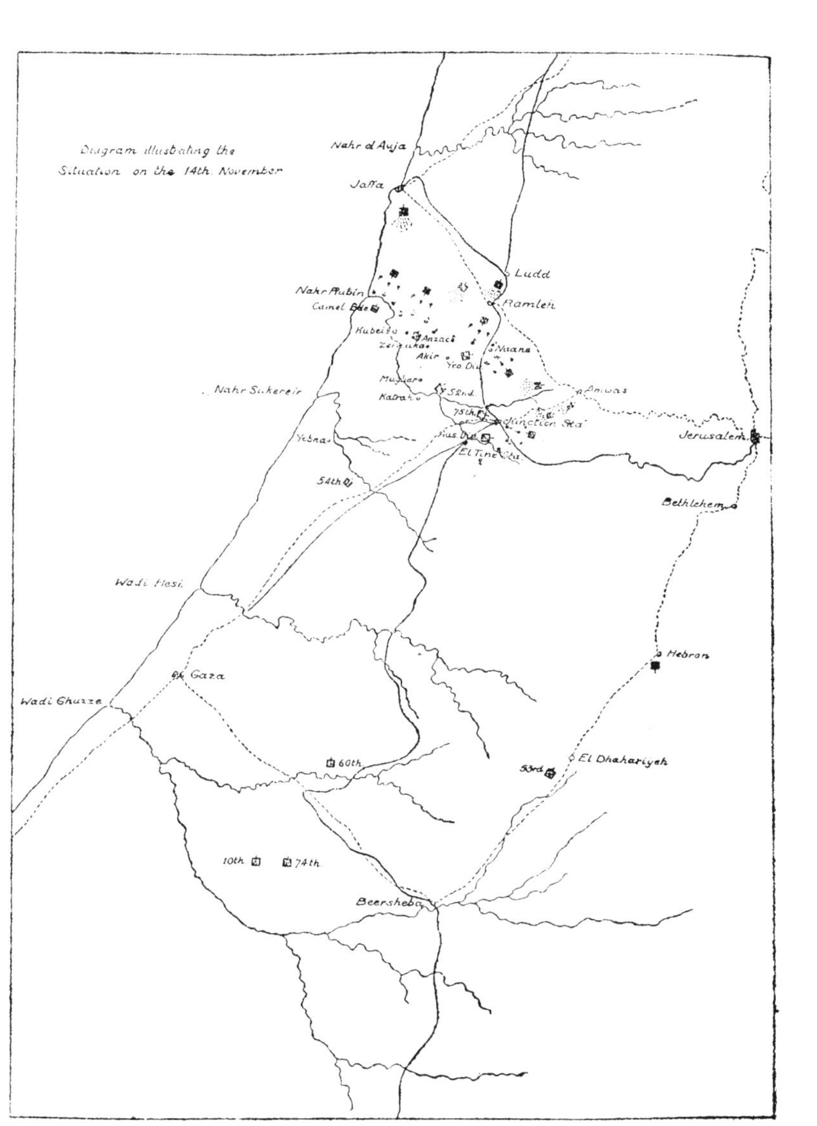

Diagram illustrating the
Situation on the 14th November
Nahr el Auja
Jaffa
Ludd
Nahr Rubin
Ramleh
Camel Bde
Kubeibe
Anzac
Zernukah
Naane
Akir
Yeo Div
Mughar
Nahr Sukereir
Amwas
Katrah
52nd
75th
Junction Sta
Yebna
Bus Div
Jerusalem
El Tine Sta
54th
Bethlehem
Wadi Hesi
Hebron
Gaza
Wadi Ghuzze
60th
El Dhahariyeh
53rd
10th
74th
Beersheba

The Camel Corps Brigade occupied a support line a short distance farther south. The Yeomanry Division remained in occupation of Akir and Naane, watching the northern exits from the latter place, with the 52nd Division lying behind it about El Mughar. The 75th Division had a brigade in Junction Station, and the remainder of the division at Mesmiye, while the Australian Mounted Division held an outpost line in observation of the country to the south-east.

On the 15th the Anzac Mounted Division, moving northwards over the plain, occupied Ramleh without opposition, taking about 350 prisoners, and on the following day the New Zealand Mounted Brigade entered Jaffa, where it was received with acclamation by the populace. On the 17th the division had reached the Nahr el Auja, near its mouth, without having yet succeeded in bringing the enemy to action. Favoured by the hard ground on the plain, and assisted to some extent by the railway along which they were retreating, the Turks made the best use of the nights during this period, and never stopped till they had put the wide and deep channel of the river Auja between themselves and our troops. They were now located, entrenched along the north bank of the river, from near the sea to about Khurbet Hadrah. The Anzac Division received orders to halt opposite this line, and remain in observation of the enemy, pending the arrival of reinforcements, while the more important task of the advance on Jerusalem was taken in hand.

Meanwhile the Yeomanry division was engaged driving the right half of the enemy army into the hills. The road from Jerusalem to Jaffa runs through a deep and narrow valley in the mountains, which has its outlet at Amwas, near Latron. Here the valley opens out into the Vale of Ajalon, which slopes gently down to the level of the coastal plain. Running north and south across the western end of the Vale, a bold ridge stands up sharply from the plain, between the villages of Sidun and Abu Shusheh. The northern end of this ridge terminates at Abu Shusheh, and the southern end at the hill of Tel Jezer, the ancient Gezer, round which so many battles have been fought in the past.

The enemy had posted a strong rearguard on the northern end of the ridge, to cover the retreat of his main body up the Jerusalem road. The Yeomanry Division was ordered to dislodge this rearguard, and then clear up the foothill country from Amwas, at the eastern end of the Vale of Ajalon, to Ramleh.

The enemy's position was one of great natural strength, and was held by a force of about 4000 Turks, well supplied with machine guns and artillery. The greater part of this force was distributed in, and on each side of, the village of Abu Shusheh, but a considerable body of Turks with machine guns was stationed some distance farther south, evidently in order to outflank any attack on the village from the west. The country on that side of the position was of an undulating nature, and afforded some cover to troops advancing over it. The ridge itself rose abruptly from this undulating country, a forbidding-looking mass of boulders and scrub. In places the solid rock outcropped from the hill over large areas, and there were a number of caves among the rocks, in many of which the Turks had posted machine guns.

General Barrow directed the 22nd Mounted Brigade and the Camel Corps to attack the hill on the north-west and north respectively, and the 6th Mounted Brigade from the south-west. At seven o'clock the two former brigades were in action, advancing dismounted. In view of the open nature of the country on the west side of the ridge, and the distance to be covered, General Godwin, who had been reconnoitring the position with his regimental commanders since dawn, decided to repeat his tactics of the 13th. Had he been able to obtain a nearer view of the appalling country over which he was launching his squadrons, it is possible that he might have decided to make at least the final assault on foot, in which case we should have lost a classic example of the capabilities of cavalry when well led.

Having made up his mind to attack mounted, he sent half of the brigade machine guns, covered by a squadron of the Berks Yeomanry, to push forward dismounted, taking advantage of what cover the ground afforded, to a point west of Abu Shusheh, and as close in as possible, from which to engage the enemy machine guns on the ridge. The Berks Battery R.H.A., from a position some 3500 yards south-west of the village, assisted in this task. The Bucks Yeomanry were ordered to charge the enemy at Abu Shusheh, while the remainder of the Berks charged on the left, against a spur running out to the west of the ridge, just north of the village. The Dorset Yeomanry were held in reserve on the right, to protect that flank. The attack of the 22nd Brigade protected the left flank.

As soon as the battery and the machine guns were in action, Colonel Cripps led the Bucks Yeomanry out into the open, in column of squadrons in line of troop columns, and cantered forward towards the village, under a fairly heavy, but ill-directed, fire. As they neared the position, the Yeomanry came under severe enfilade fire from the group of enemy machine guns on the southern portion of the ridge. Leading his regiment at a gallop into the shelter of some dead ground, Colonel Cripps halted them and signalled back for support. The Dorset Yeomanry were at once sent off to make a turning movement to the south, and take the hostile machine guns in rear. Some of the guns of the Berks Battery were also turned on to this party of the enemy.

The appearance of the Dorsets engaged the attention of the Turkish machine gunners, and the Bucks Yeomanry, taking advantage of the respite, emerged from concealment, and raced at the position.

Their appearance was met by an outburst of hysterical fire from Abu Shusheh, through which they passed almost unscathed, and reached the foot of the ridge. Then, catching their horses short by the head, they put them at the slope. Slipping and sliding, scrambling like cats among the rocks, they galloped up, and went over the Turks with a cheer.

The two squadrons of the Berks galloped up on the left at the same moment, and completed the work. Once our cavalry were in the position the enemy made but a poor fight.

Meanwhile the Dorsets took advantage of the confusion caused in the enemy ranks to charge the machine guns farther south. The charge got well home, and most of the Turks were sabred; the rest surrendered.

While the three regiments were clearing the ridge of isolated parties of the enemy who still showed fight, a force of Turks appeared from among the rocks farther south, and attempted a counter-attack against the right of our troops. The Berks Battery, however, was on the watch, and at once opened a rapid and accurate fire on these Turks, driving them back with heavy losses, and breaking up the counter-attack. By nine o'clock the whole of this strong position was in our hands, with 360 prisoners, and all the enemy machine guns. About 400 Turks were killed with the sword alone, and many more were found dead on the position, as a result of our gun and machine-gun fire.

Our own losses were extraordinarily light, only thirty-seven of all ranks killed and wounded. The Berks Battery and the Machine Gun Squadron, by their effective covering fire, had helped materially to keep down our casualties; but the chief credit for this desirable result must be given to the Turks themselves, whose shooting during the attack was exceedingly bad, and appeared to be completely out of control. It is probable that among the garrison were many who had spoken with survivors from El Mughar, and we may be sure that the story of that charge had lost nothing in the telling, and probably contributed largely to the ' nerves ' of the Turks. The action earned a generous tribute from the Commander-in-Chief, who described it in his despatch as a brilliant piece of cavalry work.

The 22nd Brigade pursued the enemy towards Amwas, rounding up a few prisoners, but the majority of the Turks escaped over the rocky, inaccessible country to the east, where our cavalry had little chance of catching them.

CHAPTER VIII

AN ENTR'ACTE

THE enemy had now been driven into a tract of difficult mountain country, very favourable for defensive tactics, and most unsuited for cavalry. Reinforcements of men and guns were being hurried southwards from Aleppo to his aid; some had already arrived. In order to drive the eastern group of his forces through the mountains, and at the same time hold the northern group on the plain, more infantry would be required.

The Royal Navy was reorganising the sea-borne supply line, but the landing of stores, which had to be carried out in surf boats, depended on a continuance of fine weather, and the 20th Corps could not, therefore, be brought up with safety until our railway had been pushed considerably farther north. Relays of Sappers had been working on the line day and night since the fall of Gaza, and the railhead was moving forward at a pace that beat all previous records for railway construction in any part of the world. Even under the most favourable conditions, however, it would take at least a fortnight to reach a point from which it would be possible to supply our troops in the mountains.

The 54th Division, 21st Corps, was already under orders to march from Gaza, but, before it could start, its transport, which had been lent to the 52nd and 75th Divisions, had to be returned, and this necessitated a complete rearrangement of transport in the Corps.

Moreover, the operations had now continued for seventeen days practically without cessation, and a rest was absolutely necessary, especially for the horses. The cavalry divisions had covered nearly 170 miles since the 29th of October, and their horses had been watered, on an average, only once in every thirty-six hours during that time. The heat, too, had been intense, and the short ration, $9\frac{1}{2}$ lbs. of grain per day, without any bulk food, had weakened them greatly. Indeed the hardships endured by some of the horses were almost incredible. One of the batteries of the Australian Mounted Division had only been able to water its horses three times in the past nine days, the actual intervals between waterings being 68, 72, and 76 hours respectively. Yet this battery, on its arrival at Junction Station, had only lost eight horses from exhaustion, not counting those killed in action or evacuated wounded.

As an indication of the reduction in the fighting strength of the cavalry, due to casualties and sickness among men and horses, it may be mentioned that the G.O.C. of the 5th Mounted Brigade reported on the 16th of November that he had, in his three regiments, only 690 men mounted and fit for duty. It is true that this brigade had suffered more severely than most of the others in the Corps, but all were much under strength in men and horses, and in urgent need of a rest.

The majority of the horses in the Corps were Walers, and there is no doubt that these hardy Australian horses make the finest cavalry mounts in the world. For many years past the Australians have been buying up the well-bred failures on the English Turf, and buying them cheap ; not for racing purposes, but to breed saddle horses for up-country stations. As a result of this policy, they have now got types of compact, well built, saddle and harness horses that no other part of the world can show. Rather on the light side, according to our ideas, but hard as nails, and with beautifully clean legs and feet, their record in this war places them far above the cavalry horses of any other nation. The Australians themselves can never understand our partiality for the half-bred, weight-carrying hunter, which looks to them like a cart horse. Their contention has always been that good blood will carry more weight than big bone, and the experience of this war has converted the writer, for one, entirely to their point of view. It must be remembered that the Australian countrymen are bigger, heavier men than their English brothers. They formed just half the Corps, and it is probable that they averaged not far short of twelve stone each stripped. To this weight must be added another nine and a half stone, for saddle, ammunition, sword, rifle, clothes and accoutrements, so that each horse carried a weight of over twenty-one stone, all day and every day for seventeen days, on less than half the normal ration of forage, and with only one drink in every thirty-six hours !

The weight-carrying English hunter had to be nursed back to fitness after these operations, over a long period, while the little Australian horses, without any special care other than good food and plenty of water, were soon fit to go through another campaign as arduous as the last one.

Junction Station was the first place where we found unlimited, and accessible, water. Owing to the vigorous action of the armoured cars, the Turks had not had time to destroy the steam pumping plant there, and our engineers soon had rows of drinking troughs erected, and a steady stream of sweet clear water flowing into them. It was good to see the horses burying their heads in the water, and drinking their fill at last. The Anzac Mounted Division, about the same time, found excellent water and a steam pump at the big Zionist wine press at Richon-le-Zion.

Everything about Junction Station spoke of the methodical German. Solidly built, stone storehouses and locomotive sheds, well-found machine shops, orderly stacks of priceless timber, pyramids of drums of oil and petrol; everything in its place, and a place for everything. Neat finger-posts and notice-boards directed the stranger where to go, and where not to go, and a host of the inevitable ' Verboten ' signs bristled on every side. It was noticeable that these last were the only ones that were written in Turkish as well as German, except the name of the station, which the Germans called Wadi Surar. We found in the station two locomotives and a number of railway wagons, which were of great value to us during the ensuing few weeks, till our own railway reached Ludd.

The heavy échelons of the cavalry ammunition columns, which had last been seen at Sharia on the 7th November, advancing boldly on the enemy, turned up at Junction Station on the 19th. They had been completely lost during the intervening twelve days, and had wandered about, neglected and forlorn, in the wake of the cavalry. During all this time they had received no rations, and had been maintained entirely by the predatory genius of the gunner subaltern in command. As this officer has now returned to civilian life, and is a respected, and it is to be hoped respectable, member of society, it is, perhaps, kinder to draw a veil over his methods.

Suffice it to say that he brought his command of 600 horses and men into the Station, all fit and well, and no questions were asked. And if, sometimes, a battalion waited in vain for its rations ; if, now and then, a harried supply officer found that one of his camel convoys had delivered its supplies during the night to some unknown unit, owing to a mistake ; if guards on ration dumps are notoriously vulnerable to cigarettes and soft words, one can only reflect that war is a sad, stern business, in which ' dog eats dog ' when opportunity arises.

On the same day another wanderer returned, whose Odyssey was even more remarkable. When the headquarters of the Australian Mounted Division had been at Khurbet Jeladiyeh on the 13th, the divisional interpreter, a Greek named Theodore, had overheard certain remarks made by a man in the village, who was dressed as a native. The man was arrested, and proved to be a Turkish spy. Terrified at finding himself discovered, the miserable wretch begged for his life, and promised, if he was spared, to put us on the track of the man who, he said, was the head of the native spy organisation of the Turkish Army. He was told to say what he knew, and we would consider whether his information was worth his life. He then gave particulars of the man, who, it appeared, was *his own father*, and said that he believed him to be at Beit Jibrin.

Accordingly the A.P.M. of the division set off next day with two cars of a light car patrol [1] and the interpreter, to try and surprise the arch spy at Beit Jibrin. The party arrived at the village about nine o'clock in the morning, to find the bird flown. On making inquiries, they learnt that he had gone on—to quote the report of the A.P.M.—' to a place

---

[1] Unarmoured Ford vans carrying a machine gun each.

called Ram Allah Rakhman, which we took to be somewhere near Bethlehem, but subsequently discovered to be the same place!' The enemy's right group was at this time in the neighbourhood of Hebron, and his left group was west of Junction Station, so that Bethlehem was a good fifteen miles behind his line. But this trifling fact did not in any way deter the pursuers. What could the Turkish Army do against two Ford cars *and* two machine guns? They blithely took the track to Bethlehem.

Shortly afterwards they came suddenly upon a patrol of six Turkish cavalrymen. 'We opened fire at once,' so runs the A.P.M.'s report, 'and killed the men and five of the horses. The sixth horse unluckily escaped, but we came up with it later on and destroyed it, thus leaving no trace of the enemy patrol!' A few miles farther on, they encountered another, and larger, body of enemy cavalry. 'This time,' says the report, 'there were about thirty of them, but, as we came upon them unawares, we had no difficulty in driving them off, after killing a good few, and we then proceeded on our way.'

Late in the afternoon the cars drove into Bethlehem, where our men were received with transports of joy by the inhabitants, nearly all of whom are Christians. The poor people crowded round their deliverers to kiss their hands, shouting and weeping, and pressing offerings of food on them, much to their embarrassment.

As it was getting late, and they found that their quarry had again moved on, the hunters consented to stay and eat with some of the notables of the town, after which they got under way again, and drove a short distance along the Beersheba road, to a place where they could hide the cars for the night.

At dawn next morning they resumed their journey, and motored *right through the enemy force*, at Hebron, without being detected. Fortunately the Turks had no post actually on the road, and it is probable that a couple of cars coming from behind their lines attracted little attention. The party drove quietly on to Beersheba, where they found a canteen, and, having loaded up with stores, returned in triumph to Junction Station.

In the meantime Corps Headquarters had become seriously alarmed at their long absence, and had despatched another patrol of two cars to try and find them. These cars got to Beit Jibrin, where they found, and captured, the spy who was the cause of all the trouble, and who had doubled back on his tracks from Bethlehem. Then, hearing that the cars had started off with the intention of going to Bethlehem, they gave them up for lost, and returned to headquarters to report.

Meanwhile an aeroplane, that had also been sent to look for the first patrol, came upon the second one returning from Beit Jibrin, and at once flew back to Corps Headquarters and reported that the lost sheep were found, and were on their way back. The second patrol came in a few hours afterwards, and reported that there were no signs of the missing cars, which must have been captured by the enemy.

By now the Corps was thoroughly puzzled, and not a little angry. The result was that, when the blushing Ulysses did finally arrive, instead of receiving a ' few kind words of praise ' for carrying out an exceedingly daring reconnaissance, he got an unmerciful dressing down for giving headquarters such a fright !

On the 18th of November the populations of the enemy countries received their first intimation that all was not well in the East. Up till this date the Turkish papers, after chronicling each day the many victories won in the past twenty-four hours in France and Russia, had added gravely, ' On the Palestine front there is no change ! ' At last the Germans came to the conclusion that this bluff might possibly be carried too far, so they caused to be printed in their own papers what purported to be an official Turkish *communiqué,* though none of the Turkish papers received it till after it had been published in Berlin. This precious document stated that in Palestine ' there had been a retirement *according to plan.'* It might have been added that the plan included leaving 12,000 prisoners and more than 100 guns in the hands of the enemy !

CHAPTER IX

MOUNTAIN WARFARE

THE advance was resumed on the 18th of November. During the preceding two days there had been no movement of importance on the part of our forces. The 22nd Mounted Brigade had located the Turkish rearguard at Amwas on the 16th, and had then cleared the foothill country as far as Ramleh, without meeting any more of the enemy. On the same day the 8th Mounted Brigade had entered Ludd without opposition, rounding up a few prisoners there. The Anzac Division remained in observation of the northern group of the Turkish forces, along the Nahr el Auja, and the Australian Mounted Division moved close to Amwas, in preparation for the advance up the Jerusalem road.

In order to avoid fighting in or near the Holy Places, the Commander-in-Chief determined to try and isolate Jerusalem completely. In order to do this it was necessary to gain possession of the only road which traverses the Judæan Range from north to south, between Nablus and Jerusalem.

The Yeomanry Division was accordingly directed to move by the old Roman road from Ludd, through Berfilya and Beit Ur el Tahta, to Bire, pushing through the mountains as quickly as possible. The two available infantry divisions were to advance up the Jerusalem road, preceded by two brigades of the Australian Mounted Division, to about Kuryet el Enab, whence they were to strike north-eastwards towards the Nablus road. The 5th Mounted Brigade, moving up the Wadi Surar, would protect the right flank of the infantry during their advance. Finally the 53rd Division, now about Hebron, was to press on from that place, and secure the Jericho road, east of Jerusalem.

The city would thus be cut off from all sources of reinforcement and supply, and, it was hoped, would capitulate without further bloodshed.

On the morning of the 18th the Australian Mounted Division found a force of the enemy entrenched on the hill of Amwas, which stands square in the middle of the pass, just where it debouches into the Vale of Ajalon. The artillery of the division, assisted by some of the guns of the 75th Division, opened a vigorous fire on the enemy on Amwas Hill, to which the Turks made but a feeble reply, while the 3rd A.L.H. Brigade endeavoured to pass through the hills to the north, round the enemy's right flank.

All day the regiments struggled on among the rocks, scrambling up and down the steep hills, and making very slow progress. By four o'clock in the afternoon they had advanced barely five miles, and the order was then given to return, and leave the task to the infantry the next day. The threat to their flank had, however, been enough for the Turks, who retired during the night, abandoning four guns, the teams of which had been killed by the fire of the R.H.A.

There had been no fighting to speak of, but the action was of great interest from the associations of the place. From its position in the mouth of the valley, Amwas is, and always has been, the key of the pass to Jerusalem. Who holds this hill holds the city. From the earliest ages, all the armies that have sought to take Jerusalem have passed this way, save only that of Joshua. Philistine and Hittite, Babylonian and Assyrian, Egyptian and Roman and Greek, Frankish Knights of the Cross, all have passed this way, and all have watered the hill of Amwas with their blood.

The Australian Mounted Division handed over the further advance to the 75th Division next day, and withdrew to the mouth of the Nahr Sukereir, to get grazing for its horses. Two days later the division marched back to El Mejdel, in order to relieve the supply situation. Our broad-gauge railway had now nearly reached this place, and it was possible to draw supplies direct from railhead with the divisional train.

The 8th and 22nd Brigades of the Yeomanry Division plunged into the hills on the morning of the 18th, and soon found themselves in difficulties. In this mountain country, in which there were no wheeled vehicles, and all goods were carried on the backs of donkeys, what was known to the natives as a good road was usually little more than a goat track, winding in and out among the boulders. As far as Beit Sira there was some semblance of a road, though, even on this portion of it, the gunners were at work all day removing the biggest of the boulders from the path, before their guns could pass. Beyond Beit Sira the road was nothing but the merest footpath, leading straight down and up the numerous deep and narrow ravines that intersect the country in all directions. Sometimes it required half an hour's reconnaissance to move forward half a mile.

Under such conditions, the 8th Brigade accomplished a remarkable feat in penetrating nearly as far as Beit Ur el Tahta by nightfall. The 22nd Brigade reached Shilta the same evening, but had to send back all its guns and transport, owing to the difficulties of the country. The 6th Brigade, starting on the following morning, reached Beit Ur el Tahta about two in the afternoon.

Cavalry, as such, were really unable to operate in this country. They were confined to the roads, or the tracks that did duty as roads, and, even on these, they could often move only in single file. Consequently they were exceedingly vulnerable, and their inability to make effective use of flank guards, or even to deploy quickly when attacked, increased the dangers to which they were exposed. Horses were little more than an encumbrance, reducing the number of men available for dismounted fighting, largely increasing the amount of transport required, and adding but little to the mobility of the troops.

In the present case, however, there were several reasons for attempting to push the Yeomanry through the hills. In the first place it was known that the enemy forces had been broken into two widely separated groups, and there was thus little danger of any attack from the north, for the next few days at any rate. Moreover there was a saving of time in employing the Yeomanry instead of the 52nd Division, as the latter was a day's march farther west when the plan of advance was decided upon. Finally, native reports of the hill country had led to the belief that it was of a much easier nature than proved to be the case.

The winter rains broke with a heavy downpour on the 19th, and this added to the difficulties of the cavalry, turning the valley bottoms into a sea of viscid, black mud, and the beds of the ravines into rushing torrents. The sudden drop in temperature which accompanied the rain was a severe trial to our troops, who were dressed in light, khaki-drill clothing, and had no blankets, greatcoats, or tents.

During the morning of the 19th of November the 8th and 22nd Brigades struggled through the rain and mud along the Wadi el Sunt, towards Beitunia and Ain Arik respectively, but about mid-day they encountered a force of Turks which had come down the main road from Nablus to Bire, and then marched westwards to oppose the Yeomanry advance. Unable to make headway against the difficulties of the country and the opposition of the enemy, who was in considerable force, the brigades held their position, and awaited the arrival of the 6th Brigade.

On the 20th the division made another effort to get on, the 6th Brigade moving to the assistance of the 8th. All wheels, including the guns, had to be sent back to Ramleh, as they were unable to move, and water for horses was scarce, despite the rain. Strong, organised resistance was now encountered at Beitunia, and prisoners captured from the enemy in the course of the fighting proved to be men from fresh, well-trained units from Aleppo, part of the Yilderim force. Little headway was made during the day. Rain came on again in the night, and no supplies were able to reach the division.

Next day the Yeomanry made a final attempt to storm the high ridge of Beitunia, which had held up their advance for two days. The 6th and 8th Brigades attacked the ridge itself from the west, while the 22nd Brigade, operating farther north towards Ram Allah, tried to turn the enemy's right flank. The attacking brigades got to within a few hundred yards of Beitunia village, on the top of the ridge, when they encountered a fresh enemy force, that outnumbered them by three to one. The Turks had a number of field and mountain guns, that had come from the north along the metalled road, while our troops had only one mountain battery. The Yeomanry made several desperate attempts to force their way up the steep, rocky sides of the ridge, but were unable to reach the top. Early in the afternoon, more enemy reinforcements arrived from the north, and counter-attacked strongly, forcing our troops back into the deep ravine on the west side of the ridge. The situation soon became serious, and orders were given for all three brigades to break off the action and retire to Beit Ur el Foka. The withdrawal began after dark, and was carried out successfully.

It is almost impossible to exaggerate the difficulties of the cavalry. The country was a maze of high, rocky ridges, running in all directions, and separated by deep and narrow ravines, the sides of which were almost precipitous, and the bottoms muddy morasses. The ground was covered with a mass of boulders, among which grew sparse patches of coarse scrub. Mounted work was, of course, out of the question in such country, and all the horses had to be kept far back from the fighting line. A quarter of the whole force was thus occupied in holding the horses, and, as the division had already been considerably weakened by the fighting of the past three weeks, the actual number of rifles available for the advance was hopelessly inadequate. It was clear that the attempt of the division to reach the main road had been definitely checked, and the only thing to be done was to try and hold on to the positions already gained till reinforcements could arrive. Men and horses were short of food, owing to the great difficulty of getting up supplies in these roadless mountains during the rains.

While the Yeomanry Division was slowly fighting to a standstill in the north, the 75th Division, advancing along the main road towards Jerusalem, and the 52nd Division on the track north of this road, through Beit Likia, pressed slowly forward, against strong resistance from the enemy, to Kustul and Beit Dukka respectively. The latter division sent a brigade to the north on the night of the 21st, and seized the high hill of Nebi Samwil, the traditional tomb of the Prophet Samuel. This hill dominates all the country to the east, even to Jerusalem itself, which can be seen from its summit. It was from here that the followers of Richard Cœur de Lion first looked upon Jerusalem in 1192, and pointed it out to the King. But Richard hid his face in his casque, lest he should see it, and prayed : ' Lord ! let me not set mine eyes upon Thy Holy City till I have rescued it from the Infidel.'

Recognising the importance of this hill in operations against Jerusalem, the Turks next day launched a series of determined attacks against it, but were unable to retake it. Day after day, till within a few days of the surrender of the city, the enemy attacked the hill, and the fiercest and most sustained fighting of the campaign took place round it. But in spite of all their efforts, it remained in our hands, and became, at last, the key that opened to us the gates of the Holy City.

The next four days were comparatively quiet on the mountain front. Both sides were too exhausted by the arduous fighting they had undergone, and by the cold and wet, to make much effort, and operations were confined to minor enterprises.

During this period the Yeomanry Division held a line, running north and south, along the heights just east of Beit Ur el Foka, and extending for about three miles. On the 23rd all horses had to be sent back to Ramleh, as it was impossible any longer to transport forage to them in the mountains. The following day the division made a demonstration along the whole front to assist the attack of the infantry against El Jib, where the Turks held a position barring our advance to the Nablus road. The enemy, however, was found in too great force for the attack to be pushed home, and, after being repulsed in three desperate assaults, our infantry had to abandon the attempt.

Meanwhile, on the plain, the Anzac Division had remained in observation of the enemy along the Auja, and had been engaged in active patrol work and reconnaissances for crossing places. Four possible places had been located ; a road bridge at Khurbet Hadrah, a ford about two miles farther east, another at Jerisheh, and a third at the mouth of the river. All these crossings were held by parties of the enemy. The average width of the river was thirty-five yards, and the depth five to seven feet. The banks were in most places steep, and the bottom was very muddy.

On the 24th the Division received orders to establish one or more bridgeheads north of the river, with the object of inducing the enemy to believe that we intended to make a farther advance along the coast. At least one of these bridgeheads was to be retained if possible.

General Chaytor decided to force the passage of the river by the ford at the mouth, where the bottom was sandy, covering the crossing by demonstrations at Hadrah and at the other two fords. The only troops available for the enterprise were the New Zealand Brigade and two battalions of infantry lent by the 54th Division,[1] a small enough force, in view of the known strength of the enemy. The rest of

---

[1] This division had arrived from Gaza on the 19th, and was holding a line from the right of the Anzac Division to the village of Shilta, about five miles west of the left of the Yeomanry Division.

Arrival of Marshal von Falkenhayn in Jerusalem in 1917.
(From an enemy photograph.)

9.45 inch Austrian Howitzer on the Nablus road.
(From an enemy photograph.)

the Anzac Division was, however, required to watch the enemy forces on the right, about Mulebbis, and in the foothills farther east.

The operations commenced shortly after mid-day, the infantry advancing with much noise and display on the bridge and upper fords, while the New Zealanders made for the ford at the mouth of the river. They crossed here without much difficulty, overpowering the small enemy post covering the ford, and then galloped along the north bank to Sheikh Muannis. An armoured car battery was now pushed up to the south bank of the Auja opposite Hadrah, and opened fire on the Turks holding the bridge there. At the same time the New Zealanders swept down on the flank from Muannis, and drove off the enemy. A battalion of infantry now crossed the river, and established a bridgehead on the north bank, with half the battalion at the bridge and half in the village of Muannis. During the night two squadrons of the New Zealand Brigade were posted on the high ground north of Hadrah and Sheikh Muannis, and a third covered the ford at the mouth of the river. Under cover of the darkness the divisional engineers threw a pontoon bridge across the river at Jerisheh, which was held by the other battalion of infantry.

Just after dawn next morning, the cavalry north of the river were heavily attacked by a large force of Turks, and driven back. The enemy followed up resolutely, and attacked the bridgehead at Hadrah. The squadron at the mouth of the river, reinforced by another regiment, was ordered to move against the Turkish right, while the remaining regiment of the brigade moved up to the south bank of the Auja at Hadrah. The Somerset Battery R.H.A., the only available artillery, came into action close by, the fire of the guns being directed by the battery commander from a house in Sheikh Muannis, across the river.

At half-past eight, the bridgehead at Hadrah was driven in, and the infantry fell back across the river. At the same time the two companies in Sheikh Muannis, which were moving to the support of the bridgehead, were heavily counter-attacked, and driven back to Jerisheh, where they crossed by the pontoon bridge, covered by the two squadrons of New Zealanders. The led horses of these squadrons were sent back to the ford at the mouth of the river at a gallop. They had to run the gauntlet of close-range rifle and machine-gun fire, but got through with comparatively few casualties, and crossed the river under cover of the squadron there, which then withdrew to the south bank.

The last man to leave Sheikh Muannis was the battery commander. He remained, coolly directing the fire of his guns, till the Turks were in the village, and then made a run for it, swimming the river under fire, and got safely away. His fine work had greatly assisted the retirement of our small force.

As soon as the last of our troops had been safely withdrawn, the Anzac Division fell back to a position on the high ground overlooking the south bank of the Auja, from Yahudieh, through Nebi Tari, to the sea, and hurriedly dug in, expecting an attack. The Turks, however, seemed to be content with having thrown our troops back across the river, and made no further move.

The operations had shown that the enemy was in such force that it would be impossible to maintain a bridgehead on the right bank, without holding the whole of the high ground two miles north of the river.

As sufficient troops were not available for this purpose, the line south of the Auja, which commanded all the crossing places, was entrenched and held by the Anzac Division, supported by a brigade of infantry, until the second, and successful, passage of the river four weeks later.

CHAPTER X

THE FALL OF JERUSALEM

On November the 27th the enemy renewed his activity in the hills. The Yeomanry Division was, at the time, reduced to about 800 rifles in the line, and was holding a position nearly four miles long with this imposing force. To add to the sense of security, there was a gap of about five miles between the left flank of the division and the nearest post of the 54th Division at Shilta. Moreover, the only line of communications was still by the Beit Sira-Berfilya - Ludd road, up which the division had marched on its first advance. This road, along which all ammunition and supplies had to come, ran parallel to, and only just behind, this gap in the line, and there seemed to be no particular reason why the enemy should not walk through the gap whenever he felt so inclined, and sit down on the road. The ' line ' consisted of a few posts, held by as many men as could be spared, and a number of small, roving patrols. One of these posts, consisting of three officers and sixty men, was in a small stone building on the top of a ridge near Zeitûn. It was attacked early in the afternoon of the 27th by a battalion of Turks with machine guns and artillery. The fight went on till dark, when the Turks drew off to nurse their wounds and get their breath for another attack. The commander of the garrison, now reduced to twenty-eight all ranks, sent an apologetic signal message to the 6th Brigade headquarters to ask if a few men could be spared to reinforce him. The house which his men had been holding had been destroyed by shell fire, and every part of the top of the hill was reeking with the fumes of high explosive shell. Two weak troops were sent to the assistance of the garrison, though it was realised that the provision of this reinforcement dangerously weakened the rest of the front !

Thus strengthened and encouraged, the garrison of the Zeitûn post successfully held out all night against repeated attacks. The Turks were again reinforced during the night, however, and next morning, as it was clear that the little garrison could not hope to hold out any longer, it was withdrawn. The enemy immediately occupied the Zeitûn ridge, the possession of which gave him command over our positions, and necessitated a withdrawal of our line. On the left flank the 22nd Brigade was thrown back, covering Beit Ur el Tahta, and the line then ran from that village, through Beit Ur el Foka, to about El Tire. The right flank of the division was in exiguous and intermittent touch with the 52nd Division. The left was entirely ' in the air.'

Throughout the day Turkish troops were moving to the north, and making their way westwards towards the gap in our line west of Beit Ur el Tahta. Large parties continually attacked the Yeomanry at different points, thus preventing the division from making any effective change of dispositions to meet the threatened envelopment.

The 7th Mounted Brigade, which was in Corps Reserve at Zernuka, and the Australian Mounted Division, resting at El Mejdel, were ordered up. Both made forced marches during the night of the 27th, and the former arrived at Beir Ur el Tahta at five in the morning of the 28th, just in time to help the 22nd Mounted Brigade to repulse a heavy attack from the north.

A brigade of the 52nd Division was sent to reinforce the exposed left flank of the Yeomanry Division, but, before it arrived there, a small party of Turks with some machine guns walked quietly through the gap between the Yeomanry Division and the 54th, and took up a position overlooking the Berfilya track.   Later in the morning, a section of the Yeomanry Divisional Ammunition Column, coming up the road from Ramleh with sorely needed ammunition for the division, was ambushed by the Turks and utterly destroyed.   A motor cyclist going down to Ramleh reached the scene immediately afterwards, and, seeing the wrecked wagons and the dead men and horses on the road, swung round his machine, and raced back again as fast as the track would allow.   The Turks opened fire with their machine guns, but failed to hit him, and he carried the news back to the division that the road was cut.   A detachment from the brigade of the 52nd, which had been sent up to cover this flank, pushed ahead, and drove off this party of Turks. The brigade then attacked the village of Suffa, which was full of enemy troops, in order to try and relieve the pressure on the left of the Yeomanry Division, but the Turks were found in too great strength to be dislodged.   Fortunately, however, they made no further attempt to penetrate through the gap, probably because they were really unaware of its existence.   Positions on both sides were exceedingly ill-defined, owing to the impossibility of digging trenches in the solid rock, of which most of the hill and ridge tops were composed.   Very heavy fighting continued throughout the day, but the enemy, though continually reinforced, was unable to break our line.

The Australian Mounted Division arrived at Khurbet Deiran early in the morning, having marched the twenty-one miles from Mejdel in one night. The 4th A.L.H. Brigade at once pushed on into the hills, and came into the line in the centre, in support of the 6th Brigade, about five in the evening. The hard-worked 52nd Division contrived to spare another battalion, which reinforced the 7th Brigade on the left.

The attack on this brigade was resumed at dark, but was driven off, after prolonged and bitter fighting. As an indication of the close nature of the struggle, it may be mentioned that the headquarters of two of the Yeomanry brigades used up all their revolver ammunition during the day.

Next day the Yeomanry Division and the 7th Brigade were relieved in the line by two more brigades of infantry from the 52nd and 74th Divisions, the latter of which had just arrived from the south. These reliefs were carried out in the intervals between repeated fierce attacks by the enemy, who flung his troops against our line all day with the greatest determination. Had it not been possible to relieve the Yeomanry about this time, there is no doubt that they would have been overwhelmed. So depleted were their ranks that the substitution of two brigades of infantry for the four cavalry brigades meant six rifles in the line for every one that had been there before. This increase in strength, with the addition of the Australian Mounted Division, sufficed to hold all the enemy attacks.

On the following morning the 3rd A.L.H. Brigade relieved the brigade of the 52nd Division on the left of the Yeomanry line, near El Burj, and the headquarters and artillery of the division moved up in the evening.

On the same day, the weary troops of the Yeomanry Division withdrew to Annabeh, whence they marched to the neighbourhood of El Mughar to rest and refit, within sight of the hill which they had captured so brilliantly a fortnight earlier.

During their twelve days in the hills they had been fighting continually, day and night, not only against a vigorous and determined enemy, but against the difficulties of a roadless mountain country. Exposed to constant rain and cold, without tents, blankets or greatcoats, often short of food, and opposed at all times by greatly superior forces of the enemy, they had set an example of dogged courage and tenacity and of unquenchable cheerfulness that has never been surpassed.

These were the last operations in the East in which they were destined to take part. In the following spring, in response to the urgent call from France for more troops to stem the great German attack, the division was disbanded, and reorganised into a number of dismounted machine gun companies. After a short course of training, these companies embarked for France, there to earn fresh laurels for their old division in the last great act of the war.

Units of the division had fought in nearly every action since the beginning of the war with Turkey, and all had distinguished themselves. At Suvla Bay in the Peninsula; at Sollum and Mersa Matruh in the western desert; at Romani, Maghdaba and Rafa during the advance across Sinai; in the two first battles of Gaza; and lastly in the great ride over the Plains of Philistia, and the stubborn drive into the Judæan Mountains. Everywhere the Turks had learned to dread the long swords and the steady rifles of the Yeomen. Their comrades of the Desert Mounted Corps bade farewell to the gallant division with real sorrow.

The enemy made one more attempt to break our line at its weakest part on the night of the 30th. About two o'clock in the morning a battalion of picked assault troops from his 19th Division was launched against the position held by the 3rd A.L.H. Brigade. The Turks were well supplied with hand grenades, which were not carried by our cavalry at that time, and pushed their attack in the most resolute manner. Our line was forced back a few hundred yards, and a small, but important, hill was lost for a time. A squadron of the Gloucester Yeomanry (5th Mounted Brigade) and a company of infantry from the 52nd Division reinforced the 3rd Brigade, and the Turks' attempt to break through was finally defeated, but only after the complete destruction of the enemy battalion. Three times during the night, between 2 A.M. and 6 A.M., this gallant regiment flung itself against our positions, pressing on each time with the most reckless courage. Each attack was repelled with heavy losses to the enemy, and in the end the battalion was wiped out: 172 Turks, many of them wounded, remained in our hands as prisoners; the rest were killed.

The 5th Mounted Brigade rejoined the Australian Division from the 21st Corps on the 1st of December, being replaced by the 10th A.L.H. Regiment, which remained on the right flank of the 60th Division, and gained touch with the 53rd Division on the 7th December.

The Australian Mounted Division remained in the mountains till the end of December, when it was withdrawn to Deir el Belah to rest and refit. It had little fighting during the period spent in the hills, but the awful weather fully made up for any lack of activity on the part of the enemy. During the whole time rain fell almost incessantly, and the cold winds that swept up and down the narrow valleys were exceedingly trying to men who were nearly always in wet clothes.

But, if the conditions in the hills were execrable, those in the coastal plain, where all the horses of the division were kept, were nearly as bad. The rains broke late this year, and, when they did come, fell with unusual violence. The plain was soon transformed into a deep sea of mud. Large areas were completely under water, and the flood carried immense quantities of soil into the innumerable small wadis that intersect the plain, filling them bank full with mud. When the waters subsided a little, from time to time, these wadis were indistinguishable from the surrounding country, and became very dangerous traps. There was more than one instance of men and horses being engulfed and drowned in their horrible black depths.

Christmas Eve and Christmas Day 1917 are never likely to be forgotten by any of the troops who were in Palestine at the time. A raging storm of rain fell without intermission for thirty-six hours. The railway was washed away in several places, wagons and lorries were unable to move, and hundreds of camels in the ration convoys lay down in the water that covered the land, and died. No food or other supplies could be brought up to the troops.

A small party of Yeomanry, making its way northwards from Esdud, reached the bridge over the Nahr Sukereir about mid-day. The men halted to feed their horses on the bridge, which consisted of a single high stone arch, and was comparatively dry. After half an hour's halt, they attempted to continue their march, but found the country to the north of the river so deep in water and mud that they could not get on. They then tried to go back again, but, in the meantime, the waters had risen behind them, and they found themselves cut off on the bridge, which was now a small island in an apparently limitless sea of muddy water. Marooned on their tiny island, lashed by the rain and the bitter wind, they spent the night and the next day (Christmas Day) huddled miserably together, without food, fire, or shelter! On the 26th the waters subsided a little, and they were able to struggle back to their camp.

The horses, already thin and tired after the heavy work and short rations of the past month, went back rapidly in condition. They were standing always up to their hocks in mud, wet through nearly the whole time, and, in this treeless country, there was little or no shelter from the biting winds. Forage, too, was often woefully short, owing to partial breakdowns of the supply columns. It is small wonder that, by the end of December, when the division was relieved, they resembled ragged scarecrows rather than horses.

Much trouble was caused in the mountains owing to the impossibility of preventing information reaching the enemy from the natives. A regulation, prohibiting the inhabitants of the villages behind our lines from leaving their houses during the hours of darkness, was rigidly enforced, and any natives found at large during the night were liable to be shot at sight. Nevertheless, with a line so lightly held as was ours, and with no regular system of trenches, it was a comparatively easy matter for the villagers to pass between the lines, even in daylight, and much information undoubtedly reached the enemy in this way.

One day a small patrol of five men of the Australian Mounted Division was making its way cautiously forward towards the enemy position in the village of Deir el Kuddis. Crossing the bottom of a deep valley, the patrol came upon a solitary Arab squatting among the rocks in the bottom of the ravine. He said he had come from Deir el Kuddis, and that it had been evacuated by the enemy. Our men, one of whom spoke a little Arabic, questioned him closely, but he stuck to his story, and also showed them a path which led to the village. They left him in the ravine, and, taking the path indicated, moved warily forward towards the village. Shortly afterwards, they heard a jackal cry in the valley behind them, but, as the hills were full of these beasts, whose mournful wailing was to be heard all night long, the men paid no attention to it at the time. Almost immediately afterwards a concealed enemy machine gun opened fire on them unexpectedly, killing one man and wounding another. They withdrew, carrying their dead comrade with them, and were making their way back towards the ravine where they had left the native, when one of them was suddenly struck by the thought that he had never before heard a jackal call in the daytime. After a discussion, they came to the conclusion that the jackal cry must have been made by the Arab they had seen, as a signal to the enemy. One of them accordingly went to look for the man, and found him in the same place. As soon as he saw the soldier, the native jumped up with a cry, and attempted to run away, but was promptly shot dead by the Australian.

The body of this man lay unburied in the bottom of the ravine all the time we were there, as none of the villagers would touch it. They had taken and buried the bodies of several other natives who had been shot when found away from their villages after dark, and, as they would not give the same treatment to this man, it is possible that he was a Turk in disguise.

One of our Horse Artillery batteries in action in the mountains west of Jerusalem.
Note the bivouac shelters pitched among the guns as camouflage.

Reading the British Proclamation in Jerusalem, 11th November, 1917.
General Allenby with Allied Répresentatives in the centre.

In the latter half of November the four infantry divisions that had remained about Gaza and Karm during the pursuit of the enemy commenced to move up to the front, and, by the end of the month, were all in the line from the sea to Nebi Samwil. At the beginning of December the 53rd Division began its advance up the Hebron road, and, on the early morning of the 9th, was in touch with the 60th Division, and had one brigade fighting its way up the Mount of Olives. The latter division, pivoting on the hill of Nebi Samwil, had made a wonderful fighting wheel to the left during the past three days, and had now closed in on Jerusalem on the west and south.

At eight o'clock in the morning the keys of the Holy City, borne by the Mayor under a flag of truce, were handed to an officer of the 60th Division.

After six hundred years the Christian had returned.

.   .   .   .

General Allenby made his official entry into Jerusalem on the 11th, accompanied by representatives of the Allied Nations. This event, and the magnificent infantry fighting that led up to it, have been too well chronicled elsewhere to need recapitulation in this narrative, which is concerned only with the doings of the cavalry.

One may be permitted, however, to emphasise once more the impressive contrast between the entry of the Conqueror of Jerusalem and that of the crazy mountebank who had visited it twenty years before. The German Emperor entered on horseback, surrounded by an immense retinue, in uniforms blazing with medals and decorations. General Allenby entered on foot and almost alone, dressed in worn, service khaki, and carrying a cane. *But* he went through the Jaffa Gate, which, in accordance with ancient tradition, is opened only to a conqueror of the Holy City ; the Kaiser entered through a breach in the wall.

The Australian Mounted Division was relieved by the 10th Infantry Division on the 1st of January, and the 3rd and 5th Brigades withdrew from the hills that day, and marched south for Deir el Belah, followed a week later by the 4th Brigade. The three days' march was carried out in continual, heavy rain, changing to hail and sleet every now and then, and through a country that was nearly all under water. Once among the clean, dry sandhills of Deir el Belah, however, all troubles were over, and soon afterwards the weather improved, and clothes could be dried for the first time for seven weeks. The Yeomanry Division had moved into the same area shortly before the Australian Division arrived.

The Anzac Division remained on the Auja till the 7th of December, when it withdrew to rest at Richon-le-Zion. Cavalry operations were much hampered by the continual rain and deep mud, but the division carried out a series of daring and successful raids on the enemy, which kept him constantly on the jump, and paved the way for the final crossing of the Auja on the 21st and 22nd of December. Two brigades took part in this operation, in support of the 52nd and 54th Divisions, and, as soon as our line was consolidated on the north bank, the whole division was withdrawn, and went into camp near the coast to rest.

Between the 31st of October and the end of December the Desert Mounted Corps had advanced some eighty miles,[1] fought nine general engagements, and captured about 9500 prisoners and 80 guns.

[1] The actual distances covered by the three divisions in the period were :—Anzac Mounted Division, one hundred and seventy miles ; Yeomanry Division, one hundred and ninety miles ; Australian Mounted Division, two hundred and thirty miles.

CHAPTER XI

DOWN TO THE JORDAN

THE advance across the Nahr el Auja at the end of
December 1917, and the infantry operations north
of Jerusalem about the same time, established our
line sufficiently far north of Jaffa and Jerusalem to
secure these two places from all but long-range gun
fire from the enemy. The line was then consolidated, and a period of trench warfare set in, which,
with the exception of several minor operations, was
to last till the autumn of the following year.

For the first part of this period, the Desert Mounted
Corps remained in the neighbourhood of Gaza to
rest and train.

The horses were in a sorry state, and the remount
depots were empty, save for a few animals which
had been returned from veterinary hospitals, after
treatment for wounds or other injuries. Owing to
the shortage of shipping, there was no prospect of
any fresh remounts arriving in the country for an
indefinite time. Consequently all the horses of the
Corps had to be nursed back to condition before
the cavalry could take part in any further serious
work.

The divisions were all camped on deep sand,
among the coastal dunes—the Yeomanry and the
Australian Mounted Divisions round Gaza, the Anzac
Division farther north. The heaviest rain drained
through this sand immediately, and half an hour
of sunshine was enough to dry the surface. For the

first time in many weeks the horses had clean, dry standings, and the effect of this was soon evident in the improved condition of their legs and coats. At the end of the first fortnight, which was a period of rest for men as well as horses, there was an all round improvement. Forage was plentiful again, and of fair quality, though every one would have given a great deal for a few tons of good oats, in place of the eternal barley.

After the first fortnight, training recommenced, gradually at first, so as not to check the recovery of the horses. By the end of the month, however, brigade and divisional schemes were in full swing.

The training was varied by salvage work on the old trenches at Gaza, from which a great quantity of ammunition and stores of every description was collected. Most of the men had an opportunity of visiting Gaza, and many were the ' curios ' collected among the ruins, to be taken home to sweethearts and wives on that glorious ' leave,' that was always coming, but never quite came.

At a little distance the city appeared to be intact, except for two minarets, accidentally broken by shell fire, the jagged stumps of which stood up conspicuously. This curious, undamaged appearance was due to the great quantity of trees which grew all over the town, and which had now put on their spring coat of green. The kindly leaves hid the scarred and broken skeletons of the trees, and veiled the shapeless ruins of the houses.

Inside, however, was a scene of utter desolation. Not a living thing was to be seen in this city, which once held 40,000 souls, save an occasional, hungry pariah dog, engaged in his horrible work among the graves of the dead.

The great mosque, which had once been a noble,

Ruins of the Great Mosque at Gaza, showing one of the arches
of the old Crusader Church.

Christian church, was almost entirely destroyed, but not by our guns. The Turks had used it as an ammunition depot, with that callous disregard for the Holy Places of their own religion which was always so characteristic of them, and, when the city was abandoned, they blew up the great store of shells there, and laid the mosque in ruins. Some of the lower arches remained, and one beautiful Norman gateway, but all the rest was a heap of tumbled masonry.

The German headquarters was in the north-west corner of the town, close to the remains of a graceful little Greek church. The house in which the officers lived was screened from view on all sides, and, as it was far removed from any of the enemy defences, it had escaped serious damage. But it was satisfactory to note that both the tennis courts, which had been made with such evident pains, had been visited by eight-inch shells.

The rest of the city was a mass of ruins, stark and silent. And so it is likely to remain for all time, an awful witness to the devastation of war. Its inhabitants have neither the energy of the people of Europe, nor the incentive of a bitter climate, and they are never likely to rebuild it.

By the end of January our front had been thoroughly consolidated, and the infantry had recovered from the hard fighting and cruel weather of December. The Commander-in-Chief now determined to extend his line to the Jordan, in order to secure his right flank.

There were several other advantages to be gained by securing possession of one or two crossings over the river. The enemy was at this time obtaining large supplies of grain from the districts round Kerak, in the land of Moab, on the eastern and south-eastern shores of the Dead Sea. This grain was carried across the sea, in barges towed by motor boats, to the north end, whence it was transported to the Turkish front by the good metalled road from Jericho to Jerusalem. With Jericho and the crossings of the Jordan immediately north of the Dead Sea in our hands, we should have control of the sea, and all this traffic would be stopped. The grain would then have to be brought up to Amman, thirty miles east of the Jordan, by the Hedjaz Railway, and transported from there over some fifty miles of bad mountain track. In the extremely disorganised state of the Turkish transport, this would be likely to cause the enemy much inconvenience and delay. The control of the river crossings at Jericho would also facilitate raiding operations across the Jordan, directed against the enemy's line of communications with the Hedjaz.

The operations necessary to secure these objects were limited to the establishment of one or more bridgeheads on the east bank of the Jordan, and to an advance of our line northwards as far as the Wadi el Auja, a small, perennial stream that flows into the Jordan some nine miles north of the point where the latter enters the Dead Sea.

The watershed between the Mediterranean and the deep cleft of the Jordan Valley runs roughly north and south, through the Mount of Olives. Some description of the difficulties of the country on the west of the watershed has already been given. On the east side they are very much greater. The streams that run down from the mountains to the plain have cut gorges through the rock, often many hundreds of feet deep, which divide the eastern portion of the range into a series of parallel ridges running east and west. Innumerable tributaries of the main watercourses run in all directions, and split these ridges again into isolated masses of rocks. It is only possible to cross the main wadis in a few places, so that movement north and south on the part of any considerable body of troops is out of the question.

Going down the road from Jerusalem to Jericho, the general fall of the ground is gradual to Talaat el Dumm, the Hill of Blood, above the Good Samaritan Inn. From here the road pitches down, in a series of zigzags and hairpin turns, to the valley floor nearly 3000 feet below. Farther north, at Jebel Kuruntul, the traditional Mount of Temptation, the mountains end abruptly in a single stupendous cliff, over 1000 feet high.

Over this country the 60th Division and the Anzac Mounted Division, which had concentrated at Bethlehem on the 18th of February, were directed to move on Jericho.

The advance began on the 19th of February, in heavy rain. All day the infantry struggled forward, against strong opposition from the enemy, and by nightfall had advanced nearly three miles, to a position about a mile west of Talaat el Dumm.

Meanwhile the cavalry, moving to the south of the 60th Division, through the Wilderness of Jeshimon, had reached El Muntar, about seven miles from the Dead Sea, and some four miles south of the Jericho road.

Next day the infantry stormed Talaat el Dumm shortly after dawn, and advanced against the high ridge of Jebel Ekteif, about one mile farther south, while the cavalry moved on Jebel Kalimun and Tubk el Kuneitra. Both these places were strongly held, and the only possible lines of approach were under accurate shell and machine-gun fire from the hill of Nebi Musa, a little to the north. The cavalry had to advance in single file along a few goat paths, and they suffered considerably from the enemy fire, without being able to make any adequate reply. Shortly after mid-day, however, two regiments of the New Zealand Mounted Brigade, having left their horses under cover in a ravine, made an assault on foot against the two hills, and captured both of them after a sharp struggle.

Meanwhile the 1st A.L.H. Brigade found a way down, along the gorge of the Wadi Kumran, and debouched on to the plain, on the shores of the Dead Sea, at dusk.

At dawn on the 21st, the New Zealand Brigade, with a battalion from the 60th Division, occupied Nebi Musa without opposition, the enemy having retired along his whole line during the night. The 1st A.L.H. Brigade pushed rapidly over the plain, and entered Jericho, which was found deserted, soon after eight in the morning. From here patrols were sent out to the east and north, and located the enemy holding a bridgehead on the west bank of the Jordan at Ghoraniyeh, east of Jericho, and in position along the Wadi el Auja to the north.

A squadron of the New Zealand Brigade, patrolling east from Nebi Musa, reached Rujm el Bahr, at the north-west corner of the Dead Sea, which was the northern base for the fleet of German motor boats engaged in towing grain barges across the sea. Shortly afterwards some of our troops found one of these boats alongside the jetty, and succeeded in capturing it intact. Mounting a machine gun in the bows, they at once set out across the sea, and, soon afterwards, encountered another German boat. After an exciting chase they forced the enemy to strike his colours, and, putting a ' prize crew ' aboard, continued their voyage. In the course of their cruise they sank another boat, and drove a fourth aground ! Later on, these captured boats were taken over by a detachment of the Royal Navy, and did good service patrolling the sea, and keeping open the communications between our forces and the Sherifian troops. They achieved the distinction of being the first British war vessels to be navigated 1300 feet below the level of the ocean.

As the enemy bridgehead at Ghoraniyeh was found to be strongly held, and its capture would have entailed heavy losses, it was decided not to attempt an attack. Our infantry withdrew to a position running north and south astride the Jericho road, at Talaat el Dumm, and the Anzac Mounted Division returned to Bethlehem, leaving one regiment to patrol the valley.

Some idea of the difficulties of the country during these operations may be gathered by the fact that a battery of field artillery, unhampered by enemy action, took thirty-six hours to advance eight miles.

During the first half of March the 60th Division again descended into the valley, and, after some very stiff fighting, succeeded in establishing our line north of the Wadi el Auja, from the Jordan to the mountains. Thereupon the Turks withdrew their bridgehead at Ghoraniyeh, and retired to the east bank of the river.

This operation cleared the lower Jordan Valley of the enemy, and established a base broad enough to enable a raid to be undertaken against the Hedjaz Railway, the Turkish line of communications for the force operating against the Arabs round Maan.

The Arab forces, which were under the control of General Allenby, were based on Akaba, at the north end of the Red Sea. They were supplied by us with arms, ammunition and light guns, and largely led by British officers, chief among whom were Lieutenant-Colonels Lawrence and Joyce.

Though intolerant of anything in the nature of discipline, and constantly at war among themselves, many of the Arab tribes of the Hedjaz had joined the standard of the old Sherif Hussein, moved thereto by their hatred of the Turks. Under Hussein's energetic son Feisal, they had carried on a successful guerilla warfare against the scattered Turkish garrisons since June 1916. Their operations were directed especially against the Hedjaz Railway. Under the leadership of the daring and beloved Lawrence, train wrecking was elevated among the Arabs to the status of a national sport. Many of the wrecked trains yielded rich booty to the Sherif, and on one occasion the haul included £20,000 in Turkish gold. Eighteen months of this warfare had given the Arabs valuable experience, and numerous minor successes had induced many tribes who were wavering to throw in their lot with the Sherif.

By the end of 1917 the Emir Feisal's forces were strong enough to undertake more serious operations. In January 1918 he seized the high ground a few miles south of Maan, while another force, under a local leader, destroyed a large part of the Turkish light railway which had been built from Kalaat Aneiza on the Hedjaz line to the Hish Forest, and was used to transport wood as fuel for locomotives. Shortly afterwards another force raided a station on the Hedjaz line, some thirty miles north of Maan, destroying the station buildings and some engines and rolling stock. In this raid the Arabs took over 200 prisoners, and killed a large number of Turks. Farther north, Arabs of the Huweitat tribe captured Tafile, which is only fifteen miles south-east of the south end of the Dead Sea. A considerable Turkish force, with guns and machine guns, which was sent, towards the end of January, to recapture this place, was decisively beaten by the Arabs, with a loss of 500 killed and 250 prisoners. In March a larger body of Turkish troops, reinforced by a German battalion, reoccupied Tafile, the Arabs withdrawing to the south.[1]

[1] See Appendix II. for note on the Arab Movement.

CHAPTER XII

THE FIRST TRANS-JORDAN RAID

In view of the successes obtained by the Arabs, General Allenby now judged the time to be ripe for a raid by our troops on the Hedjaz Railway at Amman, which he had long contemplated. The immediate effect of such a raid would be to compel the enemy to withdraw the force which had recently occupied Tafile. It might, in addition, force him to call on the Turkish troops at Maan for aid, thus weakening the garrison there, and giving the Arabs an opportunity to attack the place with some prospects of success. A further result to be expected from the raid would be to induce the enemy to keep a large part of his army east of the Jordan, thus correspondingly weakening his forces in the Judæan hills. The deep and difficult valley of the Jordan, and the river itself, would, moreover, form a dangerous obstacle to communication between the two portions of his army, a fact which might be expected to assist us materially in our next general advance.

Amman was the one really vulnerable point on the Hedjaz Railway. The Arabs had frequently destroyed portions of the line farther south, but such raids only resulted in interrupting the traffic for a few days at a time. Material for repair was available at every station, and long practice had brought the Turkish engineers to a high state of efficiency in restoring these temporarily damaged places. At Amman, however, the line ran over a viaduct, and through a considerable tunnel. If these two works could be thoroughly destroyed, the resulting interruption of traffic might well be so prolonged as to compel the retirement of the whole of the enemy force in the Maan area. Such a prospect justified the acceptance of greater risks than General Allenby proposed to incur.

The Turks were well aware that Amman was the Achilles' heel of the Hedjaz Expeditionary Force, and had provided for its protection as many troops as they could spare. The town itself, which lay immediately to the west of, and covering, the tunnel and viaduct, had been garrisoned and prepared for defence. An advanced defensive position had been established astride the Jericho-El Salt road, extending from El Haud to Shunet Nimrin, and a third position was in course of preparation on the east bank of the Jordan, opposite El Ghoraniyeh.

The Anzac Mounted Division, with the Camel Corps Brigade attached, and the 60th Division were detailed to carry out the raid, which had as its sole object the destruction of the viaduct and tunnel. The town of Amman, which is the principal Circassian settlement in Syria, lies some thirty miles east-north-east of the north end of the Dead Sea, and is connected with Jericho by an indifferent metalled road, passing through El Salt, which the Turks had constructed during the war. From the Jordan at El Ghoraniyeh, 1200 feet below the level of the sea, to Naaur, sixteen miles farther east, at the edge of the plateau on which Amman lies, the ground rises 4300 feet. Nearly the whole of this rise occurs in the last ten miles before Naaur is reached, and the intervening country is a maze of rocky hills, intersected by deep ravines, and traversed only by a few narrow footpaths.

In the course of the ages the Jordan has cut a deep trough through the valley, varying in width from a few hundred yards to a mile or more, and lying about 100 feet below the general level of the surrounding country. The bottom of this trough is a flat plain covered with a dense jungle of tamarisk, and the banks are, in most places, perpendicular. The present channel winds about down the trough, and is only about forty yards wide in normal weather, but the river is deep and very swift, and liable to a rapid rise after heavy rain.

The main watercourses descend from the hills on the east in a series of deep gorges, which traverse the narrow strip of flat country between the foothills and the old channel, and form a succession of barriers to movement along this strip, north and south. Many of these gorges can only be crossed by a single track, which runs from near Beisan, fifteen miles south of Lake Tiberias, to El Ghoraniyeh.

The plan was for the 60th Division to force the passage of the river, drive the enemy from his position at Shunet Nimrin, and then advance up to Jericho-Amman road, as far as El Salt, which was to be seized and held. Meanwhile the rest of the cavalry and the Camel Brigade were to move direct on Amman by the tracks through Naaur and Ain el Sir. After blowing up the viaduct and tunnel at Amman, and destroying as much of the railway line as they could, they were to withdraw on the 60th Division, and the whole force would then recross the Jordan, leaving permanent bridgeheads on the east bank.

The operation was thus purely a raid. Our cavalry would again be engaged in a country that was at least as unsuited for mounted work as was the Judæan Range, of which we had already had such unfavourable experience. The only information available about the Amman hills, other than that of natives, which was always quite unreliable, was contained in a memorandum written for the Commander-in-Chief by two mission fathers who had spent many years in the country east of the Jordan and Dead Sea. This document was an admirable ethnographical and geographical treatise, but, from the military point of view, which requires the utmost detail of description as regards the terrain, it left much to be desired. It appeared, however, that cavalry might be expected to be able to move with some speed up the Naaur-Ain el Sir track to Amman, in fine weather, and thus carry out the necessary demolition on the railway, and make good their retreat, before the enemy should have time to reinforce his troops east of the Jordan.

During the night of the 21st of March a party of swimmers of the 60th Division succeeded, after many fruitless attempts, in getting a line across the Jordan at Makhadet Hajlah, some six miles south of El Ghoraniyeh, and bridge building began at once. Our infantry and engineers suffered severely from the enemy's fire, but the bridge was completed by eight in the morning, and by mid-day a brigade of infantry was over the river, and forcing its way through the dense tamarisk jungle on the east side.

Meanwhile, similar attempts to cross at El Ghoraniyeh during the night had been frustrated by the strength of the current. The efforts had to be abandoned during the daytime, owing to the activity of the enemy, but were renewed during the night of the 22nd. These attempts again failed, and it was not until the morning of the 23rd that a raft was got across here. At four o'clock in the morning a regiment of the New Zealand Mounted Brigade crossed the river by the pontoon bridge at Makhadet Hajlah, and, galloping along the bank to the north, cleared the enemy from the east bank opposite Ghoraniyeh, thus facilitating the crossing of our infantry at that place. By mid-day this regiment had seized the high ground commanding El Ghoraniyeh, capturing about seventy prisoners and several machine guns.

They were followed across the Jordan by a regiment of the 1st A.L.H. Brigade, which cleared the enemy from the country south of Hajlah, and gained touch with a party of infantry which had crossed the Dead Sea in motor boats, and landed on the east bank of the river near its mouth.

By nightfall a second pontoon bridge had been thrown across the Jordan at Hajlah, and three more had been completed at Ghoraniyeh. The whole force detailed for the raid had safely crossed the river before daylight on the 24th.

As soon as it was light enough to see, the advance on Amman commenced. The 1st A.L.H. Brigade moved up to El Mandesi, about three miles north of Ghoraniyeh, to cover the left flank of the 60th Division during the attack on the enemy positions astride the Amman road, at El Haud and Shunet Nimrin. El Haud was captured about three in the afternoon, after hard fighting, and its possession enabled our infantry to turn the right flank of the enemy, who then retired on El Salt. A squadron of the New Zealanders pursued the Turks, followed by our infantry, but the bad state of the road, which the enemy blew up in several places as he retired, delayed the pursuit. The rest of the New Zealand Brigade moved on El Sir up the Wadi Jofet el Ghazlaniye. At nightfall our infantry had only succeeded in advancing about four miles from Shunet Nimrin, and were in touch with the enemy astride the road.

Meanwhile the 2nd A.L.H. Brigade, followed by the Camel Corps, had been floundering up the Wadi Kefrein, south of the road, and reached Rujm el Oshir about half-past three in the afternoon. Here the track, such as it was, petered out altogether, and all wheeled transport had to be sent back, the ammunition being transferred to camels. This caused a long delay, and it was not till half-past nine at night that the march could be renewed. Heavy rain had fallen for several days prior to the commencement of the operations, and all the tracks were deep in mud.

Rain came on again during the night of the 24th, and continued during the whole of the next three days, accompanied by bitter cold. Under this downpour the tracks marked on the map revealed themselves for what they really were, the beds of mountain streams. Each of them was transformed into a rushing torrent, carrying down rocks and mud in its course. Bad as they were, however, they formed the only possible lines of advance in this mountain country, and the cavalry had to make the best of them.

Pushing and pulling their shivering and exhausted animals up the track, the 2nd A.L.H. Brigade and the Camel Corps stumbled on in the rain and darkness all night. At half-past four next morning the head of the column reached Ain el Hekr, having taken just twenty-four hours to cover the sixteen miles from the Jordan.. The whole day was spent in closing up the remainder of the column, and it was not till half-past seven in the evening that the last of the Camel Corps got in, having walked the whole way, pulling their camels after them.

As soon as they were in, the advance was continued,

via Naaur, in pouring rain.   During this part of the march the way was not so steep as in the earlier part, but the alternate deep mud and slippery rock over which the track led caused endless delays, especially to the camels, and the force was soon strung out again over a length of many miles.   At five on the morning of the 26th, the head of the column met the New Zealand Brigade at the cross tracks one mile east of El Sir.   The New Zealanders had encountered similar difficulties of country and climate, and both men and horses were in an exhausted condition.

General Chaytor now received orders to push on at once, and seize Amman !   But, as his men had been marching for three consecutive nights (including the move to the point of assembly west of the Jordan), under conditions of the utmost discomfort and fatigue, he considered that they were in no state to make an attack on a strongly held position, even if it were possible to reach Amman before nightfall, which was extremely unlikely.   He therefore asked, and received, permission to halt for twenty-four hours, and march on Amman next morning.   Outposts were placed north, east, and south of El Sir, and strong patrols of the 2nd Brigade were sent out to reconnoitre northwards, as far as the El Salt-Amman road.   These patrols encountered a body of the enemy near El Sweileh, and dispersed it, taking 170 prisoners.   They also destroyed thirty German motor lorries and a car, which they found here, stuck fast in the mud.

While the Anzac Division was struggling towards El Sir on the 25th, the infantry of the 60th Division had been marching up the main road from Shunet Nimrin towards El Salt, with the 1st A.L.H. Brigade on their left flank, on the Wadi Arseniyet track. This brigade reached El Salt about six in the evening, and was joined there, some two hours later, by a brigade of the 60th Division. A second infantry brigade arrived at midnight. The place had been evacuated by the enemy, in consequence of the threat to his rear caused by the advance of our cavalry to El Sir.

Our infantry were now quite as exhausted as the cavalry. They had been marching or fighting continually for three days and nights, over difficult mountain country, and in most inclement weather, and it was necessary to give them a day's rest. The first A.L.H. Brigade was directed to remain at El Salt, and patrol the country to the north and north-west of that place.

Thus, on the morning of the 27th, when the advance was resumed, the foremost troops of the raiding force were little more than two-thirds of the way to Amman. The delay had been of the utmost value to the Turks, who were hurrying up reinforcements by road and rail.

During the previous night General Chaytor had sent two small raiding parties, mounted on the freshest horses available, to try and blow up the Hedjaz Railway north and south of Amman, in order to entrap a considerable quantity of rolling stock which was reported to be in the station. The 2nd A.L.H. Brigade party made for the railway north of Amman, but encountered a body of Turkish cavalry, and was forced to turn back. The New Zealanders, who were directed south of the town, were more fortunate, and succeeded in reaching the railway at a point some seven miles south of Amman station. Having destroyed a considerable stretch of the line, they withdrew safely, and made their way back to El Sir.

This march, carried out at night, in unknown and

very difficult country, without guides or reliable maps, and into the heart of the enemy's country, was a striking example of the special qualities of the Australian and New Zealand Cavalry. Trained from the cradle in the art of finding their way in uncharted country, they have the bushman's almost uncanny sense of direction. Tireless as the wiry horses they breed and ride, possessed of a wonderful keenness of vision, alert, wary and supremely self-confident, they are the finest scouts in the world.

The advance on Amman was resumed on the 27th. Early in the morning a light car patrol arrived at Sweileh from El Salt, but could get no farther east, owing to the mud. General Chaytor, therefore, ordered the cars to remain at Sweileh, as a flank guard to his division during the attack on Amman. A brigade of infantry, with two mountain batteries, set out from El Salt at five in the morning, to march to the support of the Anzac Division. This brigade could not be expected at Amman till late at night, but it was hoped that the Anzac Division would be able to take the place before then. Unfortunately the delay to our troops caused by the rain had afforded time to the enemy both to improve his defence and to reinforce his garrison.

General Chaytor directed the New Zealand Brigade to cross the Wadi Amman, south-west of the town, and move against the high ground overlooking the town and station from the south. One battalion of the Camel Corps Brigade, acting on the right of the New Zealanders, was to destroy as much of the line as possible.

The 2nd A.L.H. Brigade was ordered to push forward to the railway north of Amman as quickly as possible, and cut the line, in order both to isolate the rolling stock in the station, and to delay the arrival of possible reinforcements from the north. The brigade was then to attack the enemy positions from the north-west. The Camel Corps Brigade, less one battalion, was to attack from the west.

There was no divisional reserve. It was considered that the superior mobility of our cavalry and camelry would enable them to disengage from the fight, should such a course become necessary, and fall back on our infantry advancing from El Salt. Moreover, the difficulties of the country were so great that it was doubtful if a divisional reserve could have reached any distant part of the line that was hard pressed, in time to be of any service.

The three brigades set out from Ain el Sir at nine o'clock. All three were much impeded by difficulties of terrain. Deep mud alternated with stretches of wet and slippery rock, on which neither camels nor horses could get secure foothold. The camels suffered particularly severely. Designed by nature for work in the soft and yielding sand of the desert, they are more unfitted than any other animal to march over stony country, or through mud. Many of them fell and broke their legs, and had to be shot. Many more had already met the same fate during the awful climb up to the plateau from the Jordan Valley. In several places large morasses were encountered, and much precious time was wasted finding a way round these. The wadis, too, were deep and precipitous, particularly the Wadi Amman, which was impassable save in one or two places, and then only in single file.

The New Zealanders reached this wadi about half-past ten in the morning, and were delayed so long in crossing it that it was three in the afternoon before they reached the railway.

The Camel Corps Battalion then moved south

along the line, with a demolition party, blowing up the railway. While engaged on this work, they met an enemy train, steaming slowly over the very portion of the line that had been blown up by the New Zealanders the night before ! The train was engaged with machine-gun fire, and withdrew. Our men then examined the line, and learnt a valuable lesson in the art of temporary destruction of a railway.

It was the custom at that time for our raiding parties, which could only carry a small quantity of explosives, and no tools suitable for carrying out a systematic destruction, to blow a piece out of each rail, by means of slabs of gun-cotton placed on each side of it. The gaps thus made were about a foot long. A length of several miles of line, in which each rail had a piece cut clean out of the middle, had the appearance of having been very thoroughly destroyed, and it was believed that the whole line would have to be relaid with new rails before it could be used. But the ingenious German engineers discovered that, if a hard-wood sleeper were pushed into each gap, with its end flush with the inner edge of the rail, trains could be run over the line at once, provided they were driven slowly.

As a result of this experience, Captain Brisbane, an engineer officer of the Australian Mounted Division, devised a better method, which consisted in attaching one slab of gun-cotton only to the outside of the rails at each joint. When this was detonated, the fishplates were blown off, and the ends of the two rails were bent sharply inwards. Demolitions carried out by this method could only be repaired by relaying the line completely.[1]

---

[1] At a demonstration given some months later by a small party of engineers specially trained by this officer, one mile of track was completely destroyed in ten minutes.

While the New Zealanders had been searching for a crossing place over the wadi, the 2nd A.H.L. Brigade had pushed forward on the north-west, and got to within three miles of Amman, when it was heavily counter-attacked, about eleven o'clock, by a large force of the enemy, well supplied with artillery. The attack was beaten off, after severe fighting, but more Turks appeared to the north of the brigade, and began to work round its left. General Ryrie had to form a defensive flank to meet this threat, and his advance was stopped. Meanwhile the Camel Brigade, advancing straight on Amman astride the Sweileh track, was held up by heavy machine-gun fire, on reaching the open ground west of the town, and could get no farther.

The New Zealanders fared no better. They were very heavily attacked when attempting to seize the high ground south of Amman, and forced to give ground. The Turks attacked repeatedly on the north, west and south, and in ever increasing numbers, and our small force was hard put to it to hold its own. It was soon obvious that no farther progress was possible. General Chaytor, therefore, ordered his brigades to hold their present positions as night outposts, till the arrival of the infantry, and to keep touch with the enemy by means of frequent patrols. The force was strung out over a wide front, lateral communication was very difficult, and only small, local reserves were available. Fortunately the Turks contented themselves with digging hard all night, and erecting rock sangars, and made no serious attempt to attack.

During the night a raiding party, consisting of a few men from the 2nd A.L.H. Brigade, succeeded in penetrating through the enemy in the dark, and blew up a two-arch bridge near Khurbet el Raseife, seven miles north of Amman. The gallant little party returned safely before dawn, having done damage sufficient to interrupt traffic from the north for at least forty-eight hours. Before that period had expired, it was hoped that Amman would be in our hands.

Dawn found our weary troops cramped and stiff with their long night's vigil in the bitter cold. They had been marching and fighting for four days and nights, with only one night's rest, and had been wet through the whole time. The Turkish guns opened the ball soon after daylight, and shelled our positions intermittently during the morning.

About mid-day two battalions of infantry arrived from El Salt. They had been delayed at Sweileh, the previous night, in consequence of having marched into the middle of a sort of Belfast riot between the Circassians (Moslems) of Sweileh and the Christian Arabs of El Fuheis. With two separate wars thus going on in the same area, the situation appeared too obscure for farther advance, especially as both Circassians and Arabs showed a disposition to fire impartially on all who came within range, quite irrespective of their religion or politics. The column had, therefore, halted for the night.

General Chaytor had expected to be reinforced by a brigade of infantry during the previous night, and, in anticipation of its arrival, had issued orders for an attack soon after daylight. Though disappointed at receiving only two battalions, and those not till twelve hours later than he had expected, he decided, in view of the urgency of the situation, to attack at once.

The infantry were pushed in between the Camel Corps and the 2nd A.L.H. Brigade, and ordered to advance with their right on the Sweileh-Amman road. The attack commenced at two o'clock, and the whole line pressed forward vigorously, and got to within 1000 yards of the enemy positions in the centre, when a very heavy counter-attack was launched against the 2nd A.L.H. Brigade. The cavalry were pressed back some distance under the weight of this attack, thus exposing the left of the infantry. Intense machine-gun fire was now opened on the infantry and Camel Corps, who were on the edge of a bare, open plateau, which extends for some distance west of the town. Our attack was brought to a stop, and, as it was clearly impossible to make any farther progress in face of the strong enemy resistance, and as night was coming on, General Chaytor withdrew his force a little, to positions suitable for battle night outposts, and ordered them to hold on till next morning, when the remainder of the infantry brigade was expected up.

Desultory firing continued all night, but the enemy made no attack. Parties of the 2nd A.L.H. and New Zealand Brigades were active throughout the night, patrolling up to and across the railway, north and south of Amman. They were assisted by friendly Arabs, who spent the hours of darkness sniping at parties attempting to mend the bridge which had been blown up the previous night. Others co-operated with a troop of the New Zealand Brigade, to prevent any trains approaching Amman from the south.

The rest of the infantry brigade, accompanied by two mountain batteries, joined General Chaytor's force about mid-day on the 29th. We then had two brigades of cavalry, one of infantry, and the Camel Brigade at Amman ; a cavalry brigade and an infantry brigade at El Salt, fifteen miles farther west ; and a third brigade of infantry between Shunet Nimrin and the bridgeheads on the Jordan.   There were no troops available to increase this force.

During the morning, fresh enemy reinforcements reached Amman by rail from the north, and these troops immediately developed a strong attack against the left flank of our line. The 2nd A.L.H. Brigade drove off this attack, but the Turks repeatedly assaulted the position held by the brigade during the day, and gave our weary troops no rest.

Meanwhile a further complication had arisen, owing to a considerable body of the enemy from west of the Jordan having crossed the river at Jisr el Damieh, fifteen miles north of Ghoraniyeh, on the previous day, and commenced to advance up the track towards El Salt. On the morning of the 29th, the advance guard of this force, consisting of the Turkish 3rd Cavalry Division and two brigades of infantry, was beginning to make its pressure felt against our positions at El Salt. The 1st A.L.H. Brigade, supported by some field artillery, moved out to oppose it.

The rain had continued without abatement from the commencement of the operations, and the country was now in an almost impassable state. To add to our difficulties, the Jordan suddenly rose no less than nine feet during the morning of the 29th, and the flood water swept away all but one of our bridges. The approaches to the remaining bridge were under water, and it was evident that, if the river rose any higher, it, too, would be swept away, and our force east of the river would be cut off in the enemy's country.

It was clear that, if Amman was to be taken, there was no time to be lost. General Chaytor had intended to attack as soon as the infantry reinforcements had arrived, but, in view of their exhausted state, he decided, after consultation with the brigadier, General Da Costa, to put off the attack till dark.

Such men as could be spared from the fighting had been set to work repairing the road beyond El Salt, and, by the afternoon of the 29th, it was sufficiently restored to enable a battery of Horse Artillery to start for Amman from Shunet Nimrin.

The New Zealand Brigade, with one battalion of the Camel Corps on its right, was directed to seize Point 3039, a high hill about a mile south-east of Amman town, which commanded both the town and the station. This hill was strongly held by the enemy, who occupied two lines of entrenchments, one above the other, on the southern slopes. The Camel Corps Brigade and the infantry, moving respectively south and north of the El Salt road, were to attack the town and the old citadel. The 2nd A.L.H. Brigade was instructed to make itself as offensive as possible on the north flank, so as to distract the enemy's attention from the movements of our troops farther south.

The advance began at two o'clock in the morning. It was very dark and raining hard, and the troops had great difficulty in keeping in touch and maintaining direction over the rocky ground. The New Zealanders, very skilfully led, evaded the enemy trenches at the bottom of the hill, and reached the second line, higher up the slope, which they attacked with the bayonet, and captured. When day broke the Turks in the trenches below were forced to surrender without firing a shot. The New Zealanders now got on to the top of 3039 at the southern end, where they were held up by intense machine-gun fire. The Turks followed up this fire with a determined counter-attack, just at dawn, which was beaten off, but only with the greatest difficulty.

Meanwhile the Camel Brigade and the infantry, in the centre, had met with success at first, having captured the enemy's advanced trenches, with about 200 prisoners.   About nine o'clock the Camel Brigade, then about 800 yards west of the main enemy position, came under heavy machine-gun fire from both flanks, especially from the north end of 3039, which the New Zealanders had been unable to take, and from the old citadel on the left front.   At the same time the enemy launched a powerful counter-attack against the left flank of our infantry, in the gap between them and the 2nd A.L.H. Brigade.   This attack was repulsed, but the Turks maintained a continuous and heavy pressure against this flank all day, and our troops were barely able to hold their ground.

Fresh enemy reinforcements arrived from the north about ten o'clock, and immediately launched another violent attack on the New Zealand Brigade, which was clinging precariously to the southern edge of Hill 3039.   The attack was repulsed, but only after prolonged and anxious fighting.   The Somerset Battery R.H.A., which had left Shunet Nimrin the previous day, and had been marching for thirty hours, arrived just in time to take a decisive part in repelling this attack.

The enemy then directed an intense shell fire on the New Zealanders, and attacked the Camel Corps battalion on their right, with the evident intention of outflanking our troops on the hill.   This attack was also beaten off, and, for the rest of the day, the Turks contented themselves with shelling the hill heavily, but did not succeed in dislodging the New Zealand Brigade.

Early in the afternoon the persistent enemy attacks against the left flank of our infantry ceased, probably as a result of a push forward made by the 2nd A.L.H. Brigade farther north.   The infantry took advantage of this respite to resume their dogged advance on the Amman town position. They pressed forward till they were held up by the deep fosse on the west side of the citadel. Here they came under a murderous machine-gun fire from both flanks. The few mountain guns with our force were quite inadequate to the task of keeping down this hostile fire, and could make no impression on the thick stone walls of the old citadel. Our infantry had to withdraw to shelter.

Fresh enemy troops continued to arrive from the north, and General Chaytor now reluctantly reported that he saw no hope of taking Amman with the force at his disposal, and that any further attempt would only entail useless loss of life. No reinforcements were available; indeed, during the day, a battalion of infantry had been ordered back from Amman to El Salt. This battalion was the only one that had not been engaged, and constituted the last of our reserves.

El Salt itself had been heavily attacked all day long. The enemy column that had crossed the Jordan, and advanced up the Jisr el Damieh track, drove in our advanced post on that side during the morning. The Turks continued to press their attack with the greatest determination from the west, north-west and north, and soon all our scanty reserves were involved. One battalion of infantry had been spared from the brigade that was covering the country from the Jordan to Shunet Nimrin, and one had been sent back from Amman, as already stated.

At four o'clock in the afternoon, our troops at Amman and El Salt were only just holding their own, and it was doubtful if they could do so much longer, in face of the constantly increasing strength of the enemy.   General Shea,[1] who was in command of the whole force, decided to withdraw.   The troops at Amman were to move first, breaking off the action as soon as it was dark, and retiring along the Ain el Sir tracks.

As soon as darkness fell the New Zealand Brigade and the detached battalion of the Camel Corps disengaged, and fell back to the west bank of the Wadi Amman, where they held a line of posts to cover the withdrawal of the infantry and the Camel Corps Brigade.   The infantry marched along the El Salt road, covered by the 2nd A.L.H. Brigade, as far as Sweileh, where they turned off towards El Sir, to avoid the fighting that was going on at El Salt.   The New Zealanders held their position west of the wadi till the infantry had reached El Sir, and had a sharp action with the Turks, who had followed up closely. The enemy was finally repulsed at daybreak, and the New Zealanders then fell back slowly to Ain el Sir, which they reached in the evening.   The retirement continued through the night, in the rain and darkness. Just as the rearguard troops of the New Zealand Brigade were moving out of El Sir, they were treacherously fired on by some of the local inhabitants.   A troop was at once sent back into the village, and attacked a party of Arabs caught in the act of sniping at our men.   Thirty of the natives were killed in the encounter, and this condign punishment had an instant effect.   We had no more trouble from the local Arabs.

Meanwhile the fierce attacks on El Salt had continued all through the 31st, and it was not till eleven o'clock at night that the Turks finally drew off exhausted.   During the night of the 1st of April,

____

[1] Major-General Sir J. S. M. Shea, K.C.M.G., C.B., D.S.O., commanding the 60th Division.

our troops withdrew from the village unmolested, covered by the 1st A.L.H. Brigade, having destroyed all the enemy ammunition and stores there, and the whole force was safely across the Jordan by the evening of the 2nd.

The operations had lasted twelve days, and it had rained almost the whole time. The troops were without tents or shelter of any kind, and, for the last ninety hours of the operations, they had been marching and fighting continuously, without sleep or rest. The fighting, too, had been severe, and our casualties, about 1600 killed, wounded and missing, sufficiently heavy, considering the small size of our force, and the absence of any great artillery concentration against us.

The wounded suffered severely. The nearest hospital was at Jerusalem, separated from Amman by more than sixty miles of bad mountain road. From the firing line the wounded were taken in camel cacolets [1] to a motor ambulance relay station on the road between Amman and El Salt. The tortures of this mode of conveyance to a wounded man have to be experienced to be believed. When the animal, having received its double burden, rises with its peculiar jerk forward, it nearly pitches the patients out of the cacolets. Thereafter, each lurching step of the long, agonising march stretches the unhappy victims upon a species of rack comparable to that of a mediæval torture chamber.

At the relay station, five miles east of El Salt, the wounded were transferred to ambulance motor cars, which ran them into El Salt. Here there was an advanced dressing station, where wounds were attended to, and then the victims were again loaded

---

[1] Canvas hammocks, stiffened with bamboo poles and slung one on each side of the camel, to take a man lying down.

into ambulances, and run down to the main dressing station at Shunet Nimrin.   At this station they were taken over by a fresh relay of cars, which carried them as far as Jericho, if they were lucky.   When the bridges were washed away, however, it was for a time unsafe for the cars to cross the one remaining bridge, and the men had to be carried across the river on stretchers, and put into cars on the west bank.   At Jericho there was an operating unit for serious cases, and there is no doubt that this unit saved the lives of many by an immediate operation, who would almost certainly have died had they been sent straight on to Jerusalem.   Another change of cars was made at Jericho, and another at Talaat el Dumm.   And then at last the long nightmare of the journey ended in the blessed peace and comfort of a hospital in Jerusalem.

Nearly 2000 cases, including the sick, were evacuated in this way during the operations.

German motor boat leaving Jerusalem for the Dead Sea.
(From an enemy photograph.)

Turks loading grain from Moab for transport across the Dead Sea.
(From an enemy photograph.)

CHAPTER XIII

THE SECOND TRANS-JORDAN RAID

THOUGH the raid on Amman had failed in its primary object of so damaging the railway as to compel the withdrawal of the Turkish forces in the Hedjaz, it had succeeded in drawing northwards and retaining not only the Turkish troops which had been operating against the Arabs, but also a portion of the garrison of Maan and the stations farther south. Indeed the number of enemy troops east of the Jordan, in the Amman-El Salt-Shunet Nimrin area, was doubled as a result of these operations.

Taking advantage of this weakening of the Turkish forces opposed to him, the Emir Feisal renewed his attempts on Maan, and, during the first half of April, successfully destroyed a considerable portion of the railway both north and south of it, and even captured an outwork of the town itself, within two miles of the main positions.

Apart from the help given to the Arabs, the raid had resulted in a loss to the enemy of nearly 1000 prisoners and of all his ammunition and stores at El Salt. His losses in killed and wounded were estimated to have been not less than 1700.

Moreover the bridgehead which had been established across the Jordan at Ghoraniyeh was maintained and improved, and, a little later on, another bridge was thrown over the river some four miles farther north, at the mouth of the river Auja.

These bridges were a perpetual menace to the Turks across the Jordan, and caused them great uneasiness. On April 11th they made a determined attack on the Ghoraniyeh bridgehead simultaneously with an attack by German troops on our positions west of the Jordan, north of the Wadi el Auja. The bridgehead was held at the time by the 1st A.L.H. Brigade, and the Auja positions by the 2nd A.L.H. Brigade and the Camel Corps. Both attacks were pressed vigorously throughout the day, but ended in the complete defeat of the enemy, who left some 500 dead on the two positions, and over 100 prisoners in our hands.

Towards the end of April preparations were begun for a second raid across the Jordan. After the failure of his attack on the Ghoraniyeh bridgehead, the enemy had largely increased his forces east of the river, and had improved and strengthened his entrenched position at Shunet Nimrin. At the end of April he had about 8000 troops occupying this position. General Allenby determined to try to cut off and destroy this force, and, if successful, to hold El Salt till the Arab forces could advance and relieve our troops.

The great German offensive in France in March and April resulted in the force in Palestine being called upon to send to Europe every man and gun that could be spared. Thus, during April, the Yeomanry Division and two infantry divisions, besides ten other infantry battalions and a number of siege batteries and machine gun companies, were withdrawn from the line, and embarked for France. These troops were replaced by Indian regiments, the Yeomanry by Indian cavalry from France, and the infantry partly by the Lahore Division from Mesopotamia, and partly by untrained native troops from India.[1]

---

[1] See Appendix I. a for composition of Desert Mounted Corps after the reorganisation.

It was originally intended that the raid should take place about the middle of May, when the re-organisation had been completed, and the full strength of the Desert Mounted Corps would have been available. A necessary part of the raid, however, was the co-operation of the powerful Beni Sakhr tribe of Arabs, numbering some 7000 fighting men, which was at that time in the district round Madeba, about twelve miles east of the north end of the Dead Sea. Towards the end of April this tribe reported that their supplies would be exhausted by the 4th of May, and that they would then have to move to their summer grazing grounds farther south. The Commander-in-Chief therefore decided to attack at once, without waiting for the arrival of the Indian troops, though, in doing so, he was compelled to carry out the operations with a considerably smaller force than would have been the case if he had been able to wait another fortnight.

Thus the troops available for the raid consisted only of the Anzac and Australian Mounted Divisions, with two brigades of the 60th Division, and the (Indian) Imperial Service Cavalry and Infantry Brigades.

There was good reason for the employment of this large proportion of cavalry in an operation that was to be carried out in country most unsuited for mounted work.

General Allenby was always reluctant to keep his mounted troops in the trenches, if he could avoid doing so. Cavalry are most uneconomical troops in trench warfare, since at least a quarter of them are occupied caring for the horses, and consequently are not available for the firing line. Moreover, while employed in the line, they are deprived of the opportunity of training for mounted work, and their horses generally lose condition, since there are not enough men to look after them properly.

When, however, the three cavalry divisions were not used in the trenches, there were barely sufficient troops left to hold our long line securely, and very few infantry could be spared for extraneous enterprises. Moreover, though he would not put his cavalry into the line, if he could help it, the Commander-in-Chief had no intention of allowing them to grow rusty for lack of active operations. He was a firm believer in the old prize-ring adage that the best training for a fight is fighting.

The enemy's position ran north and south, astride the Jericho-Amman road, just west of Shunet Nimrin, his left resting on the deep gorge of the Wadi Kefrein, and his right flank thrown back in a half circle across the Wadi Arseniyat track to El Haud. Both flanks were protected by detachments of cavalry. From Shunet Nimrin two roads led back to Amman ; the metalled road through El Salt, and the more direct track through El Sir. The former was the only one available for wheeled traffic, but the latter had been considerably improved by the Turks since our last raid into Gilead. The plan was for the infantry to attack this position from the west, with the New Zealand Mounted Brigade on their right flank, while the rest of the cavalry, moving along the east bank of the Jordan as far as Umm el Shert and Jisr el Damieh, turned into the hills up the tracks from these two places, and captured El Salt, thus cutting the road to Amman. The Beni Sakhr Arabs undertook to hold the Ain el Sir track. With their only two lines of reinforcement or retreat thus closed, there appeared to be a good prospect of capturing or destroying the enemy forces at Shunet Nimrin.

In order to prevent the enemy from transferring

troops from the east to the west bank of the Jordan at Jisr el Damieh, as he had done during the previous raid, one brigade of cavalry, the 4th A.L.H., was directed to seize the Turkish bridge at that place if possible. If, however, it proved too strong to be taken, the brigade was to take up a position covering the track to El Salt, and endeavour to prevent the enemy crossing the river.

Our force crossed the Jordan on the night of the 29th of April, and by dawn the cavalry were through the scrub on the east bank, and advancing up the narrow plain between the river and the mountains, led by the 4th A.L.H. Brigade. The 1st and 2nd A.L.H. Brigades were attached to the Australian Mounted Division during the operations.

The 5th Mounted Brigade, followed by the 2nd A.L.H., turned off up the Umm el Shert track, and made for El Haud, while the 3rd A.L.H. Brigade turned up the track from Jisr el Damieh towards El Salt.

The 4th A.L.H. Brigade, followed by the 1st, in reserve, continued its march towards the bridge, and was fired on, just after dawn, from a prominent hill on the east bank about 6000 yards north-east of Umm el Shert, known to us as Red Hill. The 1st A.L.H. Regiment (1st Brigade) was directed against this hill, and the 4th Brigade passed to the east of it, and reached Jisr el Damieh about six o'clock. The 11th Regiment was at once sent forward to seize the bridgehead, but found the Turks in great force and strongly entrenched, and was unable to dislodge them. A further attempt to drive in the bridgehead also failed, and it was evident that the brigade was not strong enough to carry out the task. Red Hill, however, fell to the 1st Regiment about mid-day, after some sharp fighting, and the 4th A.L.H. Brigade then took up a position facing north-west about 2000 yards west of the foothills, and covering the Jisr el Damieh-El Salt track, from the Nahr el Zerka to a point about half a mile south of the track, with the 1st Regiment on Red Hill. It was supported by the three R.H.A. batteries of the Australian Mounted Division.

Early in the afternoon, columns of enemy troops were observed marching down to the west bank of the Jordan. They were engaged by our batteries and dispersed, disappearing among the broken ground on the far side of the river. It was not known at the time that the Turks had a pontoon bridge between Red Hill and El Damieh. It was towards this bridge that they were advancing, avoiding the one at El Damieh, which they knew to be under observation by our troops, and within range of our guns and machine guns.

At three o'clock the 1st A.L.H. Brigade was directed by the Corps to follow the rest of the cavalry towards El Salt, by the Umm el Shert track, leaving only one squadron on Red Hill.

Meanwhile our infantry had attacked the Shunet Nimrin positions on the west, and captured the advanced works, but were unable to make any farther progress, in face of greatly superior numbers of the enemy.

The 3rd A.L.H. Brigade, pushing very fast up the track from Jisr el Damieh, approached El Salt late in the afternoon, and was held up by fire from some enemy works covering the town on the north-west. The 9th and 10th Regiments attacked these works at once, and stormed them with the bayonet after a stiff fight. As soon as the position was taken, the 8th Regiment, which had been held in reserve under cover, mounted and galloped into the town, which was full of enemy troops. The Turks, surprised by this sudden charge, fought without cohesion, and the hustling tactics of the Australians broke up all attempts at reorganisation. By seven in the evening the whole place was in our hands, with some three hundred prisoners, a large number of machine guns, and all the papers and documents of the Turkish IVth Army headquarters, which was located in the town. The commander of the army, indeed, only just made good his escape. One regiment picketed the approaches of the town on the north, while the position was being cleared and the prisoners collected.

A squadron of the 8th Regiment pursued the enemy some distance down the Amman road, and captured a considerable number of prisoners. On its return, about eleven o'clock at night, the 10th Regiment was sent out along the road in the dark, to make good the junction of the Amman-Ain el Sir roads, some seven miles east of El Salt. The enemy was located in position astride the road at Ain Hemar, just west of the junction, and, as it was impossible to ascertain his strength in the darkness, the regiment threw out pickets, and remained facing the Turks till daylight.

The 5th Mounted and the 2nd and 1st A.L.H. Brigades, with the headquarters of the Australian Mounted Division and two mountain batteries, were overtaken by night on the Umm el Shert track. They had to lead their horses in single file up a very steep goat path, and made but slow progress. The head of the column reached El Salt early in the morning of the 1st of May, and the 2nd Brigade at once pushed on along the Amman road to Ain Hemar, drove off the small force of Turks there, and occupied the road junction. The 3rd Brigade held an outpost line north-west and north of El Salt, and the 1st

Brigade a similar line to the west, astride the El Shert track. The three brigades thus formed a cordon round El Salt on the east, north, and west. The 5th Brigade was ordered to move down the main road towards Shunet Nimrin, and attack the enemy's rear vigorously.

Meanwhile, down in the valley, the 4th A.L.H. Brigade was in difficulties. All night long the enemy had been crossing the river unseen, by the pontoon bridge mentioned above. About half-past seven in the morning some 4000 Turkish infantry deployed from the broken ground east of the Jordan, and advanced in open order, with their right flank directed on the gap between the left of the 4th Brigade and Red Hill. When the 1st Brigade had been withdrawn the previous evening, leaving only one squadron on the hill, General Grant had sent a squadron from the 11th Regiment to reinforce it, and had ordered two armoured cars which he had with him to watch the gap. One of these cars was put out of action very soon by a direct hit from a Turkish shell, but the other remained in action, and did much to stem the first rush of the Turks, until it was forced to retire, owing to casualties and lack of ammunition.

Our three batteries at once opened a rapid and accurate fire on the advancing Turks. They were immediately engaged by enemy batteries on the west bank of the Jordan, and heavily shelled, but continued in action, and caused severe casualties to the enemy.

Simultaneously with the attack from the west, about 1000 Turkish infantry and 500 cavalry, who had made their way up the Nahr el Zerka, debouched from the river bed, and attacked the right flank of the 4th Brigade. This attack was driven off, after a very sharp fight, but the Turks still continued to advance over the open ground from the west. At nine o'clock their forward lines had been annihilated by our fire, and they fell back a little, taking cover in some broken ground.

For about an hour there was a lull in the fighting. At ten o'clock a large body of the enemy, that had evidently worked south along the bed of the Jordan, suddenly appeared in the open, and swept over Red Hill, overwhelming the little garrison there. The remnants of our two squadrons withdrew to the broken ground south and south-east of the hill.

Immediately afterwards, the Turks attacked again along the whole line, rushing forward recklessly, shouting ' Allah ! Allah ! Allah ! ' Our small force, outnumbered by five to one, and hampered by its horses in the difficult country, was gradually forced back to the east against the hills, fighting desperately every step of the way. The right flank was driven back across the El Damieh-El Salt track, and the enemy entered the foothills north of the track, and began to work round to the rear. At the same time parties of Turks began to push southwards, between the left flank of the 4th Brigade and the remnants of the Red Hill garrison, now clinging grimly to their position south of the hill. Two troops, all that could be spared, were sent out to try and check this movement long enough to allow the right flank of the brigade to be withdrawn. The brigade headquarters and every man of ' B ' Battery H.A.C. that could be spared from the service of the guns were also thrown into the fight. This little handful of men fought heroically, but hopelessly, against the ever advancing waves of the enemy, and at last was pushed back across our line of retreat to the south.

When his right flank was turned, General Grant,

realising the impossibility of holding on any longer in the face of such odds, had ordered a retirement to a shorter line farther south, covering the Umm el Shert track. The right flank regiment was to retire first, followed by the regiment in the centre, and the line was to be re-formed, east and west across the valley, just north of Red Hill.

The brigade was now, however, in a very difficult position. Our troops had been forced back till they were facing due west, with their backs to the tangled maze of rocky hills, impassable for cavalry and guns. Some of the Turks were across their line of retreat to the south, though only in small numbers as yet. Others were working round the right flank of the brigade. All along the line our troops were hotly engaged at close quarters. To withdraw to a flank under such conditions was a very hazardous operation, but it appeared to offer the only chance of extricating the brigade from its desperate situation.

Two regiments of the New Zealand Mounted Brigade, which had been co-operating in the attacks on the Shunet Nimrin positions from the south, had been despatched to the assistance of the 4th Brigade, but they had fifteen miles of bad ground to cover, and could not possibly arrive in time to save the position. The most they could hope to do was to form a rallying point for the 4th Brigade to fall back upon.

The 4th A.L.H. Regiment, on the right flank, held on till the enemy closed to within 200 yards, in a desperate effort to cover the retirement of our guns. 'A' Battery H.A.C. was in this sector of the line, the Notts Battery R.H.A. near the centre, and 'B' Battery H.A.C. at the south end. The position of the two northernmost batteries was quite hopeless. Driven back to the verge of the impassable hills, they were in action in the open in the front line, and the only way of retreat feasible for wheeled vehicles was to the south, down the line of our troops, and in full view of the enemy at a few hundred yards distance.

Nevertheless the two batteries fought steadily on, attempting the impossible task of retiring by sections to the left flank. Each time a Turkish attack broke and melted away before their fire, the enemy dead lay a little closer to our guns. Each time a short retirement was made, the heavy pressure of the enemy pushed the guns farther into the hills; and each time there were fewer men and horses to move them. At last they were forced into a position from which there was no way out, and here they made a final stand, fighting till all their ammunition was exhausted, and the Turks were within two or three hundred yards on three sides of them. Even then a last effort was made to find a way out, but the teams were mown down by machine-gun fire, and the guns had to be abandoned. The remaining men and horses scrambled up the hills to the east, and succeeded in reaching the Wadi el Retem. The Australian troopers accompanied them, fighting grimly and silently, as an old dog fox, run into by the hounds, turns on his pursuers, slashing right and left, and dies with his teeth locked in a hound.

' B ' Battery H.A.C., having a shorter distance to go, succeeded in retiring to the south, through the enemy, and came into action again near the Umm el Shert track, to cover the withdrawal of the rest of our troops. During its retirement a gun was overturned in the bottom of a deep wadi, and had to be abandoned. A party of men, under an officer, descended into the ravine, and made a fine effort to right the gun and get it away; but the Turks appeared on the banks above, and opened fire on them with machine guns, killing nearly all the horses, and the attempt had to be abandoned.

Scrambling hurriedly through the foothills, our troops reassembled on the new position about mid-day, and took up a line along the south side of a small wadi, facing north, with Red Hill, which was occupied by the enemy, slightly to their left rear. General Chaytor, of the Anzac Division, now arrived in a motor, and assumed command. He at once decided to make a further retirement to a position immediately north of, and covering, the Umm el Shert track. This withdrawal was carried out successfully, with the assistance of the two New Zealand regiments, and a line was established along the Wadi el Retem, from the Jordan, to the foothills. Three times during the day the enemy attacked this position in a most determined manner, but the line stood fast, and each attack was repulsed with heavy losses to the Turks. When night fell, the vital Umm el Shert track, which was now the only way of communication with El Salt, was still open. Late in the afternoon touch was established with the 1st A.L.H. Brigade in the hills.

While the 4th Brigade was fighting desperately to keep open our communications with El Salt, the infantry were heavily engaged in another attack on the enemy's position at Shunet Nimrin. Fighting continued all day, but very little headway was made. Our light field guns could make no impression on the rock-hewn trenches of the Turks, and the wire, protected and partly concealed by the innumerable boulders in front of the positions, could not be effectively cut.

In spite of the weakness of our force, and the strength of the enemy's position, the attack might have been successful had the Beni Sakhr carried out their part of the bargain. Unfortunately, either through cowardice or treachery, they played us false, and never put in an appearance at all. Consequently the track through Ain el Sir remained open to the enemy, and, towards evening, reinforcements began to arrive at Shunet Nimrin by this road.

The 5th Mounted Brigade had set out from El Salt, soon after dawn, to co-operate with our infantry by attacking the enemy's rear about El Howeij. So great were the difficulties of the country, however, that it was not till nearly one o'clock that the brigade got in touch with the enemy, near the road bridge at El Howeij. The Turks were in great force, and strongly entrenched, and the 5th Brigade was unable to make much headway. The 1st A.L.H. Brigade was ordered to assist by attacking the enemy's flank farther west, at El Haud, while still guarding the El Shert track. Little progress was made during the day, and, as soon as darkness fell, the 2nd A.L.H. Brigade was withdrawn from Ain Hemar, and sent to the assistance of the 5th. Orders were sent to these two brigades that the 60th Division would attack Shunet Nimrin and El Haud at dawn on the 2nd, and that they were to co-operate in this attack by endeavouring to seize the high ground about Arkub el Khaluf.

In view of the precarious position of the 4th A.L.H. Brigade, down in the valley, the 1st Brigade was ordered to employ its whole strength in protecting the Umm el Shert track from all directions, and to keep touch with the 4th. These dispositions left only the 3rd Brigade to protect El Salt on the east, north, and north-west.

Our cavalry were now in a very precarious position. The strong force at Shunet Nimrin barred the main road, and the Wadi Arseniyat track, on the south-west. The Turkish 3rd Cavalry Division and part of an infantry division, having cleared our troops from their line of advance from Jisr el Damieh, were advancing on El Salt from the north-west ; and a third force was closing in on the east from Amman. The only line of supply or retreat still open was by the difficult Umm el Shert track.

Ammunition and food were running short, and fresh supplies had to be sent up to El Salt before morning. No vehicles could get up the Umm el Shert track, and, as the journey had to be done in the night, camels were equally out of the question. Each of the cavalry regiments had at this time a few donkeys, which were used by cooks and batmen, who did not usually accompany their units into action. About 200 of these were collected at Ghoraniyeh in the evening, loaded with ammunition and stores, and sent off in charge of a subaltern of the gunners.

Marching all night, they succeeded in reaching El Salt, which was then being hotly attacked by the enemy, on the morning of the 2nd, delivered their sorely needed ammunition, and returned safely to Ghoraniyeh. The distance covered on the double journey was forty miles, over an appalling country, and with the prospect of stumbling into the enemy at any moment. The men of the convoy had had no sleep for the two previous nights, and, being cavalrymen, were unaccustomed to marching. That they carried out their task in the face of such diffi- culties, with no greater mishap than the loss of a number of donkeys, which strayed from their half- dead drivers on the way back, is a fine tribute to the hardihood and determination of the men and the skill of the young officer in charge.

The 60th Division began the attack before dawn,

but made very slow progress up the rocky steeps of Shunet Nimrin, in face of the strong force of Turks, well posted on the heights above. The 5th Mounted Brigade commenced its advance on the Turkish right flank at El Howeij about eight o'clock, having been delayed in coming to grips with the enemy, owing to the extreme difficulty of the country. Even after the advanced troops of the brigade had engaged, it was estimated that the attack would take three hours to develop. At half-past ten, however, the whole brigade was in action against the first objective, the Howeij bridge position. The 2nd Brigade, which had farther to go, had not yet reached El Haud.

Early in the morning, the enemy column that had advanced from El Damieh, after driving in the 4th Brigade, reached El Salt, and developed a strong attack on the position held by part of the 3rd Brigade, north-west of the village. Under the weight of this attack, our line was pressed back a little, and, at eleven o'clock, a regiment from the 1st Brigade had to be despatched to the aid of the 3rd. Half an hour later a second regiment was withdrawn from the 1st Brigade, for the same purpose. The donkey convoy, carrying 100,000 rounds of small-arm ammunition and about 300 rounds for the mountain batteries, arrived at a most critical moment. The 3rd Brigade machine guns, which had almost been reduced to silence, awoke again, and the Turkish attack was temporarily driven back.

Just at this time, the brigadiers of the 2nd and 5th Brigades telephoned to El Salt that the country was so difficult that they saw no prospect of gaining their objectives before dark. General Hodgson directed them to push on as fast as they could, and attack the enemy with the utmost vigour, in order to assist our infantry in their attempt on the western slopes of the Shunet Nimrin positions.

Half an hour later General Kelly, commanding the 5th Brigade, reported his left flank in danger from a force of the enemy at El Fuheis, south of El Salt. This was most disquieting news. With a large force of Turks attacking El Salt on the north and north-west, and another force reported advancing on the east from Amman, General Hodgson had no troops to spare for defence on the south side. The cavalry were labouring under the inevitable disadvantage of having a quarter of their number occupied in holding the horses of the remainder, since all fighting in such country had to be done on foot. A whole brigade of cavalry was, therefore, barely equivalent in rifle strength to a single infantry battalion.

There was a gap of five miles of jagged, mountain country between the small force at El Salt and the 5th Brigade, which was fully occupied at El Howeij, and it appeared probable that the enemy troops at El Fuheis might penetrate through this gap. In that case the position of the 5th Brigade, and pro-bably also of the 2nd, would be hopeless. General Hodgson, however, could send no help. The only chance lay in driving in the enemy's flank at El Howeij and El Haud, and thus giving our infantry the opportunity to assault Shunet Nimrin from the west with some prospect of success. He ordered the 5th and 2nd Brigades to push on at all costs.

Half an hour later, however, the advance of the enemy force from Amman had become so threatening that he telephoned to the Corps Commander, asking if the attack of these two brigades could be stopped, in order that he might have them in hand for the defence of El Salt. Our infantry at this time were closely engaged on the west of Nimrin, fighting their way desperately up the hills, and there still appeared to be a chance of carrying the position, provided the cavalry continued to press against the enemy's right flank. General Chauvel, therefore, decided that the attack of the 2nd and 5th Brigades must be continued, but allowed one regiment of the 2nd to be withdrawn for the defence of El Salt. Shortly afterwards he consented to a second regiment being withdrawn from this brigade. This left only the 5th Brigade, already reduced in strength by casualties, and one regiment of the 2nd Brigade, to carry on the action at El Howeij.

By two o'clock these troops had progressed, with infinite difficulty and no little loss, to the edge of a tributary of the Wadi Nimrin, just north of El Howeij. At half-past two the 1st Brigade was ordered to send another regiment at once to join the two regiments of the 2nd Brigade at El Salt, who were hard pressed. There was now only one regiment of the 1st Brigade left on the west side of the village, and this was the only regiment of the force in the line not in action with the enemy. The 3rd Brigade, holding a line north-west and north of El Salt, was heavily engaged all along the line. Two regiments of the 2nd and one of the 1st Brigade were fighting on the north-east and east, and the remaining regiment of the 1st was in divisional reserve in the village.

At half-past four General Kelly reported that he was unable to advance at all. A body of Turkish cavalry was threatening his left flank and rear, and he was anxious about his led horses. General Hodgson had no troops to spare, and indeed was hard put to hold his own at El Salt. He directed General Kelly, while protecting his flank and rear as best he could with the 6th A.L.H. Regiment (2nd Brigade), to put in his reserve regiment in one last attack on El Howeij. If this attack failed, he was to remain in contact with the enemy, and attract as much attention as possible.

General Kelly formed a defensive left flank with the 6th A.L.H. Regiment, and threw in his reserve regiment to the attack. Scrambling painfully up the steep, rocky slope, the three regiments struggled forward with the utmost gallantry, against a murderous fire. Worn out by three days and nights of continuous marching and fighting, reduced by casualties, and with no supports to give their attack depth, they had no chance of reaching the enemy's position. The Turks, strong in numbers, and well posted in trenches and behind sangars, swept the slope with a hail of bullets, through which our little force could make no headway. The attack failed completely. The brigade re-formed, and took up a fire position on the north side of the wadi, facing the Turks.

On the west the attack of our infantry had also failed, and, in the evening, our troops drew off a little, and remained in observation of the Turks during the night. The enemy had been greatly reinforced at Shunet Nimrin during the day, and it was now clear that the operations would have to be abandoned. The problem was how to withdraw the cavalry from the mountains. All day long the Turks had been closing in on El Salt from the east, north, and north-west. From midnight onwards the enemy's fire had been very heavy on the front of the 2nd Brigade, and, in the early hours of the morning, his troops had worked up to within fifty yards of the 3rd Brigade at Kefr Huda. At the first sign of dawn on the 3rd, a squadron from this brigade made a desperate bayonet charge on this force. The

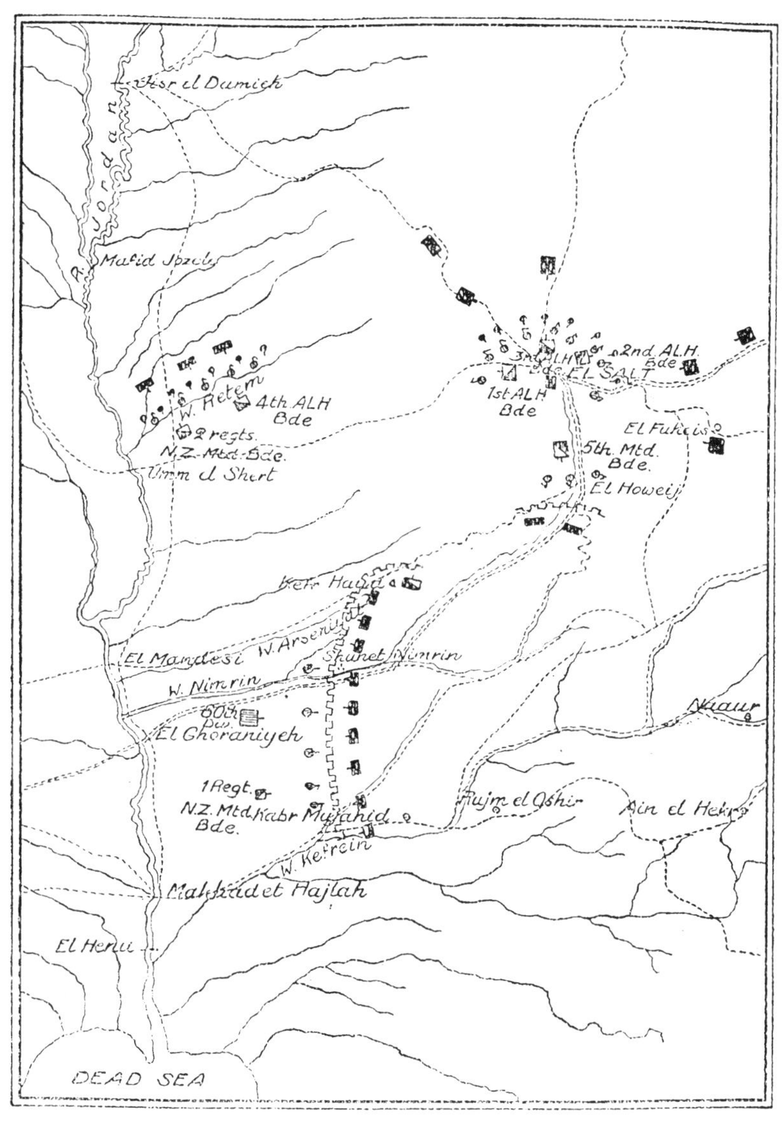

Diagram illustrating the situation on the 3rd. of May 1918.

Australians crashed into the Turks, just as they were massing for an assault, fighting like tigers, and drove them back more than half a mile, killing over a hundred of them.

This charge relieved the pressure on the north side for a little while, but another large enemy force now appeared on the Amman road to the east, and at once attacked the 2nd Brigade. Our troops were forced back by the weight of the attack, and, for a time, it looked as if our line would be broken. The situation was cleared by the action of Major Shannon, commanding the 8th A.L.H. Regiment (3rd Brigade), which was temporarily attached to the 2nd Brigade. He despatched a single troop, all that he could spare, with instructions to work round the Turks' right flank, unseen by the enemy if possible, and charge them from the rear. This desperate expedient was completely successful. The troop succeeded in getting behind the Turks just as they were preparing for another attack, and charged them with the bayonet, while the remainder of the 8th Regiment attacked in front. There were only twenty-five men in the troop, but they swung into the enemy with magnificent dash and a great deal of noise, and the sudden and unexpected attack from behind so disconcerted the Turks that they were thrown into confusion. The 8th Regiment, charging in front at the same time, completed the discomfiture of the enemy troops, who were driven back disorganised, and left 300 prisoners in our hands.

This success held up the enemy's offensive for some time, but, about seven o'clock, the Turks were seen to be again massing for an attack, and it became necessary to withdraw the 6th A.L.H. Regiment from El Howeij to support the 3rd Brigade. Shortly afterwards the 5th Brigade was called on to send a regiment to El Salt. The remaining two regiments, a mere handful of men, were directed to watch the rear of our force at El Salt, and endeavour to prevent the enemy from advancing up the road from Shunet Nimrin. Our infantry on the west assisted in this task by keeping up a sharp fire fight.

Arrangements were now put in hand to evacuate the wounded and such of the camel transport as was not required with the fighting troops, down the El Shert track, preparatory to the withdrawal of the whole force. Camels are slow and obstinate beasts, even in their native desert. Moving in single file down the precipitous goat path to Umm el Shert, they made barely half a mile an hour. Frightened by the slippery rocks, their feet cut and bruised by the sharp stones of the path, groaning and protesting in the manner of camels at every step, the unwieldy beasts lurched perilously down the track. Every now and then one of them would stop short, blocking the way for those behind it, and refuse obstinately to move on. What the wounded men in the cacolets must have suffered during this terrible journey can scarcely be imagined. It was past mid-day before the last camel had cleared El Salt.

Since the failure of their first attacks in the morning, the enemy troops had maintained a heavy fire on our positions east and north of the town, but had made no further serious attempt at an assault. Parties of them were, however, working round to the south, and the situation was becoming increasingly grave.

At half-past twelve a force of about 3000 Turkish infantry was observed advancing up the El Damieh track, the head of the column being then about three miles from El Salt. Two hours later this force had deployed, and was attacking the 3rd Brigade. At the same time the enemy renewed his pressure on the east. As the wounded were now well on their way down to the valley, the Corps Commander ordered General Hodgson to withdraw to a position south-west of El Salt, covering the El Shert track. As soon as this withdrawal began, the enemy pushed forward, and engaged our troops most severely. One of our posts on the north-west was driven in, but, before any counter-attack could be organised, a message was received from Corps Headquarters ordering the cavalry to withdraw altogether from the hills, *if able to do so.*

The 1st Brigade was now in position across the El Shert track, south-west of El Salt, and facing east. The remainder of the force withdrew through this line, by regiments, after dark, and marched down the track during the night. As they could only move in single file, daylight found them strung out for several miles along the path. The evacuation of El Salt was completed by half-past two in the morning, but the Turks did not discover this fact till dawn. They at once pushed on through the village to attack the 1st Brigade. At the same time enemy guns heavily shelled the rearguard of the brigade, and several hostile aeroplanes bombed our troops in the defile, causing a number of casualties. The Turks continued to press the 1st Brigade rearguard till it was three miles west of El Salt, when they drew off, evidently fearing to venture farther towards our troops in the valley.

By half-past ten the whole of our force was clear of the hills, and moving in extended order down the valley towards El Ghoraniyeh, covered by the 4th A.L.H. Brigade and part of the New Zealand Brigade. These two brigades had been in action almost continuously since they had taken up the position covering the Umm el Shert track on the 1st. They had, however, succeeded in repelling all attacks, with heavy losses to the enemy. On the evening of the 3rd the Turks, abandoning the attempt to break our line in the valley, had withdrawn to the north, and followed their comrades towards El Salt. The dogged fighting of the 4th Brigade and the New Zealanders had saved the situation. Had they given way, the Turks would have reached the Umm el Shert track, and the whole of our cavalry force in the hills must then, almost certainly, have fallen into the hands of the enemy.

By nightfall the whole of our force had withdrawn behind a brigade of infantry which had been brought across the Jordan from the west to form an extended bridgehead. During the night the troops recrossed the river, and the force was all safely on the west bank before morning on the 5th. The Ghoraniyeh bridgehead was restored, and the Australian Mounted Division took over the left sector of the Jordan Valley defences, along the river Auja, including a new bridge and bridgehead which had been thrown across the Jordan, at its junction with the Auja, during the operations. The Anzac Mounted Division took over the right sector of the valley defences, including the Ghoraniyeh bridgehead.

Although the raid had failed in its primary object, which was the destruction of the enemy force at Shunet Nimrin, it had not been altogether unsuccessful. In the first place the Turks had been very roughly handled, and, besides having many of their troops killed and wounded, had lost nearly 1000 prisoners. The really important result of the operations, however, lay in the fact that the raid finally convinced the enemy that, in our next general advance, our cavalry would be directed on Amman and Deraa Junction.

Under the influence of this idea, he was led to place practically the whole of his IVth Army east of the Jordan, which was thus separated by the river, with its deep and difficult channel, from the remainder of his forces in the Judæan Hills. It was this fact that enabled us, in the following September, to envelop and completely destroy the VIIth and VIIIth Armies, before the IVth Army could intervene.

The River Jordan at Ghoranigeh.

Shunet Nimrin and the Amman Road. Looking east, towards the
positions held by the enemy.

CHAPTER XIV

THE VALLEY OF DESOLATION

THE Commander-in-Chief had now to decide whether or not he should hold the Jordan Valley during the summer. Local authorities declared emphatically that it was impossible for Europeans to exist there during the summer months, owing to the intense heat and the prevalence of malaria of a most virulent type. They pointed to the fact that even the native Arabs move out of it to the hills during the hot weather, and that Jericho itself is deserted. The only inhabitants of the district during the summer are the small and miserable tribe of the Abid Miriam, a people of negroid origin, descendants of African slaves imported by the Arabs in former times. These live about Ain el Duk, where they carry on a rude form of irrigation by means of a few of the old, Roman water channels that still exist.

The official military handbook of Palestine confirmed the local opinion by the statement that ' Nothing is known of the climate of the lower Jordan Valley in summer time, since no civilised human being has yet been found to spend a summer there ' !

On the other hand, there were several strong reasons for continuing to hold the valley line if possible. Some of these have been indicated at the beginning of Chapter XI., but there was now another, and stronger, reason for holding it, which was to confirm the enemy in his belief that we intended to strike east of the Jordan in our next big advance.

Moreover, since it was clear that it would be necessary to occupy the valley and the river crossings, when the next advance was commenced, it was considered less costly to continue to hold it during the summer than to have to retake it later on.

After careful consideration, General Allenby resolved to hold the valley line permanently, and, as several of the German staff documents which we had captured assumed that we would strike in that part of our line near which the cavalry was stationed, it was decided to put them there.

The line was accordingly organised in two sectors. The left sector extended from the foot of the Judæan mountains, along the north bank of the Wadi el Auja, to its junction with the Jordan, and included the bridge and bridgehead there. A rocky ridge, several hundred feet high, ran north and south through this position, from Tel el Sultan, near Jericho, and extended north of the Auja, along the hill of Abu Tellul, ending in an abrupt bluff at Musallabeh.   This ridge was held by us, so that this portion of the line resembled a fist with the first finger extended, the finger representing the ridge, and the Wadi el Auja the line of the knuckles.   Abu Tellul and Musallabeh overlooked a dreary expanse, part swamp, part stony plain, covered with large patches of dense scrub, and intersected by innumerable deep wadis.   The Turks were able to move unseen among the scrub and wadis all round the salient in our line, a fact which caused us much annoyance all the time we were in occupation of the valley.   It was, however, necessary to hold Abu Tellul and Musallabeh, both to preserve the water supply of the Auja for ourselves, and to deny it to the enemy.

The right sector extended from the mouth of the Auja, along the right bank of the Jordan, to the

Dead Sea, and included the bridges and bridgehead at Ghoraniyeh.

The reorganisation of the cavalry was completed by the middle of May, and the Desert Mounted Corps now consisted of the Anzac and Australian Mounted Divisions and the 4th and 5th (Indian) cavalry divisions.[1] The valley line was held by two cavalry divisions, one in each sector, supported by a brigade of Indian infantry, and two battalions of the British West Indies Regiment. This organisation permitted of two divisions at a time being withdrawn to rest in camps established in the cool hills near Bethlehem, so that each cavalry division had alternatively a month on duty in the valley, and a month at rest in the hills. For the gunners of the Corps, however, there was no relief, owing to the shortage of artillery in the force, and they had to pass the whole summer in the valley, till the end of July, an experience which none of them is ever likely to forget.

In past ages the Dead Sea covered a much greater area than it does at the present day. The lower Jordan valley is, therefore, the bottom of the old sea, and is covered with a layer of white marl, several feet deep, which is strongly impregnated with salt. In spring the land supports a little thin grass, but the fierce sun of early summer scorches it in a few days to brittle dust. Under the feet of men and horses the marl of the valley floor soon broke up into a white powder, as fine as flour, which lay everywhere, in places over a foot deep. Every morning, after a breathless night, a strong hot wind arose from the north, and swept the dust down the valley in dense, choking clouds. About eleven o'clock in the morning the wind used to die down as suddenly as it had arisen, and for about half an hour there was

---

[1] See Appendix I. *a.* for detail of cavalry.

a period of deathlike stillness, accompanied by the most intense heat of the day. Then the wind recommenced violently, but blowing from the *south*, and continued till about eight in the evening. Innumerable, violent air currents swept about the valley, often carrying along ' dust devils ' of immense height. It was no uncommon thing for one of these devils to tear up a tent, and lift it bodily high into the air.

There was a tiny patch of green cultivation at Ain el Duk, about five miles behind our line, and another at Jericho, and a few dusty thorn trees grew along the Wadi el Auja. The rest of the valley was a barren and awful wilderness of dust, stones, and boulders, inhabited, before we came, only by snakes and scorpions.

The average maximum daily temperature during July, as taken at the R.A. Headquarters on the top of the Tel el Sultan-Abu Tellul Ridge, was 113·2° F. in the shade. The highest reading recorded during the month was 122° and the lowest 107°. At the foot of the ridge the temperature was about 3° higher, and at Ghoraniyeh it reached 130° on several occasions. During August the temperature rose still higher, but no daily record was then kept of the thermometer readings. The tremendous evaporation of the Dead Sea keeps the atmosphere moist, and adds to the discomfort caused by the great heat, while the increased air pressure, due to the depth of the valley floor below sea level (1200 feet at Ghoraniyeh), induces a feeling of lassitude against which it is difficult to fight.

The effect of the climate on the horses was most remarkable. After about three weeks in the valley, they became so tired and dispirited, though they had little or no work to do, that they could scarce drag themselves the mile or so to water and back again.

An unceasing campaign was carried on by the medical staff of the Corps against the malaria-bearing mosquitoes which infested the valley, and this undoubtedly did much to lessen the incidence of malaria, especially of the malignant type, among the troops. In spite of all efforts, however, the sick rate was high, as it was bound to be under such conditions. Deaths and evacuations of sick to hospital averaged together about one per cent. of the total strength per day, which meant that the whole force in the valley would have to be replaced every three months. Actually, however, the alternate month in the hills enjoyed by the cavalry enabled many men, who had been sent to hospital, to recover in time to do another tour of duty in the valley. Curiously enough the Indian troops suffered more severely than did the British.

In this climate, and under such conditions, His Majesty's troops, white, brown, and black, held the line throughout the summer of 1918, and it is safe to say that few other troops in the Great War endured greater hardships and discomfort than did the Jordan Valley force.

There was but one action of importance during the summer. On the 14th July two Turkish divisions, supported by three battalions of German infantry, attacked our positions at Musallabeh and Abu Tellul from the west. Under cover of darkness the German troops, having cut our wire, penetrated between two of our posts, and actually reached our second line on the top of Abu Tellul, which was not occupied, owing to lack of troops.

The 1st A.L.H. Brigade was holding this sector of the line at the time, supported by a miscellaneous collection of artillery—horse, field, mountain and siege. The attack was preceded by a very heavy enemy bombardment, which cut all our telephone wires. The batteries were thus, early in the fight, out of touch with their observers, and, as the latter had in some cases to move hurriedly from their posts to avoid capture, it was some time before communications could be re-established. In the meantime the batteries continued to fire on their S.O.S. lines.

The commanding officer of the 2nd A.L.H. regiment, against which the brunt of the attack fell, narrowly escaped capture, but succeeded with his staff in reaching a post in the second line on Abu Tellul. In the uncertain light just before dawn, he observed a large body of troops coming up the hill towards him, and at first took these for some of his own men retiring from the outer posts. When they reached the wire, however, and began to cut it, he realised that they were the enemy, and at once gave the order to open rapid fire on them. This had the effect of driving the Germans, who were ignorant of the fact that there were only twelve men in front of them, away to the right, where they occupied a post near the end of Abu Tellul, known as the Bluff.

Meanwhile the artillery officer with this section of the defence, who had had both his signallers wounded, succeeded in getting a runner back to one of the Horse Artillery batteries, with news of the state of affairs. An officer at once set out from his battery with two signallers, and, riding as far as the foot of Abu Tellul, under very heavy shell fire, dismounted, and set to work repairing the telephone wires. Having got into communication with the battery, the officer went forward on foot with his signallers, running out a fresh wire, and reached the top of Abu Tellul just after daylight. Here he found two officers and twelve men of the reserve regiment of the 1st A.L.H. Brigade, who were on their way to counter-attack the Bluff, a strongly entrenched position in which there were, at the time, some eighty German infantry ! The party moved forward cautiously, taking advantage of the cover afforded by the numerous rocks, but had not gone far when an enemy shell burst among them, killing and wounding six. One of the officers thereupon went back for reinforcements, and the remaining nine, including the gunners, continued their advance. After going a short distance farther, they observed a number of the enemy near the Bluff, some 200 yards distant. Fortunately the telephone line still held, so the fire of the battery was directed on the enemy. The little 13-pounder H.E. shell burst with excellent effect among the rocks of the position, and the Germans very soon had enough of them, and surrendered. They were collected, to the number of forty, disarmed, and put in charge of two of the Australians, while the ' counter-attack,' now reduced to seven, moved forward again. Another body of the enemy was soon discovered occupying the end part of Abu Tellul. The battery opened fire on these, and after a few minutes, believing that they were cut off, they too put up a white flag and laid down their arms. There were six officers and eighty men here, and their chagrin was great on discovering that they had surrendered to seven men. However, they were told that the rest of their force had been repulsed, and that our battery was quite ready to open fire again, if need arose. The two parties were quickly hustled away to the rear, being liberally shelled by their own gunners on the way.

While this little comedy was being enacted at the end of the Abu Tellul Ridge, daylight had come, and the enemy's only chance of capturing the position had passed. Our outer posts, though surrounded, had all held out, and turned the fire of their machine guns with good effect on the enemy on the southern end of Abu Tellul. Some of these worked south to the part of the ridge overlooking the Wadi el Auja, and suddenly found themselves looking down on a battery of mountain howitzers that were firing in the opposite direction, at some Turks who were attempting to cross the wadi. The howitzers were immediately turned end for end in their pits, and fired up the hill straight into the faces of the astonished Germans, who retired discomfited, to hide among the rocks and trenches farther north till gathered in by our troops later on.

By now the 5th A.L.H. regiment and the New Zealand Mounted Brigade, which had been sent up in support, had arrived on the scene. Pushing along both sides of the Abu Tellul Ridge, they quickly drove out the rest of the enemy, and restored the position.

The two Turkish divisions, which were to have attacked on each side of the German troops, had waited for daylight to make their assault, with the result that they were easily driven off. The southern force, indeed, only attacked once, and that but half-heartedly, but the division on the enemy's left made three attempts on Musallabeh, only to be driven back each time with heavy loss by a murderous machine-gun fire. The Turks left about 200 dead on the positions.

By ten o'clock in the morning the whole position was completely restored, and our prisoners (380 Germans and about 200 Turks) were on their way back to headquarters.

At this juncture there occurred an incident so typical of the Hun that it is worth recording. As they were marching back, a number of the German officers and men commenced to show evident signs of distress, and presently began to drop insensible by the wayside. As they had only light field service caps on their heads, it was thought that they had been overcome by the sun. Ambulance carts were sent for, and the sufferers were conveyed to a field hospital near by, attended on the way with the most solicitous care by their Australian escort. On arrival at the hospital, however, it was discovered that they were merely speechlessly drunk, whereupon the incensed Australians soused them unceremoniously with water, and sent them on their way to the prisoners' compounds without more ado. It transpired afterwards that several small parties of Germans had been detailed to cut our telephone wires as soon as they had penetrated our lines. While engaged on this work they had stumbled on a tent, pitched in a little gully, in which were stored several cases of beer and one or two of whisky, which had been brought up at very great trouble for the men of the 2nd A.L.H. regiment. Unable to resist this liquor, the Germans, officers and men, abandoning their task of wire cutting, fell upon the cases, and, knocking off the heads of the bottles, poured the contents down their throats. When they had drunk all they could hold, they smashed the rest of the bottles, and staggered away, to be captured disgracefully by our troops. Had any of them been on the scene when the thirsty Australians repaired to the tent after being relieved from the trenches, they would undoubtedly have shared the fate of the bottles !

During the attack on Musallabeh and Abu Tellul the enemy was observed to be massing for an attack east of the river Jordan, opposite El Henu ford, about half-way between Makhadet Hajlah and the Dead Sea. The Imperial Service Cavalry Brigade immediately moved out from Ghoraniyeh to attack.

Taking advantage of the cover afforded by the broken ground and scrub on the east bank, the cavalry arrived within charging distance before they were observed. They charged at once, and routed the Turks, killing ninety with the spear, and taking about 100 prisoners and several machine guns.

During the remainder of the period spent in the Jordan Valley, action on both sides was confined to artillery activity, in which the enemy, owing to the freedom of movement he enjoyed, had the advantage of us, and to patrol work, in which our troops, more especially the Indian Cavalry, had it all their own way. The only sources of water, other than the Jordan, were the Wadi el Auja, which was used by the troops and horses in the left sector, and the Wadi Nueiameh, which arose at Ain el Duk, and flowed into the Jordan at El Ghoraniyeh. The latter wadi was used by the Headquarters of the Valley Defences and by the field ambulances and supply and ordnance troops. The east side of the Tel el Sultan-Abu Tellul Ridge, which was only about 7000 yards from the Jordan, was occupied by horse lines, ammunition column camps, and field hospitals. Early in July the enemy, who had received considerable artillery reinforcements, pushed a number of field guns and heavy howitzers southwards, east of the Jordan, and commenced a systematic shelling of these troops. Camps and horse lines had to be moved, and scattered about in sections, in most inconvenient situations, along the bottoms of small wadis running down from the ridge into the plain. Some protection was obtained by these measures, but there was not sufficient room in the wadis for all the units, and those which had to remain in the open suffered under a constant, galling shell fire, and had to shift their camps every few days.

The whole of the Wadis el Auja and Nueiameh was under the enemy's observation either from Red Hill and other high ground east of the Jordan, or from the foothills west and north-west of Abu Tellul. The Turks took full advantage of this to shell our watering parties almost every day. The drinking-places were frequently changed, and every effort was made to distract the enemy's attention, during the hours when horses were being watered, by shelling his positions vigorously. But the dense clouds of dust raised by even the smallest parties of horses on the move, generally gave the game away, and we had constant trouble and numerous casualties among men and horses.

About the same time as the Turks became aware of the possibilities of artillery on the east bank of the Jordan, they got a six-inch long-range gun in position in the hills north-west of our line in the valley, and shelled Ghoraniyeh, Jericho, and other back areas at a range of some 20,000 yards. The gun was nicknamed ' Jericho Jane ' by our gunners, and the name found its way eventually into the Corps' Daily Intelligence Report. But when the enemy brought up two more such guns into about the same position, and the three were referred to in the daily report from one of the R.A. Headquarters as ' Jericho Jane and her two wicked sisters,' the powers that were decreed that such slang was inappropriate in official reports !

For the first week ' Jericho Jane ' confined her unwelcome attentions to Jericho, into which she put about thirty shells, and to various camps and horse lines in the neighbourhood. But, when her wicked sisters arrived, they at once commenced to pay court to the 13th Cavalry Brigade, which was in reserve at the time, and was camped about Ain el Duk on the west side of the ridge. This position had hitherto been deemed the only safe spot in the whole horrible valley, and it was a sad blow to the 13th Brigade, who had a comfortable camp close to water, to find their sanctuary invaded by these outrageous viragoes.

The first shot hit the top of the Mount of Temptation, just above the rock-hewn hermitage of a community of Greek monks. The line of fire then moved slowly down the mountain side, the thunderous crashes of the bursting shells sending the good monks to the shelter of their rock cells quicker than ever the prayer bell had done. Meantime the cavalry were breaking camp in record time. Before the first shell burst in the camp, the whole brigade was mounted and moving southwards into the Wilderness, homeless as the Children of Israel. The ' safe ' camp, the envy of all the valley, with its outlook over a beautiful patch of vivid green at Ain el Duk, was abandoned to the snake and the scorpion, and the indignant troops had to find such shelter as was available here and there in the bottoms of arid, dusty wadis.

The three sisters were eventually spotted by aeroplanes, and silenced by some of our heavy artillery in the mountain sector. In the valley itself, it was almost impossible to locate the enemy guns. Owing to the very broken nature of the country, the damp atmosphere and the constant dust, our aeroplanes were unable to spot them, even when firing, and they caused us constant annoyance, while remaining almost immune from our fire. Flying over the valley was at all times most hazardous work, owing to the innumerable vortices and pockets in the air, and there were many bad accidents.

The Australian Mounted Division left the valley finally on the 1st August, followed shortly afterwards by the 5th Cavalry Division. The two divisions were relieved by the 4th and the Anzac Divisions. Marching by easy stages during the night, and remaining hidden by day among vineyards and olive groves, they crossed the mountains to the coastal plain, and went into camp in the neighbourhood of Selmeh and Ludd.

The blessed coolness of the nights, and the clear and comparatively bracing air of the plain, soon began to have a good effect on the jaded troops and horses, worn out by their long periods in the dismal Valley of Desolation. Training recommenced at once, and continued till the middle of September, when the two divisions marched into positions of hiding, preparatory to the Great Drive. The 4th Cavalry Division, having left the valley on the 11th September, joined them on the 17th.

The Anzac Division remained sweltering by the Jordan till after the commencement of the September operations, suffering greatly from sickness, but 'carrying on' with the cheerfulness and courage typical of the Australians.

Just before leaving the valley, the writer heard an Australian trooper sum up the all-pervading horror of the place in a characteristic sentence. After gazing for some time at the hideous expanse of white dust and blistering rocks at his feet, he remarked slowly: 'Well, I reckon God made the Jordan Valley, and when He seen what He done, He threw stones at it!'

CHAPTER XV

PREPARATIONS FOR THE GREAT DRIVE

At the end of August 1918 the 5th and Australian Cavalry Divisions were encamped near Khurbet Deiran and Ramleh respectively; the 4th Division and the Anzac Mounted Division were still in the Jordan Valley. The new 5th A.L.H. Brigade, which had only two regiments, was completed by the inclusion of the French ' Régiment Mixte de Cavalerie.' This was a four-squadron unit, consisting of two squadrons of regular French cavalry and two of Algerian Spahis, and was commanded by Colonel Le Bon, an officer who had had many years' experience in the East. The Spahis, with their picturesque half-Arab uniforms and their enormous curved sabres, which they carried under the flaps of their saddles, added a note of colour to the division, and caused endless diversion to the Australians. They were mounted on good-looking barbs, which could march indefinitely, if allowed to go at their own rate, but the pace of our big horses was rather too hot for them, as was proved by the subsequent operations.

As there were only ten batteries of Horse Artillery available, one battery (' B ' H.A.C.) was withdrawn from the Australian Mounted Division in August, and joined the 5th Cavalry Division. These two divisions had thus only two batteries each.

During the first half of September preparations for the Great Drive were pushed forward energetically. Our broad-gauge railway had now been carried forward as far north as Ludd, and the old Turkish line from Ludd to Jerusalem had been re-laid for broad gauge. Light railways had been built along the coastal plain, from Ludd up to our front line; tracks had been improved, and roads made behind the line in the mountain sector, and, from Jiljulie to the sea, the gunners were working ceaselessly, like a legion of ants, preparing positions for the considerable force of artillery that was to assist in forcing the enemy defences here.

The Turkish line west of the Jordan ran east from the coast, at a point just north of the old Crusader fortress of Arsuf, over the coastal plain to Jiljulie, near the railhead at Kalkili. Here it entered the mountains, and ran a little south of east, passing roughly through Mesha, Furkha and El Lubban, to the Jordan at Umm el Shert.

Forty miles north of this line lie the Plain of Esdraelon, or Armageddon, and the Valley of Jezreel, which cut a gap right through the mountain range from the sea to the river Jordan. Esdraelon is shaped roughly like a broad-bladed arrow head, having its point at Haifa on the sea coast, and the extremities of its blades at Mount Tabor on the north, and at the little town of Jenin on the south. Midway between these two lies the village of Afule, whence the Valley of Jezreel, forming the shaft of the arrow, runs down to the Jordan at Beisan, which is about fifteen miles south of the Sea of Galilee, and four miles west of the Jordan.

From Deraa Junction on the Hedjaz Railway, about thirty-five miles east of the Sea of Galilee, a branch line runs westwards to Semakh, at the southern end of the lake, and thence southwards down the Jordan Valley to Beisan. From here two roads lead south down the valley, one on each side of the river, and a third goes south-west through the mountains to Nablus. Leaving Beisan, the railway continues in a north-westerly direction up the Valley of Jezreel, through Afule, to Haifa. From Afule a branch line runs south to Jenin, and thence to Samaria and Nablus ; and from Messudieh, near Samaria, another branch winds through the mountains to Tul Keram on the coastal plain, and thence south to Kalkili.

Thus, to quote the Commander-in-Chief's despatch: [1] ' Afule, Beisan, and Deraa were the vital points on the enemy's communications. If they could be seized, his retreat would be cut off. Deraa was beyond my reach, but not beyond that of mobile detachments of the Arab Army. It was not to be expected that these detachments could hold this junction, but it was within their power to dislocate all traffic.'

The coastal plain, consisting of rolling downland, is about ten miles wide at Arsuf. From this point northwards it gradually narrows, till it is shut off altogether at Haifa, where the Mount of Carmel, an offshoot from the main Judæan range, falls in steep cliffs to the sea. The only track over the Carmel Range into the Plain of Esdraelon that is possible for wheeled traffic is by the famous Musmus Pass, from Kerkur to Lejjun on the river Kishon, over which Thothmes III. led his army, ' horse behind horse and man behind man,' to the great victory of Megiddo, in 1479 B.C.

The pass, which carries the age-old caravan road from Egypt to Mesopotamia, leads through a narrow, rocky defile, in steep and difficult mountain country, and, near the top of the range, is enclosed in places between sheer cliffs. Skilfully handled, a small body of troops could hold it for a long time against a greatly superior force.

---

[1] Dated October 31, 1918.

The enemy VIIth and VIIIth Armies held the line from the sea to the Jordan Valley. His IVth Army was disposed in the valley and east of the Jordan. A fairly good, metalled road runs from Jiljulie, through Tul Keram, to Nablus. From here two bad mountain tracks lead down to the Jordan, one through Beit Dejan, and the other by Ain Shibleh and down the Wadi Farah. These two tracks join one another at El Makhruk, four miles west of the river, and then continue over the Jordan at Jisr el Damieh, and on to El Salt. This was the enemy's only lateral communication, and the portion between Nablus and El Salt was so difficult that the IVth Army was practically isolated from the rest of the force.

The Turkish armies opposed to us, including reserves and lines of communication troops, numbered some 90,000 men, of whom perhaps 5000 were cavalry, with about 400 guns. Their Commander-in-Chief was the German Marshal Liman von Sanders, who had his headquarters at Nazareth. Our own troops numbered about 120,000, including 25,000 cavalry, with 540 guns.

The *morale* of the enemy troops, both Turkish and German, was lower than it had been at any time since the beginning of the campaign. Many of the Turkish soldiers were ill-trained and of poor character. Disheartened by a long series of successful small raids, carried out by our infantry during the past two months, utterly weary of a war the objects of which they little understood, racked with disease, and imbued with a bitter hatred of their German masters, who despised and bullied them, they were in no state to withstand the onslaught that was preparing. The ill-feeling between Turks and Germans, which had existed from the very beginning of the war, had now reached an acute stage.   The Germans, with characteristic stupidity, failed to do anything to allay the irritation caused by their overbearing manner, and openly expressed contempt for their allies.

Numerous documents, subsequently captured by us at the enemy G.H.Q., testified to the deplorable state of internal strife and suspicion to which the enemy army was now reduced.   Indeed, with the exception of a few senior officers, the Germans seemed to take a delight in ill-treating and insulting the unhappy Turks.

These factors must be borne in mind in estimating the tactics adopted by the British Commander-in-Chief.   His plan was one of the boldest and simplest ever conceived by a great captain, and will live in the text-books of the soldiers of all nations, as a model of the use of cavalry, as long as war is waged.   Such risks as he took in the carrying out of that plan, and they were numerous, were justified by the state of the enemy armies opposed to us, and were, in every instance, triumphantly vindicated by the success of the operations.

In broad outline, the plan was to concentrate an overwhelming force of infantry and guns in the coastal sector, together with three divisions of cavalry: for the infantry to attack the enemy positions from Jiljulie to the sea, and, having captured them, to wheel to the right, pivoting on Jiljulie, and bend back the enemy's right wing into the hills, exactly like opening a door.   Through this open door the cavalry were to dash, and ride up the coast and over the Musmus Pass into the Plain of Esdraelon. Once in the plain, their task was to seize Afule, and then ride down the Valley of Jezreel to Beisan and the Jordan, and cut the railways at these two places, while an Arab force cut it farther east at Deraa. Later on Haifa was to be occupied, and thus a net of cavalry would be drawn from the sea to the Jordan. As soon as the cavalry were well through the gap on the coastal plain, our infantry were to attack all along the line in the mountain sector, while the troops that had opened the door endeavoured to roll up the enemy line from his right flank. Our force in the Jordan Valley was to advance simultaneously, and seize the bridge over the Jordan at El Damieh. The two Turkish armies west of the Jordan would thus be caught in a trap, with the sea on their right and the Jordan on their left, and, with all their communications cut, would be forced back into the cavalry net behind them.

Once the crossing over the Jordan at Jisr el Damieh was in our hands, the Turkish IVth Army east of the river would find itself isolated, with its communications cut (at Deraa), and exposed to the converging attacks of our force in the valley, which would hold the river crossings, and of the Arab forces on the east. At the beginning of September a mobile column of the Arab Army, accompanied by armoured cars and a mountain battery, was assembling at Kasr el Azrak, in the desert fifty miles east of Amman, under the energetic direction of Lawrence.

The first essential for the success of the plan was to conceal from the enemy the considerable concentration of troops on the coastal plain, especially that of the three cavalry divisions.

It is doubtful if there has ever been a greater master of the art of deception in war than the British Commander-in-Chief. No detail was too small, no dodge too insignificant to engage his full attention. The two trans-Jordan raids had given the enemy the impression that we intended to attack either up the

Jordan Valley, or east of it, at Amman and along the Hedjaz Railway, and General Allenby now set himself to foster this belief by every possible means.

To this end he ordered Major-General Chaytor, who was in the Jordan Valley, in command of a mixed force consisting of the Anzac Mounted Division and eight battalions of infantry, to make a series of demonstrations, with the object of inducing the enemy to believe that an attack east of Jordan was intended. The camps in the valley vacated by the cavalry were left standing, and other camps were pitched there, and occupied by a few men, to show signs of movement, and to make tracks about, and leading to, the camps, in order to deceive enemy airmen. New bridges were thrown across the Jordan, miles of Décauville railway were laid, and thousands of dummy horses were erected on dummy horse lines in the dummy camps. Every day, for some considerable time, a battalion or two of infantry marched down the Jerusalem-Jericho road from Talaat el Dumm, and occupied one or other of these camps. During the night they were brought back to Talaat el Dumm, in returning empty motor lorries, ready to march back again next day. These troops could be plainly seen, marching down into the valley, by the enemy at Shunet Nimrin, who was thus induced to believe that a considerable concentration was taking place in the valley. This unpleasant daily promenade fell to the lot of the British West Indies regiments.

For the benefit of the native population, elaborate bogus preparations were made for the removal of G.H.Q. to Jerusalem. One of the hotels there was cleared of its occupants, much to their disgust, and staff officers busied themselves installing office furniture and telephone equipment, and painting the names of a multitude of departments on the doors of the rooms.

Lastly, lest a chance word should reach a native enemy spy within our lines, everything was done to further the belief among our own troops that we were likely to attack on the east flank. The writer remembers receiving a visit one day from his Divisional General, and being told to do nothing to discourage the idea that the cavalry would once again find themselves in the Valley of Desolation. He also remembers vividly the lurid language that arose on all sides when this report spread about the camps!

No orders were committed to paper other than those issued by G.H.Q. and the three Corps. Secret conferences were called in turn at the various Divisional Headquarters, when the scheme was explained to staffs and commanders of brigades, each of whom then prepared his scheme, and submitted it verbally to his immediate superior.

The three cavalry divisions on the left of our line were hidden securely from the eyes of enemy aeroplane observers ; the Australian Mounted Division in the immense, old olive woods round Ramleh, the 4th Cavalry Division in the orange groves near Selmeh, and the 5th Division, which had left the Jordan Valley on September 11, in those north-west of Sarona.

Shortly before the operations commenced, the 60th and 75th Infantry Divisions were brought across to the coastal sector, where they remained, unseen by the enemy, till the attack was launched.

During all the period of concentration, the magnificent work of the Royal Air Force played a dominant part in keeping the enemy in ignorance of our movements. The Commander-in-Chief paid the force a well-deserved compliment in his despatch when he said : ' The chief factor in the secrecy maintained must be attributed, however, to the supremacy in the air which had been obtained by the Royal Air Force. The process of wearing down the enemy's aircraft had been going on all through the summer. During one week in June 100 hostile aeroplanes had crossed our lines. During the last week in August this number had decreased to eighteen. In the next few days a number were shot down, with the result that only four ventured to cross our lines during the period of concentration.' [1]

On the 18th of September, the day before the attack, a large force of bombing aeroplanes was directed over Nablus, where it was known the enemy had his main telephone and telegraph exchange. This was completely destroyed, a fact which played an important part in enabling our cavalry to reach the Plain of Esdraelon next day, before the enemy G.H.Q. knew they had broken through.

The striking success of these measures was afterwards proved by captured enemy documents. Among these was the German Intelligence Service map, issued on the very day before our attack commenced. This map shows three cavalry divisions still in the Jordan Valley, and only one in the coastal sector. Only two infantry divisions are shown in the coastal sector instead of five, and the whole map points to an attack in, or east of, the Jordan Valley. A German air reconnaissance report, dated 17th of September, and found among Liman von Sanders' papers at Nazareth, stated that ' far from there being any diminution in the cavalry in the Jordan Valley, there are evidences of twenty-three more squadrons there.'

The Turkish line on the plain consisted of two defensive positions, well constructed and heavily

---

[1] Despatch dated October 31, 1918.

wired. The first, 14,000 yards in length and 3000 in depth, ran along a sandy ridge in a north-westerly direction from Bir Adas to the sea. It consisted of a series of works connected by a continuous network of fire trenches. The second, or El Tire system, 3000 yards in the rear, ran from the village of that name to the mouth of the Nahr el Falik. On the enemy's extreme right the ground, except for a narrow strip along the coast, was marshy, and could only be crossed in few places. The defence of the second system did not, therefore, require a large force.

The attack of these positions was entrusted to the 21st Corps (3rd, 7th, 54th, and 75th Divisions), to which were also attached the 60th Division, the French Infantry Detachment, and the 5th A.L.H. Brigade (Australian Mounted Division), together with a large number of heavy guns and two brigades of mountain artillery. This force was to break through the enemy's defences between the railway and the sea, in order to open the door for the cavalry, and, at the same time, to seize the foothills south-east of Jiljulie. The Corps was then to swing to the right, pivoting on Jiljulie, as already explained, on to the line Hableh-Tul Keram, and advance in a north-easterly direction, converging on Samaria and Attara (on the Jenin-Samaria Railway about five miles north-west of the latter place), so as to drive the enemy up the two roads from Messudieh Junction and Samaria to Jenin, into the arms of the cavalry on the Plain of Esdraelon. The 5th A.L.H. Brigade was to cover the outer (left) flank of the Corps during this turning movement, capture Tul Keram station, and then raid and cut the Messudieh-Jenin Railway, near Ajje.

As soon as the infantry had broken through, the three cavalry divisions were to advance rapidly up the plain, the 5th Division along the coast road, through Mukhalid, the 4th *via* Tabsor and Mughair, and the Australian Mounted Division following the 4th.

The enemy had partially prepared an entrenched position across the plain from about Jelameh, through El Mejdel and Liktera, to the sea near the mouth of the Nahr Mefjir, and this was known to be held by a few troops. The 4th Division had orders to seize the portion of this line between Jelameh and Liktera, while the 5th dealt with the western half from Liktera to the coast.

Having made good the line of the Nahr Mefjir, they were to turn north-east and cross the Carmel Range, the 4th and Australian Divisions by the Musmus Pass, and the 5th by a little-known track from Sindiane to Abu Shusheh, and enter the Plain of Esdraelon. Arrived on the plain, the 4th Cavalry Division was to seize Afule and then push rapidly down the Valley of Jezreel to Beisan, occupy the Jordan bridges there, and send a force to hold and, if necessary, destroy the bridge at Jisr Mejamieh, twelve miles farther north. This programme entailed a ride of ninety-seven miles on end, and included the crossing of a mountain range by a difficult pass.

The 5th Division was directed on Nazareth (seventy miles) to capture the enemy General Headquarters, which was located there, and, if possible, Liman von Sanders himself, and then clear the plain as far east as Afule. The Australian Division was to remain on the Plain of Esdraelon at El Lejjun, sending a force to Jenin (sixty-eight miles), to intercept the Turks retiring from Samaria, when that place had been captured by our infantry.

As these immense distances had to be covered in

one ' bound,' speed was essential. The 4th and 5th Divisions, were, therefore, ordered to move up the coast on a wide front, and sweep over the Jelameh-Liktera positions with the sword and lance. If unexpectedly strong opposition was encountered there, the Australian Division was available, immediately in rear, to reinforce. The crossing of the Carmel Range was to be carried out as rapidly as possible, as it was recognised that our troops could only move in very narrow columns over the mountains, especially through the Musmus Pass, and flank guards would be out of the question. The 5th Division was, however, directed to drop a small force on the Sindiane-Abu Shusheh track, at the top of the range, to protect the left flank of the other two divisions, while they were passing through the defile.

The 20th Corps, in the hills north of Jerusalem, was ordered to attack all along its front on the day after the attack in the coastal plain, and drive the enemy northwards into the arms of the cavalry, while, in the Jordan Valley, Chaytor's Force had first to seize the bridge over the river at El Damieh, and then to cross the Jordan for the third and last time, and advance on Amman.

CHAPTER XVI

ARMAGEDDON

By the evening of the 18th of September all troops were in readiness for the attack. The 4th, 5th, and Australian Cavalry Divisions were hidden in the orange and olive groves at Sarona, Selmeh, and Ludd respectively. Their Horse Artillery batteries had moved up into the line on the night of the 17th, to take part in the preliminary bombardment.

Before daylight on the 19th the three divisions commenced their march up to the front, the 5th Division riding along the sea shore, at the foot of the high cliffs that fringe the coast in this part, the 4th *via* Jelil and El Haram, and the Australians on Tabsor. The two first-named divisions sent dismounted pioneer parties from each brigade forward with the infantry, to cut gaps in the wire, and to flag passages through it for their brigades. Their horses were led as close behind them as possible, and *liaison* with their brigades was maintained by gallopers.

At 4.30 A.M. the 400 guns concentrated on the front of attack opened an intense fire on the Turkish positions, and the five infantry divisions dashed forward to the attack.

The enemy was taken completely by surprise, and our infantry broke through the Turkish lines with hardly a pause, the guns maintaining a creeping barrage in front of them till they were through the first position. About 50,000 shells were put over during the short time that the bombardment and barrage lasted. At eight minutes past five the whole of the front line was reported taken, and by eighteen minutes to six the whole of the first position was in our hands, and our line began to wheel to the right.

The 5th Cavalry Division, being sheltered from view by the high cliffs of the sea shore, was able to ride right on the heels of the infantry, and the 13th Brigade, acting as advance guard, was across the Nahr el Falik by half-past eight, and riding hard up the plain towards Mukhalid. A strong patrol from this brigade was sent forward to reconnoitre Liktera.

The 4th Division, being in the open, had to wait till the El Tire-Nahr el Falik line had been cleared, so as not to interfere with our infantry, and thus did not cross the Falik till about ten o'clock. The 12th Brigade led through the enemy positions, but, as soon as they were clear of the wire, the 10th and 11th Brigades came up on the left, and the division advanced in line of brigade columns, each finding its own advance guard. The Australian Division was then about five miles farther back, passing through the enemy defences at Tabsor. Each division had picked up its artillery on the way.

The advance of the infantry had been so rapid that there had been very little time to collect prisoners, and as the cavalry advanced they came across numerous small parties of Turks, wandering about disconsolate and bewildered. They were quite disorganised, and did not attempt to interfere with our troops, and later on were all gathered in by ' mopping up ' parties, and taken to the collecting cages in rear. Farther east, disorganised parties of the enemy were streaming across the plain towards Tul Keram, pursued by the 5th A.L.H. Brigade, but these were out of sight of the rest of the cavalry as they crossed the line. Looking at the strong defences as we passed through them, deserted and quiet, it was hard to believe that, only a few hours before, these positions had been held by a numerous and well-organised enemy.

While the 5th Division was crossing the Nahr el Falik, the patrol which had been sent on towards Liktera reported a small force of enemy cavalry some two miles in front. This force at once made off in a north-easterly direction, and was not seen again. About the same time, a contact aeroplane reported some enemy infantry holding a position near Birket Ata. The 9th Hodson's Horse, which was vanguard to the 13th Brigade, reached this position about half-past ten, and at once charged and dispersed the enemy, taking about 250 prisoners and four guns. Pressing on at once, the regiment reached Liktera, half an hour later, where the Turkish Commandant surrendered at discretion, with his small garrison. The first objective having thus been secured without difficulty, the division closed up and halted on the line of the Nahr Mefjir, to water and feed. A squadron, supported by two armoured cars, was sent ahead to reconnoitre the Sindiane-Abu Shusheh track.

The 4th Division, which had been somewhat delayed finding a way through the enemy's wire, crossed the Nahr Iskanderuneh about 11.30, and, shortly afterwards, the leading regiment of the 11th Brigade, the 36th Jacob's Horse, came under fire from some Turks holding a portion of the enemy's entrenched position, just south of Zelefe. The regiment charged immediately, and the Turks broke and fled, leaving 200 prisoners in our hands. About the same time the 6th Cavalry, leading the 12th Brigade on the right, encountered a small enemy rearguard near Jett. This force was likewise promptly charged and dispersed. A marked map, found on a prisoner captured here, indicated that the enemy intended to hold a line from Arara, through Kefr Kara and Kannir to Mamas, covering both routes over the mountains. The 10th Brigade was, therefore, sent on at once with an armoured car battery to seize the Musmus Pass, the rest of the division remaining at El Mejdel and Tel el Dhrur to water and feed.

The Australian Mounted Division was ordered to halt for a time near Jelil, till word was received that the infantry, advancing to the line Hableh-Tul Keram, were progressing satisfactorily. This information came in about mid-day, and the division was then directed by the Corps Commander to push on at once towards the Nahr Iskanderuneh. The advanced guard reached the river at ten o'clock at night, without encountering any opposition, and the rest of the division, with the advanced Headquarters of the Corps, got in about an hour later. Horses were watered and fed, and the march was resumed at one o'clock in the morning.

The two leading divisions had marched again about six in the evening. The patrol from the 5th Division, which had gone ahead to reconnoitre the Sindiane track, reported that it was unfit for wheels. The divisional transport was, therefore, directed to cross by the Musmus Pass, in rear of the Australian Mounted Division, the 15th Brigade to remain at Liktera for the night, and cross by the Sindiane track, with the artillery of the division, the following day. The rest of the division, led by the 13th Brigade, reached Sindiane long after dark, and was soon involved in a tangle of hills, with no defined track visible, but innumerable, shadowy paths leading in all directions. Our maps showed a fairly direct track, which had been reported by natives as feasible for cavalry and light guns.   Their information was, however, merely hearsay, as we had not been able, before starting, to find any natives who actually knew the track.

Fortunately the 13th Brigade had in its commander[1] an officer who had had ten years' service in the Egyptian cavalry, and spoke Arabic fluently.   From time to time, during the night, he came across a few Arabs from whom he was able to get some information.   His long experience of marching in uncharted country, and a natural aptitude for finding his way, stood him in good stead, and he successfully led the two brigades over the range in the dark, marching in single file most of the time.   Two squadrons were dropped at Jarak, as left flank guard for the remainder of the Corps, while passing the Musmus defile.

The two brigades reached Abu Shusheh about half-past two in the morning, and continued the march across the plain in the darkness, crossing and cutting the Afule-Haifa Railway near Warakani, about half an hour later.   The moon was nearly full, and the light good.   On arriving at the foothills, the 14th Brigade halted till daylight, and the 13th pushed on up the track *via* Jebata and El Mujeidil, towards Nazareth.

On nearing El Mujeidil, a native guide, who had been picked up on Mount Carmel, stated that the place was Nazareth.   Though feeling sure that he was either mistaken or funked going any farther, the Brigadier decided to seize the place.   He directed the 18th Lancers to surround it, which they did, and, having blocked all exits, sent a couple of troops into the village.   By now it was clear that it was much too small a place to be Nazareth, but it was thought

---

[1] Brigadier-General P. J. V. Kelly, C.M.G., D.S.O., 3rd Hussars.   He commanded the Egyptian troops in the brilliantly successful little Darfur Campaign of 1916.

worth while to search it hurriedly, as a result of which 200 sleepy Turks were dug out of a large house. The brigade then passed on up the main road, the Gloucester Yeomanry taking the lead.

Shortly afterwards the houses of Nazareth appeared in front, gleaming white and silent in the moonlight. The advanced guard now halted, and the troop leaders were given their instructions. The town lies in a cup-shaped hollow, and straggles up the steep and rocky hills surrounding it. The principal houses, in one of which the enemy G.H.Q. would probably be located, are situated in the centre of the town at the bottom of the hollow, and on the northern slopes. The only information we had as to the exact location of G.H.Q. was that it was near a big motor-lorry park. Two troops were directed to make for the centre of the town, find the lorry park, and rush any big houses near by. Others were directed to gallop on, and seize tactical points on the northern slope, and block the roads leading north-east to Tiberias and north-west to Haifa.

Just as day was breaking the regiment drew swords and galloped into the town, causing the most indescribable confusion amongst the enemy troops, mostly German, there. Liman von Sanders himself only just made his escape in time. His housekeeper, whom we questioned later, declared that, at the first alarm, he dashed down the stairs of his house and out into the street in his pyjamas, and made off in a car along the Tiberias road.

The brigade had some hard street fighting, after the enemy had recovered from his first consternation, but the Germans and Turks were driven out of the town to the north-east. Here, however, a number of them got into some houses on the Tiberias road, and put up a good fight.

Several machine guns, mounted in a big convent which overlooked the centre of the town from the northern slope, made things very unpleasant, and it soon became evident that a deliberate dismounted attack would be necessary to dislodge them. Meanwhile the troops detailed for the duty had found and entered the enemy G.H.Q. They made a hurried search of the premises, covered by the rest of the regiment on the north and north-east, and by Hodson's Horse standing by, and seized all the more important documents. As soon as this work was finished, the advanced troops fell back fighting, and the brigade withdrew down the Afule road, taking with it 1200 prisoners. Before leaving, our troops put out of action all the motor cars of the enemy G.H.Q., and the lorries of the German lorry park. These were all afterwards repaired and used by us. On reaching the plain again, the brigade occupied Junjar, Tel Shadud and Jebata, holding the southern exits from Nazareth.

The 14th Brigade was occupied after daylight clearing the north-western portion of the plain of small parties of enemy troops, and entered Afule later on in the morning.

The 15th Brigade, with the guns and transport of the division, left the Nahr Iskanderuneh soon after dawn on the 20th, and marched by the same route to Afule. The gunners had a very rough passage over the mountains, and had to spend many hours making a roadway for the guns, so that they did not reach the station till about eleven at night.

The 4th Division left the Nahr Mefjir about the same time as the 5th, the 10th Brigade having gone on in advance to secure the Musmus Pass. The 2nd Lancers and an armoured car battery, acting as vanguard, entered the Pass, and reached Khurbet Arah without encountering any opposition. They placed outposts covering the cross roads here, and sent back a report to the 10th Brigade. Unfortunately this brigade had lost its way in the darkness, before moonrise, and was now somewhere north of Kerkur. On learning the state of affairs, General Barrow ordered the 12th Brigade up to the support of the 2nd Lancers, and himself motored up to Khurbet Arah, and directed the regiment to push on at once through the defile to Lejjun. This place was reached without opposition about eleven at night, the 12th Brigade arriving some hours later. The 11th Brigade, followed by the 10th, which had regained the road, came in at five o'clock in the morning.

As soon as it was light enough to see, the troops commenced to move out into the Plain of Esdraelon. They were none too soon. As the 12th Brigade, forming the advanced guard of the division, debouched from the defile, a Turkish battalion, with several machine guns, was deploying in the plain below.

The 2nd Lancers were leading, accompanied by the armoured cars. Taking in the situation at a glance, Captain Davison, commanding the regiment, ordered the cars to engage the enemy in front with their machine guns, supported by one squadron of his regiment. Taking the other two squadrons with him, he galloped along a slight depression to the right, and charged the Turks on their left flank. The two squadrons went right through the enemy from left to right, killing forty-six with the lance. The survivors of the battalion, about 500 in all, were taken prisoners. The Turks fought well, firing steadily till they were ridden down, but the rapid work of the cavalry gave them no chance. The whole action did not take more than five minutes, and furnished a perfect little example of sound shock tactics—movement and fire at right angles to one another.

Had our cavalry been a few hours later, this battalion would have been at the defile at the top of the pass, and might have caused a delay that would have been fatal to the success of the operations.   The battalion came from Afule, and had been ordered to cross the mountains and move down the coast to the support of the enemy right wing.   The Turks knew that their line had been broken on the coast, but they had absolutely no idea that our cavalry were through the gap.

Without a pause the 12th Brigade poured out of the pass and cantered across the plain towards Afule. The leading troops charged into the station at eight o'clock, capturing the place with little opposition. A squadron from the 14th Brigade (4th Division) rode in from the north about the same time.   The garrison of the place having just been disposed of at Lejjun, few enemy troops were found here, but the Germans had an aerodrome close to the station, and this was captured intact, with three aeroplanes and their pilots and all the mechanical staff.   A fourth aeroplane succeeded in getting away in the general confusion.   So unconscious was the enemy of the fact that our cavalry were on the plain, that, shortly after this, an enemy aeroplane, returning from a reconnaissance, actually landed on this aerodrome, and was promptly captured intact with its pilot and observer !

Afule proved a valuable prize.   In addition to ten locomotives and fifty railway trucks, which were found standing in the station, there was a fully equipped hospital, with a quantity of excellent drugs. One of the most valuable finds was a great store of petrol, which was discovered in an underground cave.

While the 12th Brigade was 'mopping up,' the armoured cars were having the time of their lives chasing twelve German motor lorries down the track leading to Beisan. They captured them all, and brought the drivers back to the station. Unfortunately no men could be spared to guard these lorries, and, when the 5th Division arrived shortly afterwards, and tried to drive them back to the station, it was found that the natives had been there in the meantime, and cut open every petrol tank to get the spirit. They were afterwards repaired, however, and did good service for us later on.

Having sent the prisoners back to Lejjun under a small escort, the 4th Division pressed on towards Beisan, after cutting the railway east, west, and south of Afule.

Riding fast all day down the Valley of Jezreel, the division reached Beisan about half-past four in the afternoon, having rounded up another 800 prisoners on the way. The Lancers made short work of the small garrison they met with here, galloping over the Turks, and taking 100 prisoners and three 5·9-inch howitzers. These guns were in position to defend the town against an attack from the *east*, an eloquent testimony to the manner in which the enemy had been deceived. Our troops then occupied the bridge over the Jordan at Jisr el Sheikh Hussein, and placed outposts south and east of Beisan.

The division had now marched eighty-five miles in thirty-four hours, fought two skirmishes, and captured 1400 prisoners, but its day's work was not yet quite finished. At six in the evening, after having watered and fed, the 19th Lancers (12th Brigade) set out in the dark, along a difficult mountain track west of the railway, to Jisr Mejamie, the railway bridge over the Jordan, twelve miles north of Beisan.

This they reached and seized at dawn next morning, having covered ninety-seven miles since the commencement of their march.

The Australians, who had left the Nahr Iskanderuneh at one o'clock in the morning, reached Kerkur and Beidus just after dawn, and thus made the crossing of the Carmel Range in daylight. They were rewarded by the magnificent view from the top of the pass, across the Plain of Esdraelon to Mount Tabor and Nazareth, and over the Nazarene hills to the great mass of Mount Hermon, poised against the sky sixty miles to the north-east. Scattered along the track were a number of derelict Turkish transport wagons, which had been abandoned as they were being driven over the pass, when the 4th Division came upon them in the dark. Many of the Turks who had accompanied these wagons, came back to the track after daylight, preferring capture by the British to facing the tender mercies of their inveterate enemies, the local Arabs. In this way the division had collected about 100 stragglers by the time it reached Lejjun. Near the top of the pass a large gang of natives was discovered at work on an excellently graded road, which was being built to the village of Umm el Fahm. It appeared that the Germans had intended to build a sanatorium there, in connection with their hospitals at Afule and Jenin. The natives employed making the road had gone to work as usual that morning, all unaware that the Germans and Turks were no longer masters in the land. When they learned the true state of affairs, their first thought was for their wages, which had not been paid, and they were not at all grateful to us for having driven their paymasters out of the country !

The division reached Lejjun at eleven o'clock, and

Before! German motor lorries at Nazareth.
(From an enemy photograph.)

After! The same lorries near Afule, after our armoured cars had finished with them.

got water for man and horse in the beautiful little Wadi el Sitt, the ' Lady's Brook,' a tributary of the river Kishon, hard by the ruins of an old Roman fort and aqueduct.

Shortly after mid-day the 3rd A.L.H. Brigade, with ' A ' Battery H.A.C., resumed the march to Jenin, to intercept the enemy troops that were expected to retire down the Dothan Pass from Nablus and its neighbourhood. The brigade reached the town in the early afternoon, and the leading regiment, the 10th, at once charged straight into it, galloping over an entrenched position, and through the streets of the town. The enemy was completely demoralised by this unexpected attack from the rear, and made little resistance. Such opposition as was encountered was speedily crushed, and nearly 2000 prisoners fell into our hands. None of the troops in the place had the faintest idea that our cavalry had even broken through their line, much less that we were actually in the plain. The German officers, of whom there was a number in the place, absolutely refused to believe that our troops had ridden the whole way, and declared that we must have been landed at Haifa, covered by our ' Wonderful Navy,' as they called it.

As soon as the prisoners had been got away, and lodged in a little valley out of sight of the town, the hills to the south were picketed, to prevent information getting to the enemy at Nablus, and the remainder of the brigade was disposed by squadrons in hollows and folds in the ground on each side of the Jenin-Afule road. The battery came into action north-east of the town, covering the Nablus road.

As was expected, after dark the enemy began to retire from his positions at Nablus and Samaria, and all night long his battalions marched down the road, through Jenin, and out on to the plain. These were not fugitives, but formed bodies of troops, retiring to the Nazarene hills, where they had a partially prepared defence line extending from the sea to Lake Tiberias. It was rather an eerie experience to watch these troops, trudging wearily along the road in the bright moonlight, all unconscious of the keen eyes of their enemies on every side of them. As each detachment got well out into the plain, at a given signal, the waiting squadrons sprang from their hiding places, and charged down upon it. One can imagine the terror of the Turks, nodding with half-closed eyes as they trudged along, when their senses were suddenly assailed by the thunder of hoofs all round them, and by the sight of wild horsemen, exaggerated in size by the moonlight, charging down upon them from every side. Small wonder that there was little resistance. Many flung themselves on the ground, shutting eyes and ears to the horrid nightmare, and calling on Allah to deliver them. Others threw down their rifles and held up their hands.

Each lot was quickly hustled out of sight, and the squadrons returned to their lairs, to await the coming of the next. Only one battalion, a German one, tried to put up any fight, and succeeded in getting a machine gun into action, but it was ridden down at once. None of the other German troops did any better than the Turks.

Some time during the night, information of the state of affairs at Jenin evidently got back to the enemy in the hills about Nablus, for the supply of prisoners suddenly ran dry. By this time the brigade had got over 8000, and needed help in handling them. In response to a message sent back to the divisional headquarters at Lejjun, the 4th A.L.H.

Brigade, with a section of the Notts Battery R.H.A., left that place at half-past four on the morning of September the 21st, and marched to Jenin. An extraordinary sight met the brigade on its arrival. The whole plain seemed to be covered with prisoners, motor cars, lorries, wagons, animals, and stores, in an inextricable confusion. In and out of this mass the sorely tried Australian troopers pushed their way, sweating and swearing, every now and then riding savagely at the hordes of natives hovering on the outskirts of the crowd like a flock of vultures, and looting the stores that strewed the ground; anon pressing into the throng again, to round up a group of straying prisoners. Over all presided the stocky figure of the brigadier,[1] like the leader of a gigantic school picnic, unhurried and efficient.

Jenin was the enemy's main supply and ordnance depot for his VIIth and VIIIth Armies, and very large quantities of valuable stores of all sorts were captured here, together with several well-equipped workshops and three hospitals. There were twenty-four burnt aeroplanes, and one intact, on the aerodrome, and a number of engines and a quantity of rolling stock in the station. In some caves near by were found large stores of German beer and wine, and a lot of excellent tinned food, and, in a wagon abandoned on the road, there were nearly £20,000 in gold. The two troopers who were detailed to guard this money sat on the boxes of bullion all day, without knowing what was in them, and have been kicking themselves ever since! This gold was of the greatest use to the Corps later on, when we were living on the country, and had to buy all our food and forage. Among the minor captures was a quantity of photographic negatives belonging to the

[1] Brigadier-General L. Wilson, C.M.G., D.S.O., A.I.F.

official photographer with the German forces, one of which depicted some of our guns which were lost in the second Amman raid. Also a British motor cycle, captured from us at the first battle of Gaza, eighteen months before.

The chief medical officer of the German hospital in the town volunteered the information that all ranks there, German as well as Turkish, were secretly glad to be captured. For the past ten days, he said, British aeroplanes had hovered over the place almost continually, and a rain of bombs had fallen all the time on the station, aerodrome, and workshops. Most of the troops left the town every day before dawn, and spent the hours of daylight in caves in the hills. All work was practically at a standstill, and none of the German aeroplanes had ever ventured to leave the ground. He was very puzzled by the fact that we had never bombed the town itself, and, when one of our officers replied that it was not the British custom to bomb undefended native villages, he shrugged his shoulders and remarked that such ideas were inadmissible in war. The Germans never brought themselves to believe that we were serious in our determination to observe the rules of civilised warfare in this respect. They realised, however, that we never bombed hospitals, a fact of which they were not slow to take advantage. Later on, when Nazareth was reoccupied, it was found that every house that harboured German troops, which is to say nearly every house of substance in the town, had a red cross, or its Turkish equivalent a red crescent, painted on the roof.

CHAPTER XVII

DÉBÂCLE

WHILE the cavalry were racing for the Plain of Esdraelon on the 19th September the 21st Corps, continuing its wheel to the right, drove the enemy into the hills. The 5th A.L.H. Brigade, riding on the left flank of the Corps, and some distance in advance of it, approached Tul Keram about mid-day.

The orders to the brigade were to seize the town, if possible, or, failing that, to engage the enemy there, and endeavour to prevent him withdrawing his troops and guns till the arrival of our infantry. Knowing the moral effect on the Turks of a threat to their rear, General Onslow decided to throw a portion of his brigade across the Tul Keram-Nablus road, the only exit from the town to the east. He despatched the 14th A.L.H. regiment and part of the brigade machine-gun squadron, with instructions to find a way through the hills north of the town, and descend on to the road some two miles to the north-east. With the remainder of his brigade he approached the town from the north-west, and was met by a very heavy fire from the enemy there. Tul Keram was a railway and store depot of considerable importance. It had been fortified, and now served the enemy as a strong point, on which his troops, defeated in the coastal plain, might rally, and so save his right flank. He was, of course, still in ignorance of the fact that three divisions of cavalry were already well on their way up the coast.

As the 5th Brigade approached the town, the Royal Air Force swept down out of the blue sky, and commenced an intense and systematic bombing of the enemy positions around the town, and the closely packed column of transport and guns slowly retiring along the road to Nablus. The utmost confusion broke out in the enemy ranks. About three [o'clock the 14th A.L.H. Regiment, which had moved with extraordinary rapidity, descended on the Nablus road about two miles from Tul Keram. The Turks were now faced simultaneously with the three things they most feared. Their retreat was cut off; they were being heavily attacked from the air; and they were threatened on both sides with a cavalry charge. The demoralisation on the road was complete. Not knowing the strength of the cavalry force which had suddenly appeared on the road in front of them, and evidently deceived by the volume of fire poured on them from our machine guns and automatic rifles, the enemy troops and transport on the road made no attempt to break through, but turned back towards Tul Keram. The persistent attacks of our aeroplanes soon destroyed all semblance of discipline in the column, and a disordered mass of fugitives streamed back into Tul Keram, increasing the confusion there. The Turks in the positions surrounding the town, however, still fought on gallantly enough, and General Onslow, unable to advance his brigade over the open ground without encountering losses which would not have been justified, contented himself with holding the enemy in check on the north, east and west, and awaited the arrival of our infantry. A brigade of the 60th Division came up about half-past five, having marched and fought over sixteen miles of heavy country since dawn, and rushed the town from the south-west.

General Onslow now reassembled his brigade, and succeeded in watering all the horses, which was something of a feat, considering the darkness and confusion. At two in the morning the brigade started off for its second objective, the Messudieh-Jenin Railway east of Ajje.

Regarded merely as a march, this expedition, carried out in the dark and without guides, over unknown and almost trackless mountain country, ranks as one of the finest episodes of the campaign. Unable to use the road or railway, along which Turkish reinforcements were known to be hurrying towards Tul Keram, the brigade struck straight across the mountains to the north-east, and passed through Deir el Ghusn, Ellar, Kefr Ruai, and Fahme. From the last-named place a moderate pack road led through Ajje to the railway, which was reached at seven in the morning by the brigade headquarters and a demolition party, who blew up a section of the line.

Dawn found the brigade strung out over fifteen miles of country. Its work was done, and, as it would have taken several hours to reassemble the regiments at Ajje, the Brigadier at once turned back along the track by which he had come, picking up his scattered units on the way, and returned to Tul Keram. It was seven o'clock in the evening before the whole brigade was again concentrated there.

In accordance with the Commander-in-Chief's plan, the 20th Corps had taken no part in the advance during the first day, beyond seizing one or two tactical points, to facilitate its operations on the following day, but on the 20th it was thrown into the battle, and the whole line became hotly engaged. The enemy fought stubbornly, especially in the centre of his line, where most of the German troops were concentrated. His positions were of great natural strength, and had been excellently entrenched and wired during the summer. By nightfall, however, his resistance had been broken all along the front, and our infantry had advanced as far as the line Anebta (five miles east of Tul Keram)-Beit Lid-Funduk-Kefr Harries-El Lubban (on the Nablus-Jerusalem road, eleven miles south of Nablus) to Dome. The enemy had thus been turned out of nearly all his entrenched positions.

Owing to the breakdown of their communications, and the virtual destruction of their air force, the Turks had not yet realised that our cavalry were behind them, and that all their lines of retreat to the north were thus closed. The only way of escape still left open for their trapped armies was by the two difficult tracks from Nablus and Ain el Subian (on the Nablus-Beisan road) to Jisr el Damieh. Chaytor's Force was fighting hard in the Jordan Valley to reach and block the lower end of these roads.

Our infantry resumed the attack at daylight on the 21st. The 20th Corps made rapid progress, and, by nightfall, had established itself across the Nablus-Jisr el Damieh track about Beit Dejan.

On the 21st Corps front, the advance was slower. The enemy in this part of the field was not yet demoralised, and his rearguards put up a stubborn fight, especially about Nablus. The 5th A.L.H. Brigade, moving along the main road from Tul Keram, with an armoured car battery, was usefully employed protecting the left flank of the Corps during the day. General Onslow turned the Turks and Germans out of a series of strong rearguard positions astride the road, by using his machine guns and armoured cars on the road, to hold the enemy in front with their fire, while dismounted parties from the brigade worked round his flanks. The French regiment particularly distinguished itself in this fighting, and earned generous praise from the Australians.

In the early afternoon some of the guns of the 3rd (Lahore) Division succeeded in reaching a position overlooking Nablus from the south-west, and their vigorous shelling, coupled with the converging attacks of the 10th and 53rd Divisions, drove the Turkish rearguards out of their positions. The 5th Brigade rode into the town hard on the heels of the retreating enemy, and took 700 prisoners. One squadron pushed on down the Jerusalem road, and gained touch with the 20th Corps cavalry regiment, the Worcester Yeomanry, about Balata. The following day the brigade marched to Jenin to rejoin the Australian Mounted Division, having accounted for 3500 prisoners during the three days.

Both at Tul Keram and in Nablus great quantities of valuable stores, which the enemy had been unable to remove or destroy, fell into our hands. Especially welcome were the many railway engines and trucks found intact at the former place, which were very soon employed on the repaired railway, carrying ammunition and stores to our troops. Here, too, a troop of the 15th A.L.H. Regiment rounded up and captured a detachment of the Turkish Field Treasury, with about £5000 in gold and a quantity of notes.

Throughout the day complete confusion had reigned in the enemy rear. Camps and stores were hurriedly abandoned or set on fire. Many heavy guns were dropped over precipices to save them from falling intact into the hands of the British. Driven out of their organised positions, and unable to keep touch with one another in this difficult, mountain country, the enemy regiments retired independently. Most of them made either for Beisan or Jisr el Damieh, but every wadi leading down to the Jordan was congested with troops. The confusion was increased by the repeated attacks of our aeroplanes, especially along the Nablus-Beisan road, which was packed with a dense column of troops and transport. Part of this column continued along the road to Beisan, where it fell into the hands of the 4th Cavalry Division. The greater part turned off at Ain el Subian, and made for Jisr el Damieh, along the Wadi Farah track. About a mile beyond Ain Shibleh, this track passes through a deep gorge. The transport at the head of the column was caught by our aeroplanes in this gorge, and heavily bombed. A general panic ensued. Drivers abandoned their vehicles, and fled into the hills; wagons, lorries, and guns were smashed or overturned, and in a short time the road was completely blocked. The remainder of the column turned off at Ain Shibleh, along a narrow track leading to Beisan. Still harassed by our aeroplanes, it broke up ultimately into isolated parties, which scattered into the hills, and were gathered in by the 4th Cavalry Division during the next two days.

Our infantry and the Royal Air Force had done their work well, in face of great difficulties. To the cavalry now fell the task of gathering up the remnants of the two Turkish armies.

There was little cavalry movement of importance on the 21st. The 4th Division established posts right across the Jordan Valley, east of the river, and pushed patrols along the roads leading south and south-west from Beisan. Shortly after dark, the first body of retiring enemy troops was encountered on the Nablus road. It was at once charged in the moonlight by the Central India Force (10th Brigade) and dispersed,

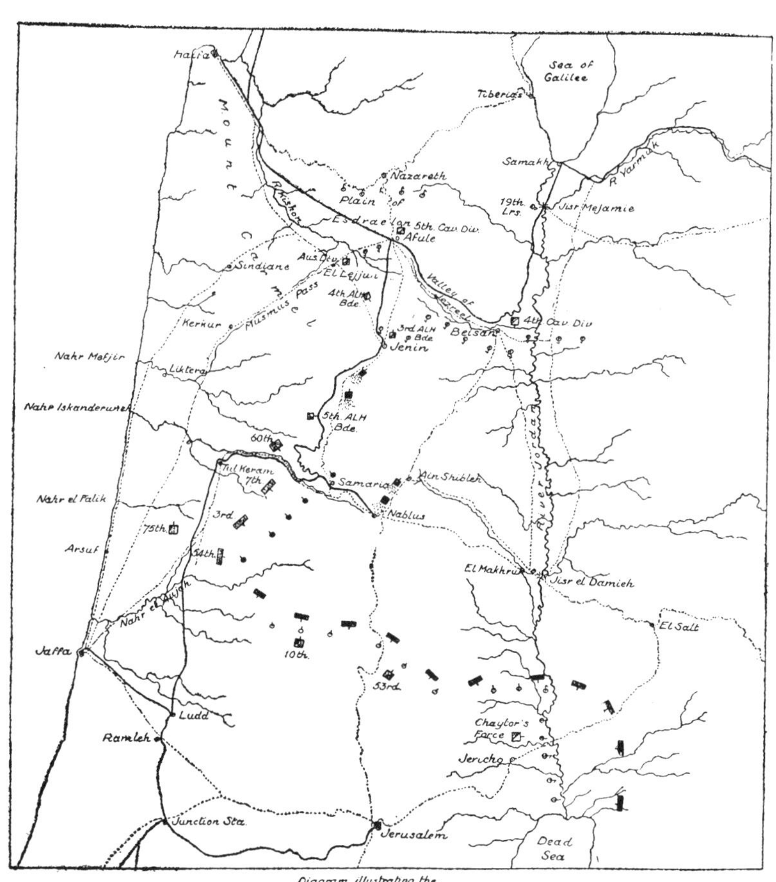

Diagram illustrating the
Situation on the evening of the 20th of November.

leaving a number of prisoners in our hands. There was no serious fighting during the night, but the division had very hard work, and got over 3000 prisoners before daybreak.

The 5th Cavalry Division had sent the 14th Brigade to Jenin, at daylight, to assist the two brigades of the Australian Mounted Division there in dealing with the large number of prisoners, and to help protect the captured enemy stores from the natives. By the afternoon, however, the prisoners had been got away under escort to Lejjun, and the brigade was able to return to Afule. The 14th and 15th Brigades then established a line of pickets along the railway to near Beisan, in touch with the 4th Division.

Meanwhile the 13th Brigade, with ' B ' Battery H.A.C., had been sent off early in the morning to reoccupy Nazareth.

The 9th Hodson's Horse marched straight up the Afule-Nazareth road with the guns, and entered the town from the south. The other two regiments, leaving the road some distance south of the town, made their way through the hills to the Tiberias road, and attacked from the east and north. All three regiments attacked dismounted. There was a good deal of fighting of a difficult nature in the narrow, tortuous streets of the town, but most of the enemy troops remaining after our raid of the previous day had already evacuated the town, and those still left were soon overpowered. By ten o'clock the 13th Brigade had possession of the town. The roads leading west, north, and east were then picketed, and strong patrols were pushed out as far as Seffurie and Kefr Kenna.

Shortly after midnight a Turkish battalion, marching from Haifa, attacked the outposts of the brigade on the Acre road. The 18th Lancers promptly charged the Turks in the moonlight, and chased them for two miles down the road, killing sixty with the lance and taking over 300 prisoners.

The Australian Mounted Division remained in the neighbourhood of Jenin and Lejjun during the day.

The large numbers of prisoners taken by the cavalry during the past twenty-four hours were a serious encumbrance, and the feeding of them became a very difficult problem. The Corps ration convoy that arrived at Jenin on the 21st had to hand over all its rations to them. As our own men carried three-days men's and two-days horses' rations on the man and horse, they did not actually have to go hungry, but the food question had become acute, and, until the prisoners could be got away, no further move forward could be contemplated. Fortunately, on the following day, it was found possible to send most of them back to Kakon, near Tul Keram, where they were taken over by a brigade of the 60th Division.

The Commander-in-Chief motored to Lejjun on the morning of the 22nd, and met General Chauvel.

' Well, how are you getting on ? ' was his greeting.

' Pretty well, Sir, pretty well,' replied the General; ' we 've got 13,000 prisoners so far.'

' No . . . good to me ! ' exclaimed the Chief, with a laugh; ' I want 30,000 from you before you 've done.'

He was to have over 80,000 from the Corps before the operations ended.

The 5th Cavalry Division concentrated at Nazareth on the 22nd, preparatory to an advance on Haifa and Acre, its place at Afule being taken by the 3rd A.L.H. Brigade. The 5th A.L.H. Brigade rejoined the Australian Mounted Division at Jenin during the day.

In the early hours of the morning an enemy column, with transport and guns, was reported by our aeroplanes to be moving north along the Ain Shibleh-Beisan track, its head being then nine miles south of Beisan. This was part of the force that had been caught and heavily bombed by our aeroplanes the day before in the gorge of the Wadi Farah, as it was trying to escape towards the Jordan.

The 4th Cavalry Division at once sent a force from Beisan along the Ain Shibleh track to intercept the column, and despatched Jacob's Horse over the bridge of Jisr el Sheikh Hussein to push patrols down the track which follows the Jordan on its east bank, so as to secure any parties which might escape across the river. At the same time the 20th Corps cavalry regiment, the Worcester Yeomanry, was ordered to advance northwards from Ain Shibleh, supported by infantry, to collect stragglers, and to drive any formed bodies into the arms of the 4th Cavalry Division.

Our airmen then proceeded to attack the column with bombs and machine guns, and, in a short time, had completely broken it up. The enemy scattered in panic into the hills in small parties, which were rounded up by the 4th Division next day. The Worcester Yeomanry rode as far as the gorge where the ill-fated column had been caught by our aeroplanes, and here its farther advance was stopped, as the track was completely blocked by overturned vehicles and the dead bodies of men and horses. On one stretch of the track just here, under five miles long, eighty-seven guns and 900 motor lorries and other vehicles were afterwards found by the infantry, when clearing up the area.

About mid-day the 11th and 12th Light Armoured Car Batteries were sent to occupy Haifa, which was believed to have been evacuated by the enemy. With them went the General commanding the artillery of the Cavalry Corps, in a large and beautiful Rolls-Royce car, with the Commander-in-Chief's Union Jack on the bonnet, and a proclamation in his pocket to read to the peaceful inhabitants.

He met with a warm reception. As the cars neared the town, several enemy batteries opened fire on them, while machine guns on Mount Carmel swept the road. The batteries had evidently registered carefully, for almost the first salvo hit the General's car, knocking it into the ditch and smashing the flag. The General himself, with his staff, had to take cover in the same ditch, and quickly too, and there they lay, getting the proclamation covered with mud, till the armoured cars succeeded in retrieving them. It was a shocking affair, and showed a sad lack of respect on the part of the enemy. The ' Haifa Annexation Expedition,' as it was irreverently called, returned to Afule in somewhat chastened mood, but fortunately without any serious casualties.

The chief movement of the day took place in the Jordan Valley. Early in the morning the New Zealand Mounted Brigade succeeded in getting astride the Nablus-Jisr el Damieh roads at El Makhruk, after a sharp fight, taking 500 prisoners, including a divisional commander. About an hour previously the 38th Royal Fusiliers, one of the two Jewish battalions with the force, had captured the enemy position covering the river ford at Umm el Shert, while, about half-past ten, the New Zealand Brigade, with a West Indies battalion, seized the bridge at Jisr el Damieh, and crossed to the east bank. In the attack on the bridgehead the New Zealanders and the ' coloured gentlemen ' both charged the Turks simultaneously, and had a severe hand-to-hand struggle before achieving their object.   The 2nd A.L.H. Brigade also crossed the river at Ghoraniyeh, and, in conjunction with the 20th Indian Infantry Brigade, drove in the Turkish outposts, and, by nightfall, was facing the main enemy position at Shunet Nimrin.

Early in the night it became clear that a general retirement of the Turkish IVth Army had begun, and orders were issued for the force to follow it vigorously on the morrow.

German aircraft captured intact at Afule. Mount Tabor in the background.

In the hands of the enemy! Some of our Horse Artillery guns captured
in the second trans-Jordan raid. (From an enemy photograph.)

CHAPTER XVIII

DESTRUCTION

NEXT day, September the 23rd, Chaytor's Force was on the move at daylight, following up the retreating IVth Army east of the Jordan. The 3rd A.L.H. Regiment (1st Brigade), with the 2nd B.W.I. Regiment, had a sharp fight at the ford of Mafid Jozeleh, half way between El Damieh and Ghoraniyeh, where the Turks had left a rearguard. The enemy was dispersed, and the Australians crossed the river at six o'clock. The remainder of the 1st A.L.H. Brigade crossed at Umm el Shert, and moved on El Salt up the Wadi Arseniyet track. The 2nd A.L.H. Brigade, having crossed the Jordan at Ghoraniyeh, pressed on up the Wadi Kefrein, and seized Kabr Mujahid at five o'clock, rounding up the small force there after a lively fight, and then turned north along the very difficult mountain track towards El Sir. Meanwhile the New Zealand Brigade, having crossed at El Damieh, rode hard up the mountain track, and occupied El Salt about seven in the evening. The only opposition met with was from a small, wired-in post on the El Damieh-El Salt track. A brigade of Indian infantry reached Shunet Nimrin in the evening, and found it evacuated by the enemy. One battalion of the B.W.I. Regiment and one squadron of cavalry were left at El Damieh, to gain touch with patrols of the 4th Cavalry Division moving down the Jordan.

Orders were issued to the force in the evening by

G.H.Q., to push on next day, harass the enemy, and try to cut his line of retreat to the north ; also to gain touch with the Arab Army advancing from the south.

The 4th Cavalry Division also had a busy day. Early in the morning our aeroplanes reported that the enemy had found a ford over the Jordan about six miles south of Beisan and was crossing the river in large numbers. The 11th Brigade, with the Hants Battery R.H.A., was at once sent off to intercept them, and moved south along both banks of the Jordan. The 1/1 County of London Yeomanry and the 29th Lancers marched along the west bank, and Jacob's Horse east of the river. At half-past eight, patrols of the 29th Lancers, approaching the ford of Makhadet Abu Naj, seven miles south-east of Beisan, were fired on by a party of Turks covering the passage of a large force of the enemy over the river. A considerable portion of this force was already across. The 29th Lancers and part of the brigade machine-gun squadron engaged the Turks on the north, while the Yeomanry pushed round the left flank of the enemy force, in order to take it in rear. The ground was very difficult, and the Yeomanry were subjected to a considerable fire from a low hill on the west bank, on which the Turks had a number of machine guns. This hill was the central point of resistance of the enemy bridgehead.

As soon as the Yeomanry were clear of the enemy's flank, the 29th remounted and charged the hill. The charge was completely successful. Large numbers of the Turks were speared, and 800 prisoners and no less than twenty-five machine guns were taken. Like all the work of these veteran Indian cavalry regiments in the campaign, this charge was admirably carried out, but that it succeeded in getting home in the face of such a potential volume of machine-gun and rifle fire is an indication of the state of demoralisation to which the enemy was now reduced.

Meanwhile, on the east bank, Jacob's Horse, which was a little way behind, rode up and instantly charged the large force of Turks on that side. This charge, however, was held up by a deep wadi, and the intense fire of the enemy compelled our troops to retire and take cover. The regiment re-formed, and again attempted to charge the enemy, but was again stopped by bad ground, and suffered severe casualties.

The Hants Battery, on the west bank, coming up just at this moment, immediately galloped into action, and opened a rapid and accurate fire on the masses of Turks across the river. It was at once hotly engaged by two concealed enemy batteries on the east bank, and in a few minutes every one of the guns had been hit. None were put out of action, however, and all continued firing most gallantly. The enemy's fire was so heavy that General Gregory ordered a troop of cavalry out into the open to try and draw the fire of the Turkish guns, and so enable the battery to withdraw and take up a concealed position. Before the guns could be moved, however, the situation was cleared by one of the Yeomanry squadrons, which had worked its way south of the enemy position. This squadron succeeded in crossing the river at Makhadet Fath Allah, and, wading across the river, charged and captured the enemy guns.

Meanwhile a squadron of the 29th had been sent across the river, a little farther north, to assist Jacob's Horse. Thus reinforced, the regiment attacked again, and this attack, coupled with the loss of their guns, broke the resistance of the Turks. Most of them surrendered. A few succeeded in escaping for the time, amid the broken ground on both banks of the river. 3000 prisoners, including a divisional commander, ten guns, and thirty machine guns fell into our hands.

After the action, the brigade continued its march south, to Ras el Humeiyir, where it bivouacked for the night, with outposts south and west, along the Wadi el Sherar and east of the Jordan.

During the night a troop of the 29th Lancers was sent off into the hills to the west, to try and gain touch with the 20th Corps, about Khurbet Atuf. This troop marched all night, along a very difficult footpath, and met the 20th Corps cavalry regiment (Worcester Yeomanry) at Atuf early in the morning. It rejoined the 11th Brigade near Ras Umm Zoka during the day.

The task assigned to the 5th Cavalry Division on the 23rd was the capture of Acre and Haifa. The 13th Brigade, with a Light Armoured Car Battery and a light car patrol, left Nazareth at five in the morning. Marching *via* Seffurie and Shefa Amr, the force reached Acre about mid-day, and captured it without difficulty, the small enemy garrison showing little inclination to fight. 260 prisoners and two guns were taken here.

The remainder of the division left Nazareth at the same hour, and reached the Kishon railway bridge, near El Harithie, about mid-day. The 14th Brigade remained here, while the 15th Brigade, with ' B ' Battery H.A.C., moved on Haifa along the Afule-Haifa road, which skirts the north-eastern edge of the Mount Carmel Range. There were only two regiments with the brigade, as the Hyderabad Lancers were absent, escorting prisoners back from Lejjun. They rejoined the brigade late in the afternoon, just after Haifa had been captured.

The Mysore Lancers, advance guard to the brigade, reached the village of Belled el Sheikh about ten o'clock, and, on emerging from the trees that surround the village, came under heavy fire from a number of guns on Mount Carmel, and from machine guns and rifles in the hills north-west of the village. Patrols sent out to the north drew fire from a large number of machine guns about Tel Abu Hawam, and concealed among trees and shrubs near the main road south of that place. It was evident that the position was strongly held.

General Harbord had arrived at Belled el Sheikh, and received the report of his advance guard. He had a difficult task before him. South of the road the rocky wall of Carmel rose steeply, 1500 feet above the plain. To the north, the country was flat and open, and afforded little or no cover for troops, except along that portion of the Nahr el Mukatta (the river Kishon) which runs east and west a mile and a half north of Belled el Sheikh, which was bordered with trees and scrub. The Wadi Ashlul el Wawy is practically dry at this time of year, but the Nahr el Mukatta is a perennial stream, the banks of which are very marshy.

The Brigadier decided that the first thing to be done was to silence the guns on Mount Carmel. He accordingly despatched a squadron of the Mysore Lancers, with a couple of machine guns, to climb the mountain by a goat path, which follows the Wadi el Tabil from Belled el Sheikh, and joins the road running along the backbone of the range. This squadron was ordered to move along this road to the north, locate the guns, and attack them. With the remainder of his force the Brigadier decided to make a mounted attack from the east on the enemy positions about Tel Abu Hawam, supported by his guns and machine guns from the south-east. ' B ' Battery H.A.C. came into action close to the road, about half a mile north of Belled el Sheikh, and the remainder of the machine-gun squadron, with two squadrons Mysore Lancers, a little farther north, along the Acre Railway. The 4th squadron Mysore Lancers was sent up the road running north from near El Harbaj, with instructions to turn westwards at Tel El Subat, and make for the mouth of the Nahr el Mukatta. It was then to push along the sea shore, so as to take the enemy positions in reverse. The Jodhpur Lancers took up a position of readiness, about 500 yards north-east of Belled el Sheikh, preparatory to making a dash for the wooded portion of the Mukatta. They were to cross this, and then wheel to the left, and charge the enemy on his left flank.

These dispositions were soon completed, and the troops then set themselves to wait until the Mysore Lancers' squadron had dealt with the enemy guns on Mount Carmel. Meanwhile our artillery and machine guns searched the palm groves and scrub about Tel Abu Huwam and along the banks of the Mukatta. Observation was difficult, as the enemy was well concealed.

Shortly before mid-day General Harbord received a welcome reinforcement in the Sherwood Rangers Yeomanry, which had been sent up from El Harithie. He at once despatched a squadron of this regiment to the assistance of the Mysore Lancers' squadron on Carmel.

Desultory firing continued for the next two hours, but there was no sign of any slackening of the enemy's artillery activity. At last the Brigadier came to the conclusion that his troops on Carmel had either been unable to fulfil their task of silencing the enemy guns, or had lost their way. Time was running on, and he decided that he could wait no longer. The Jodhpur Lancers were ordered out to the attack.

Moving off in column of squadrons, in line of troop columns, they cantered out into the open towards the stream, coming under intense fire as they crossed the Acre Railway. The fire, however, appeared ill-directed, which was probably due to the vigorous action of our artillery and machine guns supporting the attack.

Owing to the exposed nature of the ground, it had not been possible to reconnoitre the Mukatta beforehand, and, when the Jodhpur Lancers reached it, they found it quite impassable. Two ground scouts, who jumped into the bed of the stream, disappeared instantaneously into the quicksands. The regiment, was, however, now committed to the attack, and it was impossible to turn back. Changing direction left, the four squadrons charged straight at the enemy.

The leading squadron, ' B,' galloping over the two branches of the Wadi Ashlul el Wawy, dashed into the enemy machine guns, killed the crews, and opened the defile between the Wadi Selman and the mountain. The second squadron, ' D,' charged and captured the enemy guns and machine guns about Tel Abu Hawam and north of it. The remaining two squadrons galloped through the defile, straight on into the town. Meanwhile, after clearing the defile, ' B ' squadron made its way along the lower slopes of Mount Carmel, and charged into the German Colony west of Haifa, capturing several guns, and killing large numbers of Turks and Germans. ' D ' squadron, after clearing up the Tel Abu Hawam area, galloped up the east bank of the Wadi Selman and along the beach, entering the town on the north-east. All four squadrons thus entered Haifa about the same moment.

As soon as the charge got home, the two squadrons Mysore Lancers, who had supported the attack with their fire, mounted, and followed at a gallop into the town. Of the two detached squadrons of this regiment, that on the north had been held up about half a mile west of El Suriyeh. This squadron now mounted, and charged a body of the enemy in position near the mouth of the Mukatta, capturing two guns and 100 prisoners.

The squadron on Mount Carmel, after riding nearly six miles over very bad country, had at last located the enemy guns at Karmelheim, much farther north than had been expected. Dropping his machine guns and all his Hotchkiss rifles on the track, to provide covering fire, the squadron leader led the remainder of his troops away to the left to charge the guns. Owing to casualties on the way up the range, and to some of his men having been delayed by the difficulties of the track, he found that, after providing for his Hotchkiss rifles, he had only fifteen lances for the charge. Nevertheless, he decided to attack at once, rightly judging that even an unsuccessful charge would probably divert the fire of the enemy guns long enough to permit the Jodhpur Lancers to make their attack in the plain. His machine guns and Hotchkiss rifles had got close to the guns unseen, and now opened a sudden and accurate fire on them. The fifteen men then galloped in from the flank, and actually succeeded in silencing the battery. The crews of two of the guns were killed, but the battery escort then came up, and it might have gone hardly with the gallant little band of cavalry had not the squadron of the Sherwood Rangers arrived just in the nick of time to complete the work. By a fortu-

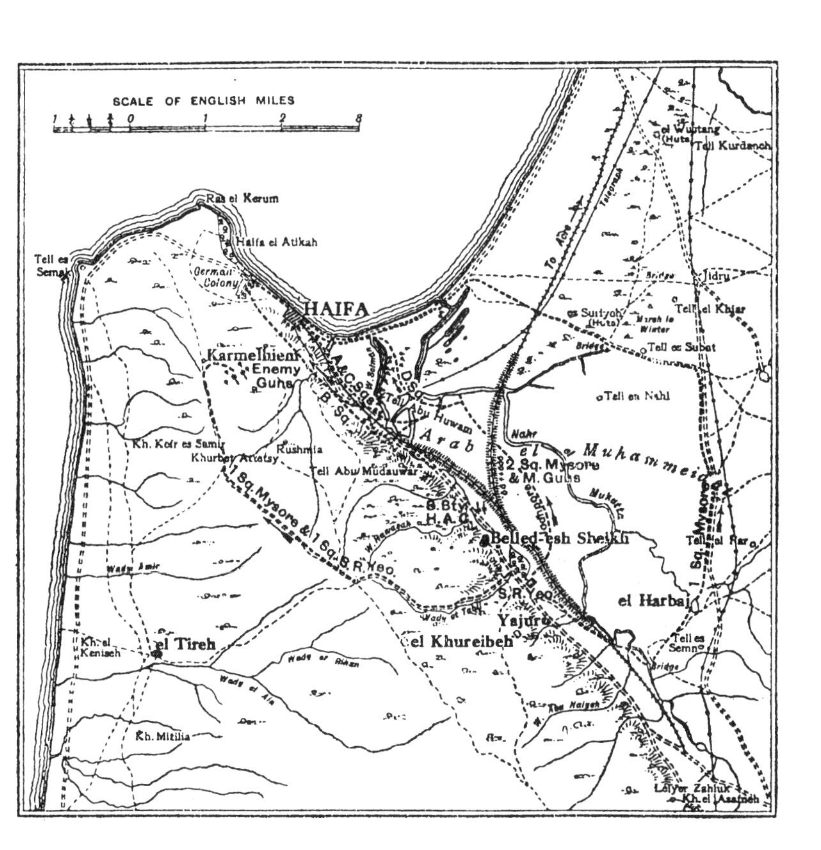

SCALE OF ENGLISH MILES
1 0 1 2 3
el Wuptang (Huts)
Tell Kurdanch
Ras el Kerum
Haifa el Atikah
Tell es Semak
German Colony
HAIFA
Jidru
Suriyoh (Huts)
Tell el Khiar
Marsh in Winter
Bridge
Tell es Subat
Karmelhieny
Enemy Guns
Tell en Nahl
Kh. Keir es Samir
Rushmia
Arab
Nahr
el Muhammeid
Khurbet Arfatsy
Tell Abu Mudauwar
2 Sq. Mysore & M. Guns
Mukatta
Tell Abu Huwam
8 Bty. H.A.C.
Belled-esh Sheikh
Tell el Far
7 Sq. Mysore & 16 Sq. B.R. Yeo
Wady Amir
S.R. Yeo
1 Sq. Mysore
el Harbaj
Kh. el Kenisch
el Tireh
el Khureibeh
Yajure
Tell es Semn
Wady et Tell
Wady el Rihan
Bridge
Wady el Ain
Abu Naigeh
Kh. Mitilia
Lotfyer Zahluk
Kh. el Asafneh

nate coincidence, this charge took place just as the Jodhpur Lancers attacked in the plain.

1351 prisoners, seventeen guns, and eleven machine guns were collected at Haifa after the action. The captured artillery included two six-inch naval guns, which the Germans had mounted on the top of Mount Carmel, to engage our warships in the event of an attempted landing.

The Turks had fought well, firing until they were ridden down, but once our cavalry were through the defile, the fight was practically over. They galloped through the town, riding down with the lance any bodies of the enemy who showed fight, and, in twenty minutes, had overcome all opposition.

The Australian Mounted Division had a day of comparative rest. The 3rd A.L.H. Brigade relieved the 5th Cavalry Division at Nazareth, and the rest of the division remained at Afule, sending patrols eastwards as far as Beisan, to bring in the prisoners taken on the two previous days by the 4th Cavalry Division. Towards evening the ' bag ' began to arrive, and, long after darkness fell, the endless column of captives was still winding its way up the Valley of Jezreel.

Most of these prisoners had marched over twenty miles since their capture, and no one knows how many more before they fell into our hands. Their dragging feet raised a heavy cloud of dust, through which they had trudged all the long, hot march, and they came in raging with thirst. In anticipation of their arrival, several large canvas tanks had been set up and filled with water, and elaborate arrangements had been made by the capable and energetic water officer of the Australian Division. Each man was to file past the tanks, have a drink, fill his water bottle, and move on to the concentration area with a gentle sigh of satisfaction. The water officer had eight orderlies. There were 8000 prisoners, and, as soon as they smelt the water, the 8000 charged the eight. The charge was successful, and the prisoners thereupon all tried to get *into* the water together. In a few seconds the tanks were trampled down, and the frenzied Turks struggled and fought with one another in the darkness round the muddy ruins. Eventually they had to be driven back at the point of the sword. More water was procured, and the prisoners were marched up to it in small parties under escort. It took all night to supply them all.

The following day the 4th Cavalry Division continued its ' mopping up ' operations in the Jordan Valley.

Early in the morning an observation post of the London Yeomanry, who were on outpost duty, observed a large force of the enemy making for the ford of El Masudi. A squadron at once galloped for the ford, but the enemy got there first, and held it up. Another squadron, coming up in support, several times charged the Turks debouching from the hills, and captured a large number of them. The Yeomen had the greatest difficulty in dealing with their prisoners, who, after surrendering and throwing down their rifles when charged, repeatedly picked them up again, and went on fighting.

The Hants Battery now came up, and got into action at close range against the enemy holding the ford. Its rapid and accurate fire completely disconcerted the demoralised Turks, and the 29th Lancers took prompt advantage of the fact to charge them. The enemy, worn out and dispirited, made but a poor fight of it, and the action was soon over. 4000 Turks, including Rushdi Bey, Commander of the 16th Division, were taken prisoner, and another

1000 were rounded up later on in the course of the day. Very few escaped.

The horses of the 11th Brigade were now in a very exhausted condition, and the ammunition of the battery was running low. General Barrow, therefore, ordered the Brigadier only to continue his southward movement as far as Ras Umm Zoka and the Wadi Kafrinji, sending patrols along the Jordan, to gain touch with Chaytor's Force.

This action completed the destruction of the VIIth and VIIIth Turkish Armies. A few stragglers escaped across the river, to wander miserably in the barren, waterless country to the east, at the mercy of hostile Arabs. With the exception of these, the entire enemy force west of the Jordan had been captured or killed, and all its guns, transport, and stores had fallen into our hands.

The IVth Army, east of Jordan, and the 2nd Corps (Hedjaz Force) about Maan, remained to be dealt with. Both these forces were in full retreat to the north, the former pursued by Chaytor's Force and the northern portion of the Arab Army, the latter harried by the southern detachment of the Arabs. As the Hedjaz Railway had been cut at Deraa, no supplies could reach these enemy forces, and they had to depend for their food on a sparsely populated country, already almost denuded of supplies by Turkish requisitions, and inhabited by bitterly hostile tribes.

As the action of Chaytor's Force formed a separate episode in the operations, it will be convenient to follow its fortunes to the conclusion of its work.

On the night of the 23rd, the dispositions of the Force were as follows :—

New Zealand Brigade in El Salt. 1st A.L.H. Brigade approaching El Salt, along the Wadi Arseniyet track. 2nd A.L.H. Brigade on the Wadi Kefrein track, a few miles west of Ain el Sir. Infantry at Shunet Nimrin. The whole force resumed the advance vigorously at daylight on the 24th. The New Zealanders encountered the Turkish rearguards at Sweileh at seven in the morning, and the 2nd Brigade at Ain el Sir at the same hour. In both places there was a sharp fight before the enemy was dislodged. The Turkish IVth Army was not yet disorganised, and was retreating in good order, fighting every step of the way.

At night the Anzac Division held a line north and south, a few miles east of Sweileh and Ain el Sir, and the infantry had reached El Salt. During the night a party from the New Zealand Brigade raided and cut the railway near Kalaat el Zerka. At six o'clock next morning the cavalry advanced straight on Amman, with orders to press into the town if possible. If unable to seize the place, they were to hold the enemy till the arrival of the infantry. At eleven o'clock the New Zealanders made an attempt to gallop the town from the north-west, but were held up by a steep cliff. Two mountain batteries arrived half an hour later, and the division then went in dismounted, in a frontal attack. It was of the utmost import- ance to keep fighting the Turks, so as to prevent them from breaking off the action and retiring. For this reason no attempt was made to outflank them, as the necessary movement to carry out a flanking attack would, in that very precipitous country, have entailed much time, of which the Turks would cer- tainly have availed themselves to disengage their forces, and make good their retreat. As it was, Amman was not captured till half-past four in the afternoon, and the time spent in clearing up the town precluded any possibility of a further movement forward that night.   The place had not fallen without a sharp fight, costing fairly heavy casualties, but, of the opposing forces, the Turks suffered far the more severely, and left 600 prisoners in our hands.

Covered by the good fighting of its rearguards, the Turkish IVth Army had now got some distance to the north of Amman. General Allenby, therefore, decided to leave it to the 4th Cavalry Division and the Arab Army, and directed General Chaytor to remain in the Amman area, and intercept the retreat of the enemy 2nd Corps from the Hedjaz.

Our aeroplanes had located this Corps on the evening of the 25th, some fifteen miles south of El Kastal, hurrying north along the railway. On the following morning, General Chaytor sent the 2nd A.L.H. Brigade southwards, to gain touch with the Turks, and to destroy as much of the railway as possible.   Patrols from the 5th A.L.H. Regiment got as far as Ziza Station, about four miles south of El Kastal, where they blew up a portion of the line. The regiment remained at Ziza for the night, and the rest of the brigade took up a position across the railway, on some high ground north of Leben Station.

Now that Amman was in our hands, the only water available for the enemy, between El Kastal and Deraa Junction, was in the Wadi el Hammam, seven miles north of Amman. The enemy had dropped a rearguard here, from the IVth Army, to secure the water supply for his Hedjaz Force. The 1st A.L.H. Brigade was despatched on the 26th to dislodge this rearguard, and occupy the wadi. The brigade had a couple of brisk fights with the Turks, and drove them off, capturing about 400 prisoners and several guns, and then took up a line along the wadi, covering the water areas.

On the morning of the 27th, therefore, the 2nd

A.L.H. Brigade was in position astride the Hedjaz Railway, north of Leben Station, with one regiment pushed out as far as Ziza ; the 20th Indian Infantry Brigade was in Amman, with the New Zealand Brigade on the Darb el Haj, east of the town ; and the 1st A.L.H. Brigade was along the Wadi el Hammam and at Kalaat el Zerka.

About half-past eight in the morning the head of the enemy corps was seen approaching Ziza. Prisoners, captured by the 5th A.L.H. Regiment during the night, had stated that the Turkish Force included the Maan garrison, and numbered about 8000 men. This information was subsequently found to have been exaggerated.

Though still retaining its cohesion, the enemy force was in a highly nervous state. During its retreat from Maan, which had been made by forced marches, it had been harried without cessation by the Sherifian camelry. Not strong enough to give battle to such a large Turkish force, the Arabs, mounted on fast trotting camels, had contented themselves with carrying out a series of raids, in which they had killed a considerable number of Turks, and captured about 300 prisoners and twenty-five guns. The tribes of the districts through which they passed flocked to the standard of King Hussein, moved partly by their hatred of the Turks, and, at least as much, by their desire for loot. Like the men of all semi-civilised races, the Arab prizes a good weapon above everything, and the news that German Mauser rifles were to be had in unlimited numbers at the expense of a few casualties, soon raised the whole country. Consequently, by the time the Turks reached El Kastal, they had, in their rear and on both flanks, a formidable force of Arab fighting men, grown bold by repeated minor successes.

Early in the afternoon of the 28th, General Chaytor summoned the Turkish force, by a message dropped from an aeroplane, to surrender by nine o'clock next morning. It was pointed out to the enemy commander, that all sources of water supply as far north as Deraa were in our hands, and he was promised a most unmerciful bombing unless he complied with the order.

No reply was received to this message till the following day, when a Turkish officer, with a small escort, succeeded in penetrating the fringe of blood-thirsty Arabs surrounding the force, and met Colonel Cameron, commanding the 5th A.L.H. Regiment, to whom he brought the surrender of the enemy commander with all his force. The Turkish General made the unusual request that his men might be allowed to retain their arms until they arrived at Amman, as he was convinced that the Arabs would attempt to rush in and murder the whole of his force if the arms were given up, and he was doubtful if the small British force on the spot could prevent this.

While this parley was proceeding, a deputation arrived from the Beni Sakhr Arabs, our quondam allies—and deserters—in the second trans-Jordan raid. These gentry now coolly demanded that the Turkish force should be handed over to them to 'protect,' as it was their right to deal with it. Misunderstanding their motives, Colonel Cameron assured them that the Turks would be well looked after by us, whereupon the sons of Ishmael became greatly excited, waved their weapons wildly, and uttered the most blood-curdling threats. Colonel Cameron temporised with them as best he could, and sent an urgent message to hurry up the other two regiments of the 2nd Brigade, which were marching towards Ziza. They arrived at five o'clock, and, as the Arabs were now openly hostile to us, the Turks were allowed to retain their arms. Under the supervision of our officers, they entrenched a line of outpost positions round the station, and these positions were then held by our men and their Turkish prisoners side by side! The Arabs made several attempts to rush the lines during the night, but were driven off by British and Turkish machine-gun and rifle fire. It would be interesting to know if there is any previous instance of prisoners of war assisting their captors to hold the latter's own allies at bay.

It is only fair to the forces of the Emir Feisal to say that the ' allies ' whom we successfully held off through the night were none of his men. As soon as the enemy force had surrendered, the Arab regulars had hurried north to rejoin their comrades pressing after the IVth Turkish Army.

The New Zealand Brigade arrived at Ziza next day, and remained in charge of the station, to guard about 500 Turkish sick and wounded and a large amount of rolling stock and captured arms and ammunition, till the railway had been repaired. The Arabs, frustrated in their amiable designs on the Turkish prisoners, drew off disappointed, and followed their compatriots towards Damascus. The 2nd A.L.H. Brigade then escorted the prisoners, just over 4000 in number, to Amman, whence they were evacuated a few days later across the Jordan.

This ended the operations of Chaytor's Force, which remained about Amman and El Salt to rest and recuperate. Since the beginning of the operations the force had contributed to the bag about 11,000 prisoners, fifty-seven guns and 132 machine guns, besides large quantities of rolling stock, ammunition, and other stores.

In the last three weeks of September the Anzac Division had evacuated just over 3000 men from sickness alone. 2700 of these were cases of malignant malaria, a terrible scourge that was with us all through these operations. The long period spent in the Jordan Valley was no doubt responsible for this heavy sick rate. The division had lost a large number of men in the months preceding September, and it was now reduced to considerably less than half its war strength. Weak and reduced in numbers as they were, and suffering from the lassitude engendered by their prolonged stay in the valley, the Australians nevertheless acted throughout the operations with the greatest energy and determination, and set an unrivalled example of toughness and cheerfulness.

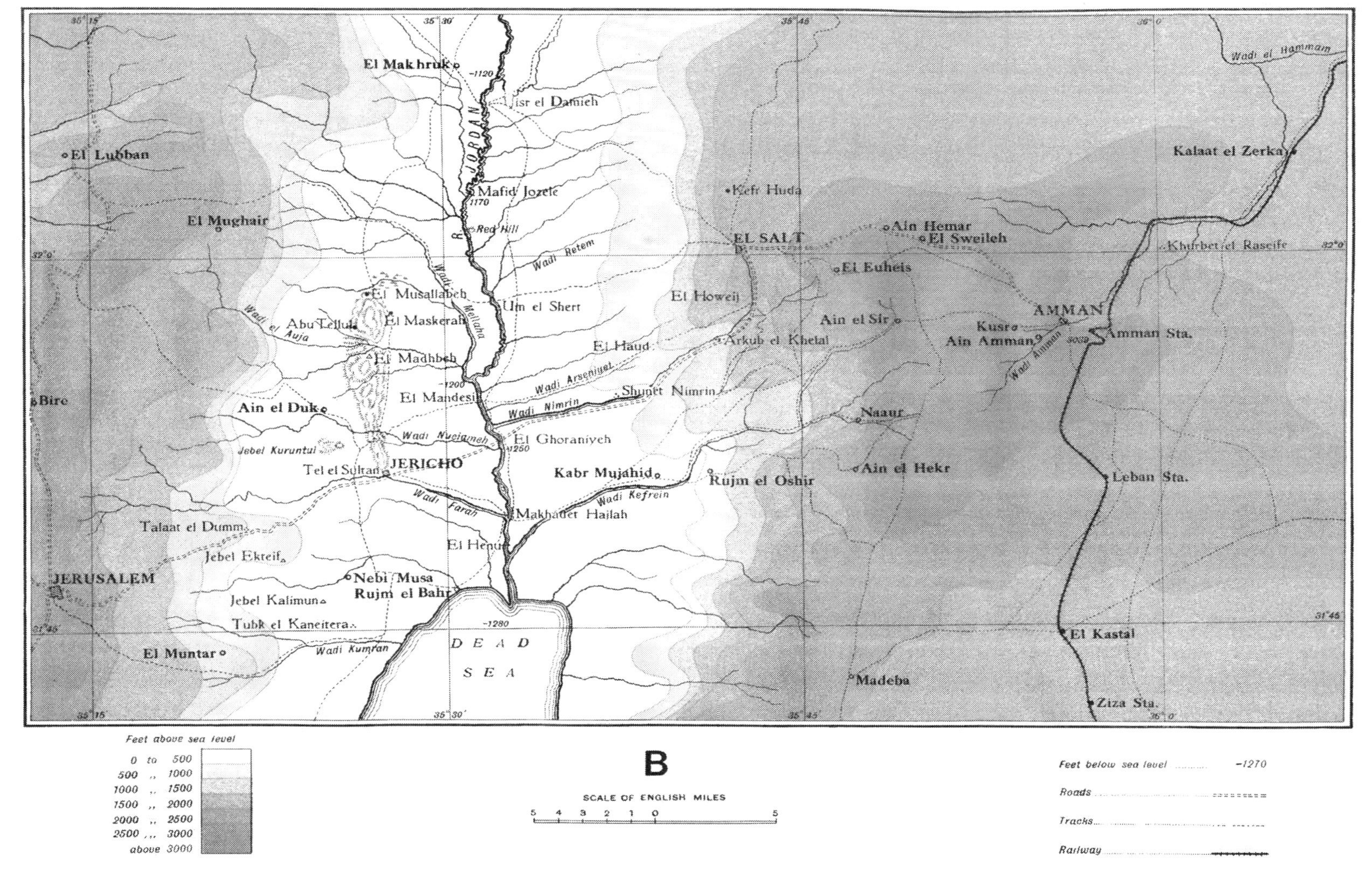

El Makhruk
-1120
isr el Damieh
Wadi el Hammain
El Lubban
Kalaat el Zerka
Mafid Jozele
1170
Kefr Huda
El Mughair
Red Hill
Ain Hemar
EL SALT
El Sweileh
Khirbet el Raseife
32°0'
El Euheis
Wadi Retem
El Howeij
Ain el Sir
AMMAN
El Musallabeh
Um el Shert
Kusr
Ain Amman
Amman Sta.
Abu Tellul
El Maskerah
Arkub el Khetal
Wadi el Auja
El Haud
El Madhbeh
Wadi Arseniyet
Shunet Nimrin
Naaur
Wadi el Auja
Wadi Mellaha
-1200
El Mandesil
Wadi Nimrin
Ain el Duk
Wadi Nueiameh
El Ghoraniyeh
1250
Ain el Hekr
Jebel Kuruntul
Tel el Sultan
JERICHO
Kabr Mujahid
Rujm el Oshir
Leban Sta.
Wadi Farah
Wadi Kefrein
Talaat el Dumm
Makhadet Hailah
El Henu
Jebel Ekteif
Nebi Musa
JERUSALEM
Jebel Kalimun
Rujm el Bahr
El Kastal
Tubk el Kaneitera
-1280
31°45'
El Muntar
Wadi Kumran
DEAD
SEA
Madeba
Ziza Sta.
35°30'
35°45'
36°0'
JORDAN R.
Feet above sea level
0 to 500
500 ,, 1000
1000 ,, 1500
1500 ,, 2000
2000 ,, 2500
2500 ,, 3000
above 3000
B
SCALE OF ENGLISH MILES
5 4 3 2 1 0   5
Feet below sea level   -1270
Roads
Tracks
Railway

CHAPTER XIX

THE ADVANCE ON DAMASCUS

As the Turkish VIIth and VIIIth Armies and the 2nd Corps had now been entirely destroyed, and the IVth Army was in full retreat, the Commander-in-Chief determined to push on with his cavalry and seize Damascus.

Apart from the moral effect likely to be produced on the Turks by the capture of this city, its occupation by our troops was a necessary corollary to the co-operation of King Hussein with our army. Damascus is an Arab, and particularly a Bedouin, city. From the time of Mohammed, it has been the focus and centre of Arab political life, constantly both reinforced and kept at the same level of civilisation by intercourse with the tribes of the desert, till to-day they form four-fifths of the total population.

It is an open secret that General Allenby had been urged by the amateur strategists of Downing Street to make a cavalry raid on the city, supported by the forces of the Emir, but he had steadily refused to commit his cavalry to this hazardous enterprise until he had dealt with the Turkish Army. Now, however, the way was clear, and he determined to push on with all speed.

The advance was to be made in two columns. The Australian Mounted Division and the 5th Cavalry Division were ordered to march *via* Nazareth and Tiberias, crossing the upper Jordan just south of Lake Huleh, and march up the Tiberias-Damascus road, across the Hauran.   The 4th Cavalry Division was to cross the Jordan at Jisr Mejamie, north of Beisan, and proceed *via* Irbid and Deraa Junction, and thence up the Hedjaz Railway, joining hands with the Arab Army about Deraa.

In order to increase to the utmost the mobility of the troops, all transport, even to the regimental water-carts, was left behind.   Only the guns and ammunition wagons and a few light motor ambulances per division accompanied the force.   The arrangements as to food and forage carried on the man and horse were the same as in the 1917 campaign.   When this two days' supply was exhausted, the cavalry were to live on the country.   Later on, after the capture of Damascus, and when our line of communications had been organised, tea, milk, and sugar were sent up by lorry to Damascus, or by sea to Beirût and Tripoli, but, except for this, the Corps subsisted entirely on the local resources of the country from the 25th September till the administration of the conquered territory was finally handed over to the French more than a year later.

The orders for the advance were received on the 25th of September, but certain preliminary movements had taken place on the previous day.   Thus the 7th Infantry Division arrived at Jenin on the 24th, preparatory to taking over Afule, Nazareth, and Haifa from the cavalry.   The 4th A.L.H. Brigade, with one regiment of the 5th Brigade, left Afule on the evening of the same day to march *via* Beisan to the village of Semakh, at the southern end of the Sea of Galilee.   The enemy had a small force here, engaged in evacuating the considerable quantities of stores at Deraa.   These were sent by rail to Semakh, and thence by boat to Tiberias, where lorry columns awaited them, and shipped them on to Damascus along the Hauran road. The Central India Horse (10th Brigade), who had relieved the 19th Lancers at Jisr Mejamie on the 23rd, had reconnoitred the village on the following day, and found it strongly held. The 4th A.L.H. Brigade was ordered to capture the place, and then rejoin the Australian Division at Tiberias.

On the 25th of September the 4th Cavalry Division concentrated at Beisan, with the 10th Brigade at Jisr Mejamie. The Australian Mounted Division, less the 4th Brigade, left Afule early in the afternoon, and had concentrated at Kefr Kenna, some five miles east of Nazareth, about ten o'clock that night. A regiment of the 3rd A.L.H. Brigade, supported by two armoured cars, was sent ahead along the Tiberias road to reconnoitre the town. The 5th Cavalry Division, which was not relieved at Haifa by the infantry till early the next morning, left that place at once, and reached Kefr Kenna about five in the evening.

The 4th A.L.H. Brigade, having bivouacked at Jisr Mejamie on the night of the 24th, approached Semakh just at daylight on the following day. At half-past four the advance guard, consisting of the 11th Regiment and the brigade machine-gun squadron, came under heavy machine-gun and rifle fire from the railway station. Patrols from the regiment located the enemy holding an entrenched position south of the village (which lies on a bare, flat plain), with posts extending across this plain to the hills on either side.

General Grant decided to attack at once, and ordered the remainder of his brigade to close up. The machine guns and one squadron of the 11th Regiment at once came into action south of the town, and opened a hot fire on the enemy positions, particularly on a sort of fort that had been built by the Germans out of railway material. The other two squadrons of the 11th charged from the east, one on each side of the railway. The charge was driven home, over the enemy positions and into the village, where the Australians dismounted, and went in with the bayonet.

On the arrival of the rest of the brigade, the 4th Regiment was sent in mounted on the west. After charging into the town, these troops also dismounted, and continued the fight on foot.

The enemy, stiffened by the large number of German troops, resisted desperately, and some of the fiercest hand-to-hand fighting of the campaign took place in this village. We learnt afterwards that Liman von Sanders had paid a hurried visit to the place in a car, after flying from Nazareth, and had given orders that it was to be held to the last man, so as to clear the ammunition and stores from Deraa for the defence of Damascus.

Gradually the defenders were driven back through the narrow streets of the village, till only the railway ' fort ' still held out. This was garrisoned chiefly by Germans, who had a number of machine guns covering all approaches. One of these guns was located in a railway culvert, and, as a troop of the 12th Regiment was working towards it, the crew suddenly stood up and held up their hands, shouting out: ' We surrender ! ' Being unaccustomed to the ways of the Hun, our men got up and walked towards the gun in the open. When they were about fifty yards away, the crew dropped to their knees, at a given signal, and opened a murderous fire on our men, killing or wounding nearly all of them. The few who escaped worked round to the other side of the railway, and, crawling through the culvert, fell upon the treacherous crew from behind, and killed them all.

About the same time, another troop of the same regiment encountered a German machine gun in charge of an officer. As our men approached, the officer stood up and waved a white handkerchief, whereupon the subaltern in command of the troop went up to him unsuspectingly. When he was about two paces away, the German pulled out his automatic and deliberately shot the unfortunate officer dead.

These two pieces of treachery met with a just retribution. The enraged Australians stormed into the fort, deaf now to all offers of surrender, and bayoneted the defenders almost to a man. About 150 Germans and several hundred Turkish prisoners were taken in the action, and some 200 corpses, mostly those of Germans, were left on the position to be looted by the natives. None of our men would put spade to the ground to bury them.

Two motor boats were lying at the pier when our troops attacked. One of these succeeded in escaping to Tiberias, where it was abandoned by the crew, and burnt. The other was set on fire by Hotchkiss rifle fire, and blew up.

As soon as the action was over, a squadron from the brigade was sent forward along the lake road towards Tiberias. This squadron gained touch with the regiment of the Australian Division advancing from Nazareth, and the two detachments captured Tiberias, which was lightly held, before dark, with about 120 prisoners.

The operations now resolved themselves into a race for Damascus between our cavalry and the Turkish IVth Army. The country about ten miles south of Damascus is favourable for defence against a force advancing from that direction, and the enemy command hoped, if the IVth Army could reach this position first, to be able to delay our troops long enough for help to arrive from Aleppo, and thus save Damascus.

The survivors of the German G.H.Q. troops and garrison of Nazareth had retired, *via* Tiberias, to the Jordan at Jisr Benat Yakub, just south of Lake Huleh. Crossing the river here, they blew up the bridge behind them, and took up a strong position on the east bank, overlooking the only known fords. They were joined, on the morning of the 26th, by a few hundred Turkish troops who had been hurriedly collected in Damascus, and sent down in motor lorries across the Hauran. If this force could hold the crossing for twenty-four hours, there was a chance of the Turks winning the race to Damascus.

The Australian Mounted Division left Kefr Kenna at midnight on the 25th, and, marching all night, reached the hill of Tel Madh, overlooking Tiberias, at dawn. Continuing the march, after a short halt to water and feed, the division arrived at El Mejdel, on the lake shore four miles north of Tiberias, in the early afternoon. In order to give time for the 5th Division to close up, and for the 4th A.L.H. Brigade to rejoin from Semakh, the Australians bivouacked here for the night. Patrols were sent forward as far as Jisr Benat Yakub, and the rest of the men spent the afternoon bathing in the lake.

Meanwhile, the 4th Cavalry Division, having crossed the Jordan at Jisr Mejamie, on the morning of the 26th, sent the 10th Brigade ahead as advance guard, with orders to push on towards Deraa as fast as the difficult nature of the ground would allow. The remainder of the division followed at a considerable distance.

After the fall of Amman, the enemy IVth Army

Nazareth, from the north.
Note the Red Crescents on the roofs of the houses.

Horse Artillery entering Tiberias, on the race for Damascus.

had hurried northwards along the Hedjaz Railway, and, by the morning of the 26th, was passing through El Remte, with a strong flank guard thrown out to the west. Late in the afternoon the 10th Brigade located this flank guard holding a position astride the Beisan-Deraa road, along a ridge from Beit Ras, through Irbid, to Zebda. The country was very difficult and broken, and intersected with wadis.

A reconnaissance carried out by the 2nd Lancers, the vanguard regiment, indicated that Irbid was held in strength, while Beit Ras and Zebda were occupied to protect the central portion of the enemy position, and were not so strongly held. The Brigadier decided to encircle Irbid from both flanks. He directed the 2nd Lancers to work round to the north of the town, between it and Beit Ras, which latter place was apparently very lightly held, and the Central India Horse to seize Zebda, and then endeavour to get astride the Deraa road behind the enemy position. The Berks Battery R.H.A. came into action just off the road, some two miles west of Irbid, with the Dorset Yeomanry in reserve behind it.

The regiments moved off at once, and commenced to work round the enemy's flanks. Half an hour later, a squadron of the 2nd Lancers attempted to charge the Irbid position from the north-west. Night was approaching, and the officer in command doubtless considered himself justified in taking the risk of a charge, in the hope of breaking the Turks' resistance before the coming of darkness enabled them to retire. But the horses were very tired, the country was broken and stony, and no previous reconnaissance of the ground was possible. The charge was met by the enemy with very heavy machine-gun fire, and was brought to a stop. The squadron suffered severely, two troops being practically wiped out before it reached cover again.

The Turks at Irbid had been retreating rapidly for three days, harassed by the Arabs, and their *morale* was not high. But they had not, as yet, suffered any severe defeat, and they were in considerably better case than the miserable remnants of the VIIth and VIIIth Armies, with which our cavalry had been engaged since the 20th of September. This fact would seem to have been overlooked by the 2nd Lancers. Moreover the enemy was in considerable strength. Natives reported on the following day that there had been not less than 5000 Turks at Irbid. This was manifestly an exaggeration, but the mere mention of such a number indicated that there had been, at any rate, a large body of them there. The failure of the charge taught a lesson that is liable to be forgotten by cavalry when pursuing a broken and demoralised foe ; namely, that, for a small body of horse to charge an enemy force of unknown strength, without previous reconnaissance of the ground, and without any fire support, is to court disaster.

The rest of the regiment continued to work gradually round the enemy's right flank. Nightfall found them some distance to the north-east of the village, where they put out pickets and remained during the night.

Meanwhile the Central India Horse, advancing more warily, occupied Zebda, after some sharp fighting, and then attempted to penetrate Irbid dismounted from the south-west. The attack was driven back by the enemy with some loss, and the regiment took up a position south of the village, and engaged the Turks with machine-gun and rifle fire. One squadron continued to work eastwards, and, by the time darkness descended, had nearly reached the Deraa road. This squadron formed a defensive post near the road, and stood to till daylight.

The 12th Brigade spent the night at El Shuni, on the Wadi el Arab, six miles east of the Jordan, and the rest of the division at Jisr Mejamie.

From the summit of the ridge near Beit Ras, just before sunset, our troops had seen the Arab Army, twenty miles away, on the far side of Deraa. After their raids on the railway at this place, between the 16th and 18th of September, the Arabs had moved east into the wild fastnesses of the Hauran. From here they had made several raids on the IVth Army, harassing the Turks' right flank, and forcing them to abandon much of their transport and artillery. On the day and night of the 26th, the Arab camelry, led by Lawrence, pushed rapidly northwards, cutting the railway at Ghazale and Ezra, ten and twenty miles north of Deraa, and reached Sheikh Saad, fifteen miles west of Ezra, on the morning of the 27th. Here they engaged and defeated an advanced detachment of the IVth Army, capturing 500 Turks and a number of German officers, and then entrenched themselves astride the Damascus road to await the coming of the remainder of the army.

At daylight on the 27th, Irbid was found to have been evacuated during the night. The 10th Brigade at once pushed on towards El Remte, with the Dorset Yeomanry as advance guard. At half-past ten, patrols from this regiment encountered the enemy in position astride the road, just west of El Remte. The position was not so strong as that at Irbid, and the country was more open.

A quarter of an hour later, the Dorsets reported the enemy to be retiring from the position to the south-east. The Brigadier directed the regiment to occupy the ridges on the left bank of the Wadi

Ratam, overlooking the village from the south-west, and to make a demonstration against the enemy, in order to cover the assembly of the remainder of the brigade, which was to advance under cover of the high ground immediately north of El Remte, and cut off the enemy's retreat to Deraa. The Berks Battery came into action west of the village, to support this move, and to take advantage of such targets as offered.

While these movements were taking place, the Yeomanry were heavily counter-attacked by the enemy troops that they had supposed to be retiring. The attack was pressed vigorously, and the Dorsets were forced back some distance. A signal message was sent to brigade headquarters asking for assistance, but, before the message could be acted upon, Lieutenant Mason, skilfully withdrawing his squadron in the advanced firing line, mounted it, and charged the counter-attack. The Turks were utterly surprised by this sudden charge. A number of them were killed with the sword, and the rest driven back in confusion into the village. The Dorsets then continued to work round to the south, but were held up shortly afterwards by heavy machine-gun fire from a fortified stone house.

Just at this moment, a body of enemy cavalry was observed galloping away from the village to the east. The Yeomanry were unable to pursue them, but they were effectively shelled by the Berks Battery, and dispersed.

The Central India Horse had by now reached a point north-east of the village, from where they espied the Turkish infantry retiring in some disorder. Charging instantly, they went through the Turks, killing many with the lance, and rounding up 200 prisoners. This charge completed the rout of the enemy force, the survivors of which scattered in all directions.

The 10th Brigade now received orders to await the arrival of the rest of the division at El Remte. The 12th Brigade came up about half-past five in the evening, and the 11th some two hours later. Patrols from the 2nd Lancers, on outpost duty, gained touch with the Arab Army during the night.

At dawn on the 28th, the brigade moved out to the hills east of El Remte to cover the assembly of the division, which then marched to Deraa. The advanced troops reached the town at seven in the morning, and were met by Lawrence and Sherif Nasir. The Arab troops had arrived there about midnight, and found the place evacuated and in flames. They at once sent mounted scouts to the north, who located the main body of the enemy forces retiring towards Mezerib, ten miles north-west of Deraa. The road from Mezerib to Damascus runs through Sheikh Saad, where Lawrence's camel corps was lying in wait for them.

CHAPTER XX

THE ADVANCE ON DAMASCUS (*Continued*)

WHILE the 4th Cavalry Division was treading on the heels of the enemy east of the Jordan, the Australians had not been idle. Leaving El Mejdel soon after daylight on the 27th, they reached the Jordan at Jisr Benat Yakub about mid-day. The news that the bridge had been destroyed, and that the crossing was held by the enemy, had been brought back by the patrols that had reconnoitred as far as the river the night before.

The division had no easy task before it. Napoleon rated the forcing of a river crossing as one of the most difficult operations in war. In this case the difficulties were increased by several factors. West of the river the ground sloped gently upwards for about 3000 yards, in a wide expanse of plough and grass land, unbroken by a single tree or bush. On the east the ground was much steeper, thus giving good command of the river, and was thickly covered with scrub and innumerable big boulders, which afforded excellent protection to the enemy. The river was deep and very swift, and the only known ford, some few hundred yards south of the bridge, was commanded by the fire of numbers of enemy machine guns. The only cover on the west bank was afforded by a small group of buildings close to the bridge, and by the insignificant ruins of the castle of Baldwin II. (Kusr Atra), a few hundred yards farther down stream.

A local native stated that he thought the south end of Lake Huleh was shallow enough to be waded by mounted men, and it was accordingly decided to send the 3rd Brigade, by a long detour, to attempt a passage here.   To the French troops was assigned the task of endeavouring to reach the buildings at the west end of the bridge, from where they could engage the enemy with rifle and machine-gun fire, and, possibly, force a passage over the river.   The remainder of the 5th Brigade was to reconnoitre for a ford farther south, and, if successful in finding one, to cross the river, and get astride the enemy's line of retreat.   One regiment of the 4th Brigade, which had rejoined the division at El Mejdel, accompanied the 5th Brigade.   The rest of the 4th did not arrive till the evening.

While the two brigades were moving to the north and south, the two batteries of the division, in action due west of the bridge, amused themselves by knocking out the enemy guns.   Having silenced these, they turned their attention to a column of motor lorries that had brought some of the Turks from Damascus, and were now waiting to take the Germans back again, when they judged it expedient to retire, and leave their allies to be captured.   Two of the lorries were knocked out, and the remainder chased out of range.   Our guns were then occupied with the more serious business of registering such of the enemy machine guns as had been located.

While thus engaged, the two batteries received orders to report to the 3rd and 5th Brigades respectively.   Following instructions from the brigadiers concerned, they limbered up, and moved off to accompany the brigades moving north and south.   Owing to the difficulties of the country over which they had to move, and the long distance they were required to go, it was nearly two hours before they were in action again.

The French regiment, moving over the open, dismounted and widely extended, reached the buildings with some loss, but was unable to attempt the ford, in face of the very heavy fire from the east bank. No artillery support was available, as our batteries were on the move.

The 3rd Brigade scouts found Lake Huleh quite unfordable, but one regiment succeeded in working its way dismounted down to the river bank south of the lake. It came under very heavy fire here—indeed the water in the river was bubbling with machine-gun bullets—but the men gradually worked south by twos and threes, towards what looked like a possible crossing just north of the bridge.

Meanwhile the regiments with the 5th Brigade, after riding for two miles south of the bridge, without finding any sign of a ford, waded boldly into the river at a likely looking place, and succeeded in struggling across. Arrived on the other side, they found themselves involved in a perfect maze of precipitous wadis running in every direction, in a formation of old lava, broken into huge, jagged boulders. They wandered about in this wilderness for the rest of the afternoon and evening, and only gained the Damascus road after dark, too late to intercept the retiring enemy. The threat to their communications, however, had had its invariable effect on the Turks, and, as soon as darkness fell, they retreated hurriedly. All the Germans, and as many Turks as could find room, piled themselves on to the lorries. The rest of the Turks had to walk.

At dusk the regiment of the 3rd Brigade on the river bank, taking advantage of the failing light, plunged into the river, and swam across. The cold plunge, and the prospect of a night in their wet clothes, induced in the men a suitable frame of mind for dealing efficiently with any Turks they might meet, and, in the ensuing bayonet fight on the east bank, they killed a large number of the enemy and took eighty-five prisoners. They then pushed on up the road as far as Deir el Saras, where they met patrols of the 5th Brigade.

Just before dark a German aeroplane flew over our troops at a great height, and dropped a couple of bombs, which did no harm. This was the first enemy aeroplane seen in the air by our cavalry since the commencement of the operations, a fine tribute to the work of the Royal Air Force.

The name Jisr Benat Yakub means the Bridge of the Daughters of Jacob. The bridge carries on its grey, old arches the oldest known road in the world, the caravan way from Egypt to Mesopotamia. All the armies of time have trod this trail. Egyptian, Assyrian, Hittite, Jew ; Saracen Arab and Christian Knight ; Turkish Janissary and soldier of Napoleon— all have crossed the sacred river at this point. So it is conceivable that the name really comes, as the Arabs aver, from the daughters of the patriarch, though a local tradition ascribes it to a massacre of some Jacobin nuns, which took place here in the twelfth century. The bridge marks the northern limit of Napoleon's advance through Syria, and it was a strange turn of the wheel of fate that again brought French soldiers here fighting the Turks, a hundred and twenty years later, but this time as allies of the English.

The action had delayed the division for the better part of a day, thus increasing the chance of the enemy army reaching Damascus first. Indeed, had it not been for the vigorous and effective action of Lawrence's camel corps on the following day, it is just possible that the Turks might have won the race.

The delay had, however, permitted the 5th Cavalry Division, which had left Kefr Kenna at dawn, to close up, and it lay that night near Rosh Pina, a Jewish village about eight miles west of the Jordan.

The Corps bridging train came up during the night, and the Sappers set to work repairing the bridge. This proved a big task, as one of the four arches had been completely demolished. At daylight on the 28th, as the work was still far from finished, the rest of the Australian Mounted Division forded the river, and at once pressed on up the road towards El Kuneitra. The passage of the guns was very arduous. The river was only about four feet deep at the ford, but there were deep holes on either side, and the current was torrential. The ground on the other side proved to be a marsh, covered with a tangle of high, stiff scrub, and interspersed with large boulders. A road had to be cut through this scrub, boggy places filled in with tree trunks and bushes, and the ford improved. All this took time, and it was nine o'clock before the first gun was across the ford, and safely on the road.

For the first two miles from the Jordan, the road climbs out of the valley in a series of steep zigzags, and the surface was atrocious. Once out of the valley, however, an excellent, metalled road stretched ahead all the way to Damascus. Four Turkish guns, three of them destroyed by direct hits from our artillery, two motor lorries, and a number of machine guns were found on the east bank.

The division made good progress, and the advanced troops reached the Circassian village of El Kuneitra, at the top of the watershed, about one o'clock. The 5th Division got in about five hours later, and the two divisions bivouacked for the night east and west of the village.

The cavalry were now over sixty miles from Nazareth, the nearest post held by our infantry, and Damascus was forty miles farther on. The whole country was, very naturally, in a most disturbed state. Bands of marauding Arabs and Druses patrolled the Hauran, ostensibly at war with the Turks, but always ready to fall on and plunder any weakly-guarded convoy. To protect our communications, therefore, General Grant, with the headquarters of the 4th A.L.H. Brigade and the 11th Regiment, was stationed at Kuneitra. The Hyderabad Lancers, who had been left at the Jordan, near Jisr Benat Yakub, were also placed under his command.

Kuneitra is the seat of government of a *Kaza*, and one of the most important of the Circassian villages that are found scattered throughout the Hauran, and as far south as Amman. Their origin dates back to the annexation by Russia of the Turkish provinces of Kars, Batoum, and Ardahan in 1877. The Circassians, being Moslems, left the annexed provinces in considerable numbers, and were planted by the Turks along the fringe of the desert, to act as a check on the turbulent Arab tribes. They were given land and favoured in other ways by the Turks, and are consequently cordially hated by the local Arab population. Our cavalry had encountered them before, during the Amman raids. They used to enlist freely in the Turkish cavalry, and should make good soldiers if properly trained. Now, however, the defeat of their protectors laid them open to the vengeance of the Arabs, whom they had always despised and insulted, and they were completely cowed. On the afternoon of the 26th, our aircraft had reported a force of enemy cavalry, estimated at 3000, in the neighbourhood of El Kuneitra. This large force made no attempt to assist in holding the passage of the Jordan, and, by the time our troops reached El Kuneitra, it had all melted away. Arms were buried or hidden, uniforms thrown away, and the big, sturdy, fair-haired louts were all wandering about their villages, with their hands in the pockets of their baggy breeches, trying to look as much like peaceful agriculturists as possible.

A party of Hauran Druses had looted the village before our troops arrived. Some of them were rounded up near by and questioned, but, as they were fighting with the Arabs, and were thus our ' allies,' albeit their methods were not ours, they had to be set free again.

While the Australians and the 5th Cavalry Division were advancing on El Kuneitra, the 4th Cavalry Division passed through Deraa, and pressed on to El Mezerib and Tafas, with the Arabs on its right flank, harassing the rear of the retreating IVth Army. The main Turkish force had got some distance farther north, but it had been delayed for many hours on the previous day at Sheikh Saad, by the skilful fighting of Lawrence's Arabs. It was this delay that finally decided the fate of the Turks in the race for Damascus. The remnants of the IVth Army did, in fact, reach the city, but our troops were close on their heels, and they got no farther. Of the units that left Deraa on the 27th, however, not one man lived to reach Damascus. Passing through Tafas on the afternoon of that day, they seized eighty Arab women and children, and butchered them in cold blood, with every refinement of torture and outrage that the bestial mind of the Turk could conceive. For this deed the Arabs exacted vengeance to the last man. Not only was every man of the Turkish rearguard killed, but two trains full of sick and wounded, which were captured by the Arabs on the railway farther north, were set on fire, and burnt with their human freight. It was a terrible vengeance, but characteristic of the Arabs, and one can hardly blame them. It is to be noted that the Turks who perpetrated this horrible massacre were accompanied by a number of German officers, who appear to have made no effort to stop the hideous work.

CHAPTER XXI

THE FALL OF DAMASCUS

AT two o'clock on the afternoon of the 29th, the Australian Mounted Division started on the last lap of the race to Damascus. The 5th Cavalry Division followed a few miles in rear of the Australians. The distance to be covered was about forty miles, and it was hoped that, if the two divisions marched all night, they would be able to surround the city soon after dawn on the 30th.

It was arranged that the Australian Mounted Division should send two brigades along the foot of the hills west of Damascus, to close the two roads leading north-west to Beirût, and north-east to Homs. The 5th Division was to send one brigade round the east side of the city, to gain touch with the Australians on the Homs road, and place the remainder of the division astride the Deraa-Damascus road, at or near Kiswe, to receive the remnants of the Turkish IVth Army, which was to be driven into their welcoming arms by the 4th Division.

It must be explained that the only available maps were very inaccurate and greatly lacking in detail. Thus, there was no indication that the steep and rocky hills, which press right on to Damascus on the west, were almost impassable for cavalry; or that the Beirût road runs along the bottom of a deep, precipitous gorge, into which it was impossible for cavalry to descend; or that, to reach the Homs road, it would be necessary to pass through the western suburbs of the city, always a difficult and dangerous operation in a hostile country, and doubly so for mounted troops.

For political reasons, strict orders had been given that no British troops were to enter Damascus, and these orders considerably hampered our subsequent operations, and made our task more difficult.

In the end, however, it was the action of the enemy that was the chief cause of our delay. A couple of armoured cars went ahead of the Australian Division to reconnoitre, and returned, shortly after the division had started, with the information that the enemy was holding a position astride the road, near the village of Sasa, a little north of the Nahr Mughaniye. The cars had drawn a considerable fire from guns and machine guns. Patrols of the 3rd A.L.H. Brigade crossed the river just before dark, and had located the enemy's position fairly accurately by the time the rest of the brigade arrived. The position had been well sited by the enemy, on a rocky ridge running about east and west. An impassable morass of unknown extent protected his right flank, north of the road, and the country to the south was a wilderness of broken lava boulders, most difficult even for infantry and in the daylight.

The 8th and 9th A.L.H. Regiments dismounted, and advanced in pitch darkness against the presumed position of the enemy's left flank. The going was so bad that it was nearly two in the morning before they got to grips with the Turks. There was a half-hour's very confused bayonet fighting among the rocks in the darkness, during which it was almost impossible to distinguish friend from foe. The Turks then broke, most of them making for the road. A pre-arranged signal of Verey lights, sent up by the attackers, apprised the division of this, and, immediately it was seen, a squadron of the 10th A.L.H. Regiment, which had been held in readiness, galloped straight down the road in the dark, to get ahead of the retreating Turks and cut them off. It very nearly came to grief over one of the enemy guns which had been abandoned on the road, but fortunately the leading horses saw it, and swerved aside just in time. The squadron was followed, at a more sober pace, by the 4th and 12th Regiments of the 4th Brigade, which now took the lead.

About 100 prisoners, three guns, and a number of machine guns were captured on the position, and, after daylight, about 250 more stragglers were gathered in, including a party of 150 Germans, who had retired before the 10th Regiment charged down the road. Our casualties had been rather heavy for so small an affair, and, by some strange chance, the Turks captured and carried off with them in their retreat eight of our men. These we came upon and rescued near the village of Sasa, shortly after daybreak.

The net result of this action was that, instead of being on the outskirts of Damascus at dawn on the 30th, our troops were still nearly twenty miles away.

Pressing on as fast as possible, the division reached Kaukab about ten o'clock, and here encountered the enemy again. At some time or other the Turks had constructed a long line of entrenchments stretching from near Katana (north of the El Kuneitra road) across the road at Kaukab, along the high ridge of the Jebel el Aswad, over the Deraa road north of Kiswe, and thence over the Jebel el Mania to near Deir Ali. It was the western portion of this line, astride the El Kuneitra road, that they were now holding. The position looked strong, and, had the Turks put up a determined fight here, they might have saved many of their friends in Damascus, to say nothing of their masters the Germans, from capture.

'A' Battery H.A.C. and the Notts Battery R.H.A., which were marching near the head of the advance guard, came into action at once, and opened a rapid and effective fire on the enemy position. After a few minutes' bombardment, the 4th A.L.H. Regiment was launched at the village of Kaukab, and the 12th at a spur of the Jebel el Aswad, against the enemy's left flank. The going here was good, and the cavalry were able to gallop right on to the position, which they proceeded to do, covered by the fire of the guns. The combination of gun fire and charging cavalry was too much for the shattered nerves of the Turks, who broke and fled, pursued by the Australians. The whole force was killed or captured.

The 5th Brigade now took the lead, and rode hard up the road towards Damascus, followed by the 3rd Brigade, which had rejoined from Sasa just after the action. The leading troops came under fire from the houses and gardens of the suburb of El Mezze. The Notts Battery came into action, and shelled the enemy satisfactorily, while the 5th Brigade plunged into the maze of hills north of the road, and made for the Beirût road. Seeing their right threatened, the Turks retired into the town, and the 3rd Brigade was free to move on. Patrols from this brigade then found that it was impossible to reach the Homs road, except by going right through the town, as the river Barada, running between rock cliffs, barred their path farther west. As the orders against entering the town were peremptory, there was nothing to be done but send back word of the state of affairs, and wait for permission to advance. This permission was not received till late at night, when it was impossible for the brigade to make its way through the narrow, tortuous streets of the town, which was still full of enemy troops.

Meanwhile the 5th Brigade was encountering great difficulties in the bare, rocky hills west and north of El Mezze, but the advanced troops reached the gorge of the Barada, above El Rabue, about five in the evening. Here they found themselves on the top of a cliff about 200 feet high, overhanging the road and railway to Beirût, and looked down upon an extraordinary sight. The whole of the bottom of the gorge, from side to side, was packed with a struggling mass of fugitives, on horse and afoot, in motors, cabs and carts, surging along like a tidal wave. There was a train on the line, packed with Germans, but it was completely blocked by the mass of people who struggled and fought along the railway, and the engine driver had long since been submerged in the tide of frenzied Turks. Even the river was full of men and horses.

There was no possible way of getting down on to the road from the top of the cliffs, but the fugitives had to be stopped somehow. A few machine guns were brought into action, and ordered to open fire on the head of the column below. General Onslow, who commanded the brigade, told the writer afterwards that he had never given an order with greater reluctance and horror. With a view to minimising the inevitable slaughter, he instructed his machine gunners to concentrate their fire as much as possible on the vehicles at the head of the column, in order to disable them and so block the road. When the firing commenced, the Turks in front tried to turn back towards the city, but the pressure behind them was so great that they were constantly pushed along into the zone of the bullets. At last, however, the growing pile of corpses and broken vehicles at the

Royal Horse Artillery fording the Jordan at Jisr Benat Yakub.

The Beirût road in the gorge of the River Barada. 1st October, 1918.

head of the column completely blocked the gorge, and the Turks realised that their escape was barred. They turned and streamed miserably back towards the city. Part of the crowd was intercepted by troops of the 3rd Brigade, who took about 5000 prisoners. The rest reached the city, and were collected next day. How many perished in the defile will never be known, but it took a large force of German prisoners ten days to dispose of the bodies. It was fitting that they, who by their insane ambition had brought the Turks to this sorry end, should have had the task of burying the victims of their lust for power.

Before dark, the 5th Brigade got a small party down on to the road, and picketed it during the night.

While the Australian Mounted Division had been pushing round west of Damascus, the 4th and 5th Cavalry Divisions had been slowly closing in on the city. The former had pursued the retreating IVth Army relentlessly all through the 29th of September, and, on the morning of the 30th, the 11th Brigade, which was acting as advance guard, reached El Ghabaghib Station, on the old French railway from Damascus to Mezerib, about thirty miles south of Damascus.

The main body of the enemy, which had been marching hard all night, was now some distance ahead of the division, but its retreat was constantly harassed by Lawrence's Arabs, who made repeated raids on the right flank of the Turks, and had by now reduced them to a state of extreme disorganisation. It must be remembered that the 4th Cavalry Division had about thirty miles farther to go before reaching Damascus than the other two divisions. Moreover, although there had been no opposition from the enemy after the action at El Remte, the division had been much delayed by the bad road from Deraa to Damascus, across the southern Hauran. The whole of this area is overlaid with the *débris* of extinct volcanoes, mostly in the form of huge boulders of black basalt, which everywhere cover the ground. Much time was spent in clearing away these boulders, to make a passage for the guns and transport of the division.   The whole country from Deraa to Damascus was strewn with the bodies of Turks that had died from exhaustion.   Dead horses, broken-down vehicles, and abandoned guns were scattered everywhere.   It was estimated that 2000 enemy dead were passed on the march, and many more than that number of dead animals.   The hot sun, beating down on the black rocks, burnt like the blast from a furnace, and the heavy air, poisoned by the unburied corpses of men and beasts, hung like a pall over the land.   There is little water to be found in the Hauran in summer, and less food, and not a single tree and scarce a human habitation soften the desolation of this horrible region.

The 5th Cavalry Division reached Sasa at about eight on the morning of the 30th, and there received a message from an aeroplane that a large body of the enemy, which was, in fact, the leading portion of the IVth Army, was approaching Kiswe, along the Deraa-Damascus road.   The 13th Brigade, followed by the 14th, was at once despatched to try and intercept this force.   Before they moved off, General MacAndrew [1] issued the following characteristic order to his brigades : ' Push on !   Kill or capture all you can, and seize Damascus.'

This day marked the end of the Turkish IVth

---

[1] Major-General Sir H. J. M. MacAndrew, K.C.B., Indian Army.   He died from burns received in an accident at Aleppo in July 1919.

Army, but, as it split up into a number of detached groups, which were attacked throughout the day by brigades, regiments, and even single squadrons of the 4th and 5th Cavalry Divisions, it is impossible to give any very concise account of its destruction. It is clear, however, that, on the morning of the 30th, the army was marching in two main bodies. The leading portion, that which had been seen and reported by our aircraft, consisted of the remains of the Turkish 3rd Cavalry Division, with such of the infantry as had been able to keep up with the mounted troops. The following portion, evidently much more disorganised, was marching some eight to ten miles in rear.

The 13th Brigade, moving along the south bank of the Wadi el Zabirani, encountered some opposition on the ridge of the Jebel el Aswad, north of Deir Khabiye, from enemy troops occupying a portion of the entrenched position that has been mentioned above. By mid-day, however, the brigade had succeeded in dispersing the enemy, taking some 700 prisoners. Meanwhile the 14th Brigade had got astride the Deraa-Damascus road, north of Kiswe. It was just in time to intercept the leading portion of the Turkish force, the advanced elements of which had cleared Kiswe, and were hurrying up the road over the Jebel el Aswad towards Damascus.

In the somewhat confused fighting which followed the encounter, the greater part of what was left of the Turkish 3rd Cavalry Division, including the divisional commander and his staff, fell into our hands. The remainder of the force was driven back, completely broken, to Kiswe.

At this time the 15th Brigade was in divisional reserve a little east of Khan el Shiha.

Shortly afterwards, about four in the afternoon,

the second portion of the Turkish army was seen approaching Kiswe, followed by the 11th Brigade of the 4th Cavalry Division. This brigade had been checked for a time at Khiyara Chiftlik, about six miles south of Kiswe, by a body of the enemy who took up a position behind the mud walls of a farm there. The brigade was rather heavily shelled from the direction of Kalaat el Nuhas at the same time. The farm was cleared by a mounted charge, and the Turks dispersed. Some escaped up the steep slopes of the Jebel el Mania to the east, but the bulk of them continued along the main road to Kiswe. On their arrival there, they joined the demoralised remnants of the leading portion of their force, that had escaped the onslaught of the 14th Brigade. Here they learnt that the road to Damascus was barred, and, looking backwards, saw the lances of the 4th Cavalry Division approaching. Caught between the two forces, they made a last despairing attempt to break through. There appears to have been a general *sauve qui peut*. Some attempted the Damascus road, and were ridden down and captured by the 14th Brigade. Others made their way north-east up the Nahr el Awaj, and attempted a counter-attack against the left flank of this brigade, but were broken up by the fire of the Essex Battery. They split up into small groups, and disappeared among the gardens of the Damascus plain east of the city, where the majority of them were almost certainly murdered by the natives. The largest body broke out to the north-west, and fell into the arms of the 13th Brigade near Sahnaya, where about 1500 prisoners were taken, and many were killed. Others again were observed trying to escape to the east. The Ayrshire Battery, attached to the 11th Brigade, galloped forward, supported by two machine guns and a few Hotchkiss rifles, and came into action at close range, causing the Turks to scatter wildly. The 29th Lancers pursued these disorganised parties up the slopes of the Jebel el Mania, and had rounded up large numbers of them before darkness put an end to the pursuit. Finally, a number remained in Kiswe, and tried to organise some sort of resistance there. At five o'clock, however, the 13th Brigade swept suddenly down upon the village and captured it, with about 700 prisoners and several guns.

It was now nearly dark, and nothing further could be done that day. The 5th Division remained for the night along a line north of the Wadi el Zabirani, from the Kuneitra-Damascus road to a few miles north-east of Kiswe. The 4th Division concentrated south of Kiswe.

Two troops of the Gloucester Yeomanry, 13th Brigade, and a troop of the 12th Regiment, 4th A.L.H. Brigade, starting from south and west of the town respectively, attempted to reach the big German wireless installation at Kadem Station in the southern suburb. The wireless plant had, however, been prepared for demolition, and was blown up before our troops reached it. Both parties had a warm time, and were continually sniped at by wandering bodies of the enemy from the houses and wooded gardens. Eventually they came upon a number of large ammunition dumps, which had been set on fire and were going off like a monstrous Brock's Benefit, and they had to beat a hurried retreat. All through the early part of the night tremendous explosions shook the air, as the fire reached fresh stacks of shells. Kadem railway station and all the houses round it were completely destroyed, but there was little other damage in the city. The Turks were too dispirited and worn out for deeds of frightfulness, and the Germans too intent on trying to make good their escape. The independence of the city from Turkish rule was actually publicly proclaimed in the Serai early on the afternoon of September the 30th, without any opposition from the Turks, although there were at the time some 15,000 Turkish and German soldiers in the town, including Jemal Pasha, the commander of the IVth Army. A number of these troops had come from Aleppo and Beirût, and the remainder were stragglers who had made their way in, by rail and road, from the south, after the *débâcle* of September the 19th and succeeding days. Nearly all of them were half starved and worn out by continual marching, and their *morale* had sunk so low that they made no protest when the whole city broke out in a blaze of Sherifian flags. Insulted and beaten by the people, who refused to give or sell them food, abandoned by their German masters in the most callous manner, diseased and starving, many of the poor wretches died in the streets that night. Many others, less fortunate, met a brutal death at the hands of the populace. Several thousand dragged themselves to the Turkish barracks, which they filled, and overflowed into the parade ground, where some 300 perished during the night. Two considerable bodies did indeed attempt to escape, one along the Beirût road, and the other towards Homs. The fate of the former has already been told. The latter body, which consisted of fresher troops, from Aleppo and Beirût, got out of the town on the north-east, and marched all night along the Homs road.

The next day, October the 1st, as soon as it was light, the 5th Cavalry Division concentrated and moved round to the east of the city, pushing the 13th Brigade as far north as the Homs road, where it got into touch with the 3rd A.L.H. Brigade of the Australian Mounted Division. This brigade passed through the city at dawn, patrols of the 10th A.L.H. Regiment reaching the Serai square about six in the morning, and being thus actually the first troops to enter the city. Passing the Baramkie railway station on the way, they found there a train just about to start for Beirût, the troops in it being ignorant of the fact that the railway had been cut (by the 5th A.L.H. Brigade) the previous night. They were speedily undeceived, and about 500 prisoners and a number of guns and machine guns were taken from the train, and handed over to the 4th and 12th Regiments of the 4th Brigade, which marched to the station later in the morning.

Hurrying through the town, the 3rd Brigade reached the Homs road, and pressed along it on the track of the enemy force that had escaped that way the previous evening. The 10th Regiment came up with part of this force about nine o'clock in the morning, on the Wadi Maraba, near Harista el Basal, and promptly charged it, killing many with the sword, and capturing about 600 prisoners and some forty machine guns. Continuing the pursuit, the cavalry came upon more of the enemy near Duma, and again at Khan Kusseir, twelve miles from Damascus, in the evening. They were engaged in continual skirmishing throughout the day, and the action at Khan Kusseir, where they were opposed by Germans, though short, was severe. The enemy troops had a number of machine guns, and put up a good fight, but were broken by a charge delivered from the cover of some vineyards and olive groves on their right flank, and all of them were killed or captured. The brigade remained at Duma for the night.

The advance troops of the Arab Army, under

Lawrence, reached Damascus about half-past eight in the morning, and established their headquarters in the Government buildings.

Meanwhile the two regiments of the 4th A.L.H. Brigade were at work collecting prisoners in the town, and evacuating them to a concentration area near Daraya. All day long the sorry business continued, and by evening nearly 12,000 had been collected. They were in a pitiable state. Many of them, the remnants of the IVth Army, had been chased for 150 miles by our cavalry and by the Arab forces. Constantly bombed by our aircraft, harassed day and night by the Arab Camel Corps and the hostile population of the country through which they passed, denied all food, and often short of water, it is one of the marvels of war that they had struggled so far. The task of getting them out of the city was a horrible one. Many fell by the wayside, and all the efforts of our cavalry failed to get them on their feet again, and they had to be left to die. All night long our over-worked ambulances toiled among them, bringing water and food and what medical assistance was possible, but they were utterly unable to cope with the numbers, and by morning over 600 were dead.

For the first fortnight, and until the rest and good food had had time to take effect, the mortality in the prisoners' camp, though decreasing daily, averaged over a hundred a day.

The whole Turkish force was riddled with disease. Nearly all were suffering from either malaria or dysentery, and there were several cases of smallpox. Venereal disease is endemic among the Turks, and, in normal times, seems to have little effect upon their general health; but, in the exhausted and weakened condition in which they now were, it laid hold on

The Emir Feisals' Headquarters at Damascus.
Note the Sherifian standards on the balcony.

Tripoli. The old Crusader Citadel.

them virulently, and took a heavy toll of lives.   An indication of the spread of this disease among the Germans was afforded by a room in the hospital at Afule, which was filled with boxes of salvarsan. This drug, we were informed by German medical officers, was reserved exclusively for the use of German troops.

The operations closed on the 2nd October with an extraordinary charge by the 3rd A.L.H. Brigade. Early in the morning, a column of the enemy was seen moving north, parallel to the Homs road, and some miles to the east.   This column had evidently hoped, by avoiding the road, to make its way unseen to Khan Ayash, where it would have entered the hills, and probably then made its escape.

The whole brigade immediately mounted, galloped six miles over the open plain, and charged the enemy with the sword.   The Turks had with them a few guns and a number of machine guns, which they brought into action and fought to the last.   The brigade galloped on, through a hot fire, and charged clean through the enemy force, killing a large number of them, and capturing 1500 prisoners, including a divisional commander, three guns, and twenty-six machine guns.   In point of distance this must be a record cavalry charge.

On the same day, detachments from each brigade of the Corps and some of the guns paraded at the village of Sbeine, south of Damascus, and marched through the city from end to end, led by the Corps Commander.   This was not intended as a triumphal march, but was a necessary display of force, to overawe the turbulent elements in the town, who threatened to create a state of absolute anarchy.

For political reasons the city was supposed to be in charge of the Arab forces, and an Arab Governor was actually appointed. But, with the best intentions in the world, the small force of so-called 'regular' Arab soldiers could do little or nothing to keep order. The irregular—highly irregular—forces of King Hussein far outnumbered the Arab Army. During the advance on the city, hordes of nomad Arabs had joined his standard, drawn thereto partly, no doubt, by their genuine and deep-rooted hatred of the Turks, but also, and far more strongly, by their equally genuine and deep-rooted love of plunder. Till they reached Damascus, the loot had consisted almost entirely of rifles and ammunition, best of all loot from the desert Arab's point of view, but now that each son of Ishmael was in possession of at least two good rifles, and was festooned with machine gun belts full of cartridges, he felt that he could toy with some more fancy trifles, should they come his way. So it was not surprising that, as soon as they entered the city, they all set to work at once to collect what Thomas Atkins would call ' souvenirs.' They were perfectly good-tempered about it, and only killed a few shopkeepers who made an unconscionable fuss about having their booths looted. No mercy was shown to the Turks, however. They were hunted down and killed remorselessly whereever found. Some of the Arabs even broke into the Turkish hospital, and set about murdering the moribund wretches whom they found there, till driven away by our troops.

The desert-bred Arabs are probably the most independent of mankind. They acknowledge no authority, and will take orders only from those who are able to exact obedience by force of arms. This the Emir Feisal was quite unable to do, even had he been willing, which is doubtful. His attitude seemed to be that boys will be boys, and it would be a shame

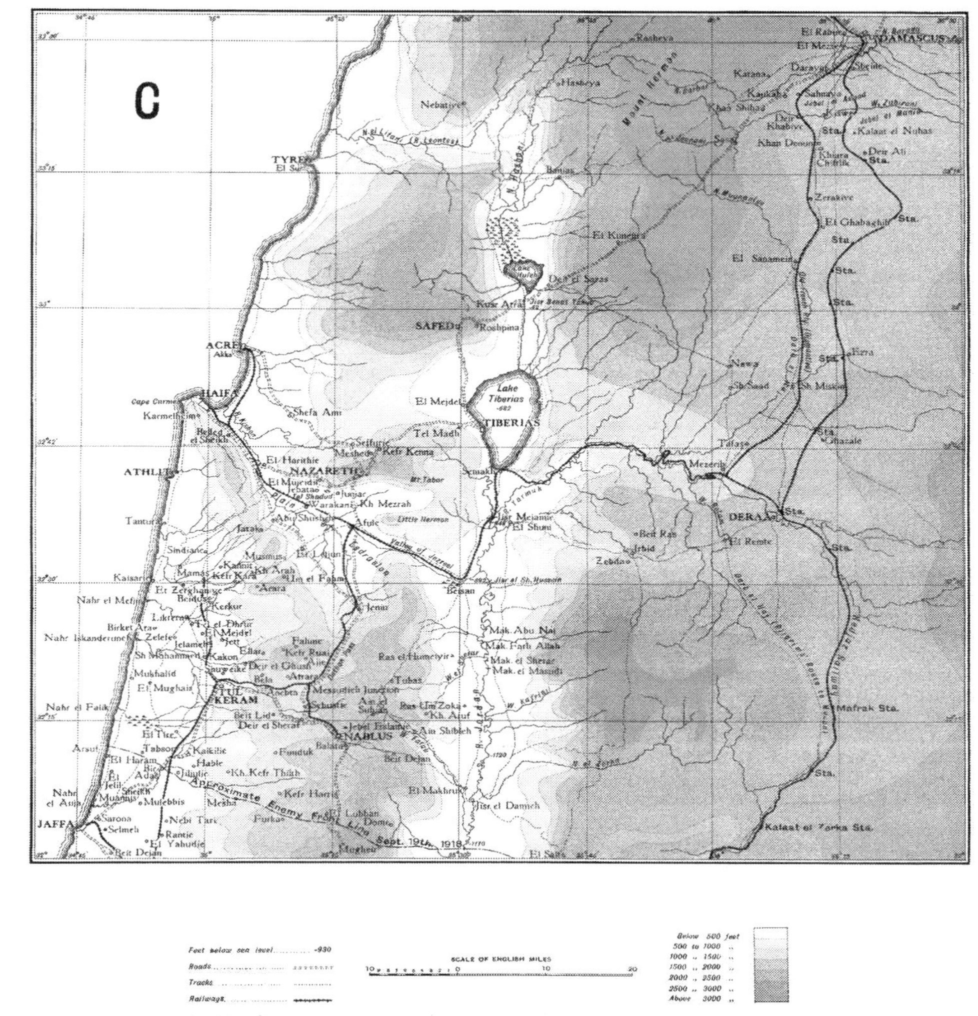
C
DAMASCUS
El Rabue
El Mezze
Rasheya
Katana
Darayat
Kaukaba
Deir Khabiye
Khan Denun
Khara Chifrik
Deir Ali Sta.
Kalaat el Nuhas
Sta.
Zerakiye
El Ghabaghib Sta.
El Sanamein
Sta.
Sta.
Nebatiye
Hasbeya
Banias
El Kuneira
Nawa
Shesad
Sh. Miskin
Kera
TYRE
El Sur
Nel Litani (R. Leontes)
SAFED
Roshpina
Kus Atra
Jisr Benat Yakub
Der el Saras
Lake Huleh
ACRE
Akka
Talase
Ghazale
Mezerib
DERAA Sta.
Sta.
Sta.
HAIFA
Cape Carmel
Karmelheim
Belled el Sheikh
Shefa Amr
El Mejdel
Lake Tiberias
-622
TIBERIAS
El Harithie
Meshed
Seffurie
Kefr Kenna
Tel Madb
Mt. Tabor
NAZARETH
El Mujeidil
Jebatao
Iuyac
Warakani
Kh. Mezrah
Abu Shusheh
Afule
Little Hermon
Semakh
Yarmuk
Meiamie
El Shuni
Beit Ras
Irbid
ATHLIT
Tantur
Jataht
Musmus
Er Juun
Zebdao
Sindiance
Kannir
Kh. Arah
Kefr Kara
Um el Fahm
Amara
Bessan
Jisr el Sh. Hussein
Kaisarie
Mamas
Et Zerghaniye
Beidusse
Kerkur
Jenin
Mak. Abu Nai
Mak Fath Allah
Ras el Humeiyir
Mak. el Sheraa
Mak. el Massidi
Nahr el Mefjir
Birket Ata
Likteraa
Jelame
Tel el Dhrur
El Mejdel
Jett
Falune
Kefr Ruai
Aiie
Tubas
Nahr Iskanderune
Zelefe
Sh. Mohammed
Kakon
Ehar
Deir el Ghusn
Mushalid
Shuweike
Bela
Atrara
Meseudieh Junction
El Mughair
TUL KERAM
Schunie
An el Sabieh
Ras Um Zoka
Kh. Aiuf
Nahr el Falik
Beit Lid
Deir el Sherat
Jebel Islamie
Ain Shibieh
NABLUS
Mafrak Sta.
El Tire
Arsuf
Tabsor
Kaikilie
Funduk
Balatat
Beit Dejan
El Haram
Bica
Hable
Kh. Kefr Thilth
El Ada
Jiltutie
Jelil
Sheikh Muannis
Mulebbis
Kefr Harris
El Makhrur
Jisr el Damieh
Nahr el Auja
Meisha
Lubban
Domie
JAFFA
Sarona
Selmeh
Nebi Tari
Rantie
El Yahudie
Beit Dejan
Furka
Mugheir
Approximate Enemy Front Line
Sept. 19th. 1918.
El Saff
Kalaat el Zorka Sta.
Hejaz Railway
Dera el Haj (Pilgrims) Route to Mecca
Old French Rly (Damascus)
Damascus Rly (Hejaz)

Feet below sea level............-930
Roads
Tracks
Railways
SCALE OF ENGLISH MILES
10 8 6 5 4 3 2 1 0   10   20
Below 500 feet
500 to 1000 ,,
1000 ,, 1500 ,,
1500 ,, 2000 ,,
2000 ,, 2500 ,,
2500 ,, 3000 ,,
Above 3000 ,,

to interfere with their simple pleasures, after the hard time they had had. One of the first things the ' Boys ' did was to open the jail and release all the ruffians therein, who added to the liveliness of the city.

After two days of something like pandemonium, the powers that were recognised the necessity of imposing some sort of restraint on the lawless elements, and two regiments of the Australian Mounted Division were stationed in the city for police duties. The Australian troopers speedily had the situation in hand, and the normal life of Damascus was resumed within forty-eight hours.

CHAPTER XXII

THE LAST PHASE

ARABIAN Syria extends northwards a little beyond
Aleppo. A study of the place-names on the map
will establish a fairly well-defined line, running from
about Jerablus on the Euphrates to the sea near
Antioch, north of which the Arabic names give place
to Turkish. From the political point of view it
was highly desirable that all the country south of
this line should be in our hands before the Turks
should have had enough, and ask for a cessation of
hostilities. But Aleppo is a far cry from Damascus,
230 miles by the Rayak road, and it is doubtful
whether the Commander-in-Chief had in his mind at
this date so extended an enterprise as the capture
of that city.

Strategically, however, an advance as far as Rayak
and Beirût offered several advantages. The possession of Beirût would give us a good, if small, port,
connected by rail and road with Damascus, thus
greatly shortening our line of supply. And, with
Rayak Junction in our hands, we should control the
important broad-gauge line that runs northwards
from this place, through Homs, Hama, and Aleppo,
to join the Baghdad line at Muslimie.

The total destruction of the Turkish armies had
ensured us freedom of movement at least as far as
the line Rayak-Beirût, and the only obstacle to an
advance lay in the weak and reduced condition of
the Corps.

In the twelve days from the 19th to the 30th of September inclusive, the three cavalry divisions had marched over 200 miles, fought a number of minor actions, and captured more than 60,000 prisoners, 140 guns, and 500 machine guns.

Long marches, especially at night, and half rations during the whole period, had rendered the horses thin and tired, and they were in urgent need of a rest. The men were in considerably worse case. In the course of the operations, the Australian Mounted Division had lain one night beside the Jordan at Jisr Benat Yakub, and the 4th Cavalry Division had spent several nights in the neighbourhood of Beisan. In both places the men were exposed to the attacks of swarms of malaria-bearing mosquitoes. Though the outbreak of malignant malaria, which was the fruit of these nights, did not begin to make its appearance till about the 5th of October, the day on which the advance was resumed, there were many cases of influenza in the Corps, and the hospitals were full of sick men, especially Indians. The 5th Division, which had not been in the mosquito districts, suffered less severely from malaria, and was thus able to continue the advance later on, at a time when the other two divisions were so weakened by the disease as to be almost incapable of moving.

After weighing all the factors of the situation, however, the Commander-in-Chief decided that the advantages to be gained by securing the port of Beirût and the railway to Damascus, justified a farther advance, and he determined to push on with his cavalry at least as far as the Rayak-Beirût line.

The 4th and 5th Cavalry Divisions were detailed for this task, the Australian Division remaining in and around Damascus, to keep order in the city and throughout the surrounding country.

The two divisions started on the morning of the 5th of October. At Khan Meizelun, eighteen miles from Damascus, their roads parted, the 4th Division moving on Zebdani, on the railway between Damascus and Rayak, the 5th making for Rayak by the main road through Shtora. Both objectives were reached without difficulty the following afternoon. In the course of the advance the 14th Brigade entered Zahle, capturing 177 prisoners and a few guns. Thirty burnt aeroplanes were found on the aerodrome at Rayak, and in the station a quantity of rolling stock and a number of engines of both the broad and the narrow gauge. Though damaged, most of these were subsequently repaired and put into use.

On the next day (the 7th) the armoured cars attached to the 5th Cavalry Division made a re-connaissance to Beirût, which they entered without opposition about mid-day. The townspeople received them with acclamation, and showed with pride a party of about 600 Turkish soldiers whom they had collected and disarmed. The 7th Indian Infantry Division, which had left Haifa on October the 3rd, reached Beirût on the 8th, and took over these prisoners.

On the 10th the cars reconnoitred northwards as far as Baalbek, without encountering any of the enemy, and the Commander-in-Chief thereupon decided to make a farther advance as far as Homs.

Unfortunately malaria had by now laid such a hold upon the men of the 4th Division, that the surviving hale scarce sufficed to carry on the ordinary duties of camp, and any further work by this division was out of the question. This left only the 5th Division, itself much reduced in numbers, to carry on the advance.

The 7th Infantry Division was directed to send a

brigade to Tripoli, where there was a small port, with jetties suitable for landing stores in fine weather, and a fairly good, metalled road running inland to Homs, which would facilitate the sending of supplies to the cavalry at the latter place. The 5th Division was then ordered to occupy Homs as soon as possible, the 4th remaining in the Zahle-Rayak-Baalbek area.

The 13th Brigade entered Baalbek on the 11th of October, and collected 500 Turks who had surrendered to the inhabitants, and who had been ' offered ' to the armoured cars the previous day.

The railway from Aleppo to Rayak was in working order, and it was quite possible for the enemy to send troops south to delay our advance. It was very important, therefore, that any further move forward, once decided upon, should be carried out as rapidly as possible.

To this end General MacAndrew organised his division at Baalbek in two columns. Column 'A,' which was to lead the advance, consisted of the divisional headquarters, three batteries of armoured cars, and three light car patrols, supported by the 15th Brigade. This brigade had only two regiments, the Hyderabad Lancers being still on the line of communications. The remainder of the division formed Column 'B.' It will be apparent that Column 'A' was little more than a raiding force, but it was considered that the heavy volume of machine-gun fire provided by the twenty-four cars would be sufficient to disperse, or at least to break up and disorganise, any body of the enemy that might be encountered. The country was very suitable for the employment of armoured cars, being open and fairly flat, with a hard surface.

A wing of the Royal Air Force was attached to the

division for reconnaissance purposes.   Throughout the campaign, the close co-operation between our aeroplanes and the cavalry had given most excellent results.   During the advance on Damascus, Air Force motor cars had accompanied the advanced headquarters of the Corps, carrying a party who selected and marked landing grounds at each halting place.   Lorries carrying petrol and stores followed a few miles in rear.   These arrangements resulted in maintaining that close personal contact between the two forces without which satisfactory work is impossible.   Moreover, the provision of a landing ground beside the advanced Corps headquarters meant that there was always an aeroplane ready at hand for instant use, if any special work was required.

Similar arrangements were now made with the 5th Division, and the subsequent assistance of the wing attached to the division was of the highest value.

At this time no orders had been received as to Aleppo, but it is evident that General MacAndrew had in his mind the probability of an advance to seize that city.   At any rate, this organisation of his division enabled him to do so when the time came, and by a piece of sheer bluff.

The march proceeded without incident up the valley of the Orontes, and the armoured cars of Column 'A' entered Homs unopposed on the 15th, where they met a force of Sherifian troops, under Sherif Nasir, who had marched from Damascus by the direct north road.   Two days previously the 20th Corps cavalry regiment had occupied Tripoli, where it was joined a few days later by part of the 7th Infantry Division, and arrangements were at once put in hand to land stores at the little port, and send them up by road to Homs.   Column 'B' arrived on the 16th.

The Commander-in-Chief now determined to complete the political part of the campaign by seizing Aleppo, and occupying all the Arab-speaking country from the sea to the Euphrates.

The only troops available for the enterprise were the 5th Cavalry Division and the armoured cars. The Australian Division was at Damascus, over 100 miles away, and could not be brought up in time. The 4th Division, reduced in strength and exhausted by disease, was incapable of any work till men and horses had been given a thorough rest and time to recover from sickness. This division and the Australian Division had suffered some 300 deaths from disease since reaching Damascus, a fortnight before. Even the 5th Division, which had suffered far less severely than the other two, was in a deplorable state. The whole division hardly mustered 1500 sabres. The two R.H.A. batteries with the division numbered between them but four officers and eighty men.

It was known that there were about 20,000 Turks and Germans at Aleppo, or south of that place, and it was believed that about half of these were combatants, though probably ill-armed and disorganised. Aleppo is over 100 miles from Homs, and 180 from Tripoli or Baalbek, the two nearest points from which any possible reinforcements could be sent.

In the face of these facts, the boldest of commanders might well have been excused for deciding to call a halt. But the political and moral advantages to be gained by a farther advance into the enemy's country appeared so great that General Allenby determined to accept the risk. On the 19th of October he directed General MacAndrew to advance to Aleppo.

The divisional field squadron Royal Engineers, covered by the 15th Brigade, at once moved out to

El Rastan, to repair the bridge over the Orontes at that place, which had been blown up by the Turks during their retreat. The following day the divisional headquarters and the cars joined the 15th Brigade at El Rastan, and, on the morning of the 21st, Column 'A' crossed the repaired bridge, and, making a long march, reached Zor Defai, five miles north of Hama, that evening. No opposition was encountered during the march.

Next morning the cars pushed off early on an extended reconnaissance. Reaching Ma'arit el Na'aman, thirty-five miles distant, about mid-day, without meeting any of the enemy, they made a short halt, and then started off again towards Aleppo. Seven miles farther north, near Khan Sebil, they sighted some enemy armoured cars and armed motor lorries. These at once turned and fled, pursued by our cars, and a nice little hunt ensued. Hounds were stopped after a fifteen mile point, as it was getting late, but not before a German armoured car, two armed lorries, and thirty-seven prisoners had been captured. Just as our cars drew off, two enemy aeroplanes appeared, and, evidently mistaking the German lorries for our troops, promptly dived, and machine-gunned them vigorously! The armoured cars had reached a point fifty-five miles from Zor Defai, and only twenty miles south of Aleppo, before they turned back. They withdrew to a point four miles north of Seraikin, where they bivouacked for the night, finding their own outposts. The 15th Brigade reached Khan Shaikhun late in the afternoon.

On the 23rd the cars pushed on again, and encountered some enemy cavalry at Khan Tuman, about ten miles south of Aleppo. These they brushed aside without much difficulty, and proceeded along

Aleppo. The old citadel.

Bedouin and Sherifian soldiers. Near the Euphrates.

the road. Some miles farther on, however, they were held up by strong Turkish rearguards holding an entrenched position astride the road, through El Ansarie and Sheikh Said. A reconnaissance of this position, carried out by the cars and some aeroplanes, indicated that it was held by a force of 2000 to 3000 infantry. It was reported locally that there were six or seven thousand more in Aleppo.

General MacAndrew thereupon determined to try and bluff the enemy into surrendering, and, to this end, sent an officer with a flag of truce into Aleppo in a car, to demand the capitulation of the city. The Turks took this officer through their defences without blindfolding him, apparently in order to show him that the position was a strong one, which it was, and adequately held. Having done so, they entertained him most courteously with cigarettes, coffee, and small talk for half an hour or so, and then handed him a reply to take back to the British General. The officer got back to Divisional Headquarters about four in the afternoon, and delivered his letter, which proved brief and to the point. ' The Commander of the Turkish garrison of Aleppo,' it ran, ' does not find it necessary to answer your note.' Fortunately for us, however, the Turkish Commander, after making this bold reply, began to get uneasy, and, in the course of the next three days, evidently came to the conclusion that discretion was the better part of valour. During the night of the 25th he commenced to withdraw his forces to the north.

At seven o'clock the cars were withdrawn into bivouac on the open plain south of Khan Tuman, so as to give them freedom of movement if attacked during the night.

The 24th was occupied in further reconnaissance of the enemy positions. The Turks were found in occupation of the same trenches, with cavalry out-posts pushed forward on to the hills north of Khan Tuman. Some of the cars were sent off in a north-westerly direction, with the object of discovering a practicable way through the rocky hills south-west of Aleppo, to the Alexandretta road. They were unable, however, to find any track that was possible for cars.

Further reconnaissances on the 25th disclosed the enemy positions more fully, and drew considerable fire from guns, machine guns, and rifles all along the line. The 15th Brigade came up in the evening, and relieved the cars on outpost duty that night. Sherif Nasir's Arabs, who had been marching at a great pace along the railway, had arrived earlier in the day, and moved east towards Tel Hasil, to attack the city from that side.

Column 'B,' which had been steadily plodding along, a day's march in rear of Column 'A,' reached Seraikin the same evening.

With the arrival of the 15th Brigade and the Arabs, General MacAndrew deemed himself strong enough to take Aleppo. He ordered the 15th to advance early next morning, through the hills west of Aleppo, *via* Turmanin, and get astride the Aleppo–Alexan-dretta road, while the Arabs and the armoured cars attacked from the east and south respectively. During the night of the 25th, however, the Arabs, assisted by friends in Aleppo, succeeded in entering the city. They enjoyed a first-rate, old-fashioned, hand-to-hand fight with the Turks, and beat them decisively. By ten o'clock in the morning the city was in their hands, and General MacAndrew motored in with the armoured cars. Sherif Nasir had lost about sixty killed, but he had inflicted far heavier casualties on his enemies, and driven them out of Aleppo full speed.

Meanwhile the 15th Brigade had started at seven in the morning, and reached the Alexandretta road, without opposition, about ten o'clock. The only definite information the brigade had received at this time, was that about 300 Turkish cavalry were on the road, eight miles north of Aleppo. Shortly afterwards a verbal message was brought in by a car, to the effect that about a thousand ' scallywags ' of all descriptions, with two field guns, had left Aleppo, going north, about half-past seven in the morning.

The brigade proceeded along the road, and, about eleven o'clock, two squadrons of the Jodhpur Lancers, who were acting as advanced guard, topped the ridge overlooking the village of Haritan from the southeast, and about a mile and a half distant. They immediately came under heavy rifle fire from the village, and took up a dismounted position on the ridge.

Rightly deeming that instant action was all important, and relying on the information he had received as to the strength and composition of the enemy force in front of him, General Harbord decided to attack at once. He ordered the Mysore Lancers to move out to the east, and endeavour to charge the enemy on his left flank. Two squadrons of the Jodhpur Lancers were directed to move in support of the Mysores, as a ' mopping up ' party, while the remainder of this regiment, with the machine gun squadron, held the Turks in front, with fire directed from the ridge on which the advance guard had first taken up its position.

Just after the Mysore Lancers commenced their move eastwards, General Harbord was reinforced by a battery of armoured cars, which had been sent out from Aleppo to join him. He directed these cars to approach the enemy positions along the road, and assist the attack with their machine-gun fire. Unfortunately something went wrong with the battery leader's car, and it was withdrawn and driven back to Aleppo. The remaining three cars, through some misunderstanding, followed it, and the brigade was thus deprived of their support.

Meanwhile the Mysore Lancers, finding that the enemy's position extended farther than was expected, moved more to the east to gain the flank. At twelve o'clock, Major Lambert, finding himself in a favourable position, ordered a charge. The ground was rather rocky, and gave some trouble to the horses, but the charge was driven well home, and a considerable number of the enemy was killed. The Turks, however, were to be found in much greater strength than had been expected, and, after driving through their flank, the Lancers were heavily fired on by Turks farther west. Many of those who had been ridden over, and had thrown down their arms, now picked them up again, and continued the fight. Seeing that his regiment had not sufficient weight to charge through the large body of Turks farther west, Major Lambert rallied his squadrons behind the Turkish line, and took up a dismounted position on the left rear of the enemy, where the two squadrons of the Jodhpur Lancers joined him.

The charge had compelled the Turks to reveal their full strength, which turned out to be about 3000 infantry and 400 cavalry, with ten or twelve guns and about thirty-five machine guns. Seeing the smallness of the force opposed to them, they now advanced boldly to the attack, but, when about 800 yards away, thought better of it, and began to dig themselves in.

The 15th Brigade remained in observation of the Turks, and desultory firing continued till about nine o'clock at night, when the enemy faded gradually and silently away. Two hours later the 14th Cavalry Brigade, which had reached Aleppo with Column 'B' late in the evening, arrived on the scene, and relieved the 15th Brigade. The casualties in the latter brigade totalled sixty-three killed, wounded, and missing, which comparatively light bill might have been very much heavier had the Turks showed any real disposition to fight. They outnumbered our men by at least seven to one, and were well supplied with artillery and machine guns, but their *morale* had sunk so low that it was only surprising that they did not all surrender, or break into helpless flight, when charged. We learnt afterwards that the Turkish Commander in Aleppo had been completely deceived by General MacAndrew, whose boldness in detaching the whole of his cavalry to cut the Alexandretta road led him to believe that we had a much larger force at our disposal than was actually the case.

On the 28th the Arab forces seized Muslimie Junction, on the Baghdad Railway twelve miles north of Aleppo, dislodging a small Turkish rearguard there, and this inglorious little action ended the war for Turkey. The few surviving Turks retired rapidly in the general direction of Constantinople, and that was the last seen of their army. The Armistice [1] came into operation at noon on the 31st of October.

In the thirty-eight days since the commencement of the operations, the 5th Cavalry Division had marched 567 miles, fought six actions, and taken over 11,000 prisoners and fifty-eight guns. The total captures of the Desert Mounted Corps in the same period were 83,700 prisoners and about 160 guns.

The Australian Mounted Division left Damascus

---

[1] See Appendix III. for terms of Armistice.

on October the 27th to march to Aleppo, a distance of rather over 200 miles. Marching by the direct road to Homs, which runs almost due north from Damascus, the division reached the small village of Jendar, eighteen miles south of Homs, at nine o'clock on the night of the 31st. Here the news of the Armistice was received by wireless, but, as there was no water available in the neighbourhood, the Australians continued the march the same night, and arrived at Homs at eight o'clock on the morning of the 1st of November. Three days later they moved down to Tripoli, on the coast, where they remained until sent to Egypt, *en route* for Australia, at the end of February 1919.

The Commander-in-Chief made his official entry into Aleppo on the 12th of December. As at Damascus, we had installed an Arab Governor here, but, in view of the disorders that had occurred at the former place, his powers were restricted to giving advice, and the whole of the policing of the city was in the hands of our troops. The 'Chief' took the occasion to give him some good advice, couched in the vigorous language for which he was famous.

One of the first things General Allenby did, when order had been restored in the country, was to direct that a day should be set aside to be observed throughout the force as one of thanksgiving for victory. Tuesday, December the 16th, was selected for the purpose, and was celebrated by the holding of religious services in the morning by all the many religions and denominations in the Corps. The afternoon was spent in such games and sports as could be organised.

CHAPTER XXIII

POLICE WORK

THE cavalry had reached their final goal, and their fighting work was over. But there was still much to be done. The Desert Mounted Corps took over the administration of the conquered country from Damascus in the south to Marash, in Cilicia, 120 miles north of Aleppo; and from the sea coast to Ras el Ain, 120 miles east of the Euphrates, an area of about 35,000 square miles. Corps headquarters was established at Homs. The 5th Cavalry Division, at Aleppo, had a brigade at Aintab, eighty miles farther north, and detachments at Alexandretta, Islahie, Marash, Arab Punar and Jerablus on the Euphrates. Later on, infantry, attached to the Corps, occupied Alexandretta, Adana, Tarsus, Smyrna, and other towns on or near the coast. The 4th Cavalry Division remained at Beirût and in the neighbourhood, and the Australian Division at Tripoli, with a brigade at Baalbek, and detachments at Shtora, Lebwe, and Rayak. At the end of February 1919, when the Australians returned to Egypt, the 4th Division handed over Beirût to the French, and was quartered at Homs, Baalbek, Rayak, and Deraa.

As was only to be expected after the events of the past four years, the country was in a most unsettled state. The crops and live stock had been mercilessly requisitioned by the Turks over large areas, and many of the peasants, left callously to starve, had taken to a life of brigandage. The whole country was infested with robber bands. Even large parties dared not travel at night, and indeed few ventured to travel at all. Those whose business or duty took them about the country crept from village to village by unfrequented bye-paths, avoiding the roads. Merchants and shopkeepers buried most of their wares, displaying in their places of business only a few miserable samples.

The direct road from Damascus to Homs was so overrun with robbers that even considerable bodies of Turkish soldiers marching along it had been attacked and massacred; so that it had been, at last, altogether abandoned as a line of communications in favour of the longer, and far worse, road through Baalbek.

Within three weeks of the signing of the Armistice, unarmed pedestrians travelled alone and unafraid through all the land. On every road were to be seen throngs of refugees returning to their ravished homes, accompanied by carts piled high with household goods. When night came on, these people pulled off the road, and slept in peace and safety till morning. Merchants brought out their wares from secret places, and buyers crowded into the cities in thousands.

During the whole time the British forces were in occupation of the country, from the end of October 1918 till November 1919, there were only two attempts to disturb the peace, and both of these were nipped in the bud at once. The first occurred on the night of November the 30th, 1918, when a notorious robber chief, who lived in an almost inaccessible village up in the Anti-Lebanon, attempted to raid one of our ammunition and store depots at Rayak. The robbers were driven off, with the loss of six men killed and

Within the jurisdiction of the Desert Mounted Corps.
The River Euphrates at Rakka.

Aintab.

twenty prisoners, and we had no more trouble of that sort.

The second attempt took place at Aleppo on the 23rd February 1919. A plot was engineered by Turkish ex-officers and local Arabs, to bring about a massacre of the hated Armenians in the city. The disturbance was quickly put down, but not before a few persons on both sides had been killed. Several prominent natives were arrested in connection with the plot, and tried by a mixed court of British and Arab officers. Those of the conspirators who were proved actually to have taken life were executed, and others were sentenced to various terms of imprisonment. These sentences had a most salutary effect, and there was no further effort to disturb the peace.

There was a detachment of the Arab Army, about 200 strong, at Aleppo, and one or two soldiers were quartered in all outlying villages of any importance. It is pleasant to be able to record that the Arab Government made a genuine, and successful, effort to assist in maintaining law and order in the country, and the Arab Governor of Aleppo was always on the 'best of terms with our officials. The Governor at this time was Gafar Pasha, who had been a general in the Turkish Army, and had fought against us in the Senussi Campaign, where he was taken prisoner, and sent to Cairo to be interned. He was liberated, at his own request, in order to join the Arab Army, in which he commanded a division with distinction from the latter part of 1917 till the end of the war.

One of the most difficult tasks carried out by the Corps was that of restoring to the Armenians their houses and property. A Reparation Committee was formed in Aleppo, with representatives at Aintab and Marash, and much useful work was done. All houses that formerly belonged to Armenians were evacuated by their Moslem occupiers, and, as far as possible, restored to their rightful owners. Very many of these had, however, been killed or had disappeared. Others, attracted by tales of the fabulous sums to be made in Aleppo by trading with the British, flocked into the city, and refused to return to their own homes. Many Armenian women had entered the harems of Turks or Arabs, and a number of these did not now wish to leave. They were well treated there, and protected, and they preferred the comfort of the harem to the prospect of starting again in the cold world outside.

The difficulties of the Reparations Committee were much increased by the intrigues and lies of the members of local branches of the Turkish Committee of Union and Progress. These people had been the chief offenders in the persecution of the unhappy Armenians, and they, more than any others, had grown fat on the plundered property. Now that their power was broken, they feared not only the confiscation of their ill-gotten goods, but drastic punishment, possibly even death, for the many murders they had committed. It was not to be wondered at, therefore, that they should seize every opportunity to hamper and embarrass our officials in their investigations. More than one prominent local member of the C.U.P. had to be removed from his position as headman of a village, in consequence of his obstructive tactics.

Notwithstanding all these difficulties, very large numbers of Armenians were restored to their houses, furniture and effects were recovered or made good, and families were re-united. Some 3000, who were awaiting repatriation, were housed in the barracks at Aleppo, fed by the British, and given work at high wages.

It must be confessed that the Armenians are, as a nation, a very unpleasant people. That this is largely due to the treatment they have received in the past does not alter the fact. Deprived of their land many centuries ago, and debarred, to a great extent, from engaging in industry, they have become moneylenders, as have the Jews in similar circumstances. Usurers in all countries are a detested class, and the Armenians are no exception to the rule. They are the usurers of Turkey, grasping and avaricious, the holders of mortgages on the peasants' land, the speculators in food, hated and despised by all classes. Small wonder that the Turk, bloodthirsty as he is by nature, needs little encouragement to start a massacre of them, whenever he has the chance.

Another important task undertaken by the Corps was the stabilising of the exchange. At the time when we first occupied Aintab, shortly after the Armistice, Turkish 100 piastre notes were worth about 4s. 6d. in Aleppo. The ten piastre notes had practically no value, and most of the merchants refused to accept them. All the Egyptian notes were accepted at about their face value. In Aintab, on the other hand, which was only eighty miles away, traders were suspicious of the Turkish 100 piastre notes, but those of ten piastres were readily accepted, and were worth nearly twice as much as the equivalent Egyptian note. Similar apparently unreasonable anomalies were to be observed in other places. A good example occurred at the beginning of February. One day a merchant of Aleppo came to General MacAndrew, and stated that he had just heard that his business in Baghdad, which was his principal source of livelihood, had been nearly ruined by an enemy. If, said he, he could get there at once, he could save it, but it was a matter of days, almost of hours. Under the circumstances, would his Excellency permit him to ride to Baghdad and back in one of the British aeroplanes, for which he would pay any sum that was demanded. He was turned over to the Intelligence Branch, who, after making inquiries, reported that he was a man of substance, much respected in Aleppo, and with considerable local influence, which might be useful to us. His request was accordingly granted, and he was taken to Baghdad in one of our aeroplanes. He only remained there twenty-four hours, and then flew back to Aleppo. He paid £160 for the trip, and seemed to think his journey cheap. A few days later the General's headquarters were besieged by a crowd of applicants, each of whom had a business in Baghdad which was on the point of being ruined by an enemy ! Further inquiries by the Intelligence Branch elicited the facts of the case. It appeared that the Russian one-rouble note was worth about half its face value in Aleppo. In Baghdad, where there was a large number of them, they were not worth the paper on which they were printed. The astute merchant, hearing of this, and realising that such a state of affairs could not last an hour, once telegraphic communication was established between the two places, determined to bring as many of the notes as he could to Aleppo at once. There was no time to be lost, as the telegraph line was nearly through, so he hit upon the plan of hiring an aeroplane, and cleared, according to repute, nearly £40,000 as the reward of his initiative !

This was the last and greatest of the many gambles in exchange that enlivened the days of the merchants of Aleppo during the early period of our occupation of the place. Gradually, by means of a vigorous publicity campaign, and by selling surplus enemy stores for Egyptian money only, the monetary position was stabilised, and, by the end of May, Egyptian paper was generally accepted all over the country.

It must not be supposed that the life of the Corps was all work and no play. At Beirût and Tripoli racecourses were laid out very soon after the cavalry occupied those places, and several capital little meetings were held. Later on an excellent course was made at Aleppo, with two grand stands, paddock, judge's box, parade ring, and everything complete, even to a fully equipped totalisator (run by the Corps cashier). Races were held every fortnight, and the social amenities were provided for by a tastefully laid out 'lawn,' and first-rate catering arrangements! Aleppo also boasted a really good polo ground and several football and cricket grounds. Both the racing and the polo were considerably better than were to be had in Cairo or Alexandretta.

There was also a pack of 'fox hounds' at Aleppo and another at Tripoli. The 'Lebanon Hounds,' at the latter place, showed some quite good sport over the comparatively flat country near the coast, but the 'Aleppo Hunt' was handicapped by the rocky nature of the country, and by the fact that most of the 'earths' were holes in solid rock, out of which it was impossible to dig a fox that had got to ground. Moreover, as they met at five o'clock on Sunday mornings only, the fields were never very large!

The 13th Brigade, at Aintab, held a series of point-to-point meetings in the vale of the Kuwaik Su, and the regiment at Marash organised a pig-sticking club, which met once or twice near the Ak Su lakes. There was not much sport, as the pigs came from the hills, which were unridable, and to which they speedily retired, as soon as they were disturbed.

Expeditions to the ruins of the Hittite City of Carchemish, near Jerablus, to the summer palace of Haroun al Rashid at Rakka on the Euphrates, 150 miles east of Aleppo, to Palmyra, the city of Zenobia, in the desert eighty miles east of Homs, and to various other historical remains, added interest to life, and, at the same time, served to give officers and men a knowledge of the country that they could have obtained in no other way.

The Anzac and Australian Mounted Divisions left for Egypt in the spring of 1919, and on the 7th June the Desert Mounted Corps was broken up. The administration of the conquered territory was taken over by the newly-created ' Northforce,' which consisted of the 4th and 5th Cavalry Divisions and two divisions of Infantry, the whole under the command of Major-General Barrow. This force found garrisons for places up the coast as far as Smyrna, and also took over the administration of the Baghdad Railway from Constantinople to the railhead east of Nisibin in Mesopotamia.

In November of the same year the administration of northern Syria was finally handed over to our French Allies, and the last of the British and Indian Cavalry marched out of the country they had conquered and held for over a year.

Inscription cut on the rock cliffs of the Dog River, near Beirût, amongst those of Rameses II, Nebuchadnezar, Senacherib and other early conquerors of Syria.

CHAPTER XXIV

HORSE ARTILLERY

Command.—Of all the matters concerning the employment of horse artillery which came under discussion during the campaign, none was more important than the vexed question of command.

The cavalry brigadier is naturally eager to have a battery attached to him permanently, and considered as part of his brigade. Apart from the conviction that a battery always on hand and under his own orders will be of more value to him than one over which he has no direct control, there is the feeling that the battery rounds off his command, and makes it, in effect, a miniature army, complete with all modern conveniences. If the powers that be would only throw in a couple of armoured cars and a private aeroplane, the cavalry brigadier would be the happiest man on earth !

Most R.H.A. battery commanders will agree with the brigadiers. Attached to a brigade, the battery commander is freer and more independent, and gets, perhaps, more of the ' fun of the fair ' and less of the drudgery than he does when acting as a divisional unit.

In spite of these opinions, however, the hard facts of this campaign go to prove that our guns invariably rendered more efficient aid to the cavalry they were supporting when employed under the orders of the divisional commander than when attached to brigades. The divisional commander must always know more of the fortunes of the battle than any of his brigadiers, and is thus generally in the better position to decide where artillery support is most needed. Moreover, if each battery is attached to a brigade, and acting under the orders of a brigadier, each brigade can only receive the support of one battery. But there are occasions, in most engagements, when one brigade needs all the artillery support available, while another, in reserve, or not yet heavily engaged, requires none. If the control of the artillery is left to one individual, fire can be concentrated quickly in support of those brigades or regiments that are most in need of it, and no gun is ever idle. There were one or two lamentable instances, in the 1917 operations, of a brigade remaining in reserve all day with its attached battery sleeping peacefully beside it.

The actions of Summeil in the 1917 operations and of Kaukab in 1918 may be taken as fair illustrations of the employment of artillery as a divisional unit. That of Jisr Benat Yakub in 1918 was an example of the principle of attaching each battery to a brigade.

With the small, three-brigade cavalry division cf the present day the former arrangement will practically always yield better results than the latter. Direct artillery *liaison* should, of course, be maintained between the divisional artillery commander and each brigade, if it is at all possible to do so.

Reserves.—There were, in the early days of the campaign, indications of an idea on the part of some commanders that a certain proportion of the artillery should be held in reserve, in the same way as a brigade or regiment. This idea probably arose from the fact that one of the essential differences between artillery and other arms had been overlooked. When once a brigade or regiment has been committed to an attack, in a moving battle, and is in contact with the enemy, it can seldom be easily withdrawn in order to be transferred to another part of the field. Guns, on the other hand, do not come into direct contact with the enemy—at least the gunners try their best to avoid doing so! They can, therefore, as a rule, be withdrawn without difficulty, if their services are required elsewhere. All guns in action may thus, in a sense, be said to be in reserve, since they can readily be moved to another part of the field if required. Except, therefore, for the purposes of conserving ammunition, guns should rarely be unemployed during the progress of an action.

Artillery with Advance and Rearguards.—At the beginning of the campaign, most divisional commanders, when moving with one brigade as advance guard, allotted one battery to it. As the operations progressed, however, the view that a larger force of artillery might profitably accompany the advance guard began to gain ground. The experience of the whole campaign points to the conclusion that, in view of the small number of guns available in a cavalry division, two of the three batteries should normally accompany the advance guard brigade. The practice may be open to the objections that it makes the advance guard column unduly long, and that some risk is involved in leaving the main body so short of artillery. Both these objections appear, however, to be outweighed by the advantages of having a large proportion of the artillery in front. Whether the enemy's resistance is stubborn or feeble, artillery fire can assist in breaking it, and the greater the number of guns available, the quicker will that object be achieved, and the less delay will there be to the advance of the main body.

The battery or batteries with the advance guard

should, of course, march as far forward as is compatible with safety. Guns must always take longer than cavalry to move a given distance, and, if they are well to the front, no time will be lost in getting them into the only formation in which they are of any use, *i.e.* in action.

The divisional artillery commander should accompany the vanguard commander. When contact is established with the enemy, he is then on the spot, and able to make a personal reconnaissance at once, and decide, subject to the orders of the advance guard commander, how his guns can best and most quickly assist the cavalry. No time will then be lost in getting the guns into action. In the final series of operations, the enemy was in too demoralised a state for his action to form a very reliable guide in future wars, but it was found that vigorous artillery fire, *delivered immediately after the first contact* of our cavalry with his rearguards, invariably exercised a powerfully adverse effect on his *morale*. The little action of Kaukab well exemplifies this fact.

The above remarks as to artillery with the advance guard apply with equal force, *mutatis mutandis*, to the artillery of a rearguard during a retirement.

Escorts.—The campaign afforded few opportunities on our side to test the efficacy of artillery escorts. The action at Huj, however, in November 1917, was an excellent example of bad escort work on the part of the enemy. Our gunners have always maintained that the rôle of an escort is to obtain information rather than to afford protection. Guns on the march are vulnerable to a sudden attack, especially from cavalry; in action they are, or should be, well able to take care of themselves. If this contention is right, it follows that escorts need not be large, and should not be kept near the guns, but should patrol the country in any quarter from which attack may be expected, search dead ground, woods, etc., and give early information to the guns of the approach of the enemy.

At Huj the enemy had two battalions of infantry and several machine guns disposed about his batteries, but he had not a single patrol pushed out to the east. Our cavalry were thus able to approach to within 800 yards of the position of the guns unseen and unsuspected. The result of the Turks' negligence was a severe disaster, and it is to be hoped that the lesson will not be thrown away on future commanders of artillery escorts in the British Army. The escort work in our cavalry in Palestine and Syria was almost invariably very good, especially amongst the Australians.

R.H.A. Howitzers.—Most officers, both of the R.H.A. and the cavalry, who served in Syria, agreed as to the desirability of having a few light howitzers attached to each cavalry division. Such a gun as the 3·7-inch mountain howitzer, if it could be mounted on a suitable field carriage, would be admirably adapted for use with cavalry. Had a few howitzers been available during the attack on Beersheba, the stone block-houses and the rocky sangars of Tel el Saba would soon have been rendered untenable by the enemy, and would not have delayed our advance as they did.

As to whether two guns in each six-gun battery should be replaced by howitzers, or a separate battery of four howitzers should be provided for each division, opinion varied amongst the gunners on the spot. The writer is strongly in favour of the latter alternative, as being simpler, and in conformity with the existing practice in field artillery.

Shrapnel and H.E.—The question of the best

proportions of shrapnel and high explosive shell to be carried in a horse artillery battery came under discussion at various times during the campaign, and opinions varied according to the nature of fighting in progress at the time. Amongst the rocks of the hill country, most battery commanders preferred a large preponderance of H.E., while, in open country, they wanted more shrapnel. One thing certain is that the Turks themselves dreaded the former far more than the latter. On several occasions enemy officer prisoners told the writer that they always had greater difficulty in getting their men to attack through H.E. shell fire than through shrapnel, even though, as they averred, the latter invariably caused them more casualties than the former. As before remarked, the behaviour of the Turks was not a very reliable guide for future wars, but it is to be noted that the same aversion to H.E. shell was observed amongst the Germans, and even amongst our own troops.

There seems little doubt, therefore, that the moral effect of H.E. is much greater than that of shrapnel. If this be so, R.H.A. 13-pounder guns, whose lethal effect is so comparatively small, should be provided with a large proportion of it. The writer suggests, on the experience of this campaign, that the due proportion lies somewhere between 50 and 75 per cent. of the total ammunition carried.

General.—The batteries serving with the Desert Mounted Corps, being Territorial units, had each only four guns. There is no doubt that cavalry divisions with four-gun batteries are seriously under-gunned, and it is satisfactory to note that, under the new Territorial War Establishments, all R.H.A. batteries are to have six guns.

Before leaving the subject of artillery, the writer

would draw attention to a fact that is often over-looked by cavalrymen. It is that, with the best will in the world, and the best of horsemanship and driving, guns cannot move as fast as cavalry. There were several instances during the campaign where a brigade, detached with a battery on some special duty, pushed along very fast for several miles, clashed with the enemy, and then reproached the gunners for not being on the spot to help. It is often forgotten that the artillery draught horse has to carry nearly the same weight as a cavalryman's and, at the same time, do his share in dragging along, ' over hill over dale, thorough bush, thorough briar,' a clumsy mass of steel weighing a ton and a half.

A consideration of this fact leads to the conclusion that, if guns are to keep up with cavalry when moving fast and far, certain advantages must be allowed them.

In the first place orders should reach the artillery early, in order to enable it to get on the move before the cavalry start, when the situation allows.

On the move, guns should march close to the head of the column. This order of march is also desirable from the fighting point of view, as has been pointed out above. The advisability of keeping the guns well to the front was generally recognised towards the end of the campaign, but, in the early days, there was a tendency to keep them too far back.

If there is a shortage of water or forage, the artillery horses should be the last to suffer from it.

Though the writer happens to be a gunner, these remarks are not set down as a special appeal on behalf of the artillery, but in the belief that, only by giving to the guns some such special privileges, will they be able to do the work that is required of them. Horse guns are the servants of cavalry as field guns are of infantry, but, unless the servant is adequately fed and looked after, he cannot serve his master properly.,

Needless to say, if a cavalry commander considers that he can carry out the task assigned to him without the help of his guns, and time presses, he is perfectly justified in pushing on at once with his cavalry, and leaving the guns to follow as best they can, as was done, quite properly, by the 5th Cavalry Division when crossing the Carmel Range in September 1918.

CHAPTER XXV

HORSES

ONE of the greatest difficulties with which the cavalry had to contend throughout the operations arose from the constant struggle to keep the horses sufficiently fit to carry on. This is, of course, always the case in war time, but the difficulties in the Syrian campaign were probably greater than in any previous one in which the British Army had taken part.

Climate.—To begin with, the climate encountered included every extreme of heat, cold, drought, and rain. For the first three weeks from the commencement of the 1917 campaign, the weather was extremely hot, the temperature running up to 110° in the shade. For two days, November the 10th and 11th, matters were rendered worse by a burning hot east wind, which raised clouds of suffocating dust. Then the rains broke, and, for the next six weeks, constant wet, deep mud and piercing cold winds were the order of the day. After a short period of good weather, the cavalry moved to the Jordan Valley, where they spent the summer of 1918, under conditions of heat and discomfort which have already been described. Finally, in the following winter, the horses found themselves sometimes standing in six inches of snow.[1]

Condition.—In the second place, the health of the

---

[1] Snow lay on the ground in the Baalbek-Rayak area for a considerable part of the winter, and on the western side of the Lebanon, in the Beirût-Tripoli area, for short periods from time to time.

horses was in an unsatisfactory state when the cavalry operations commenced.

Whatever their outward appearance might have been, and it varied considerably in different units, their internal condition was by no means good. The great bulk of them had taken part in the advance across Sinai, and had been in Egypt for a long time prior to that. Two years of unaccustomed and indifferent forage, added to the large quantities of sand they had consumed in their food while in the desert, had more or less permanently injured their digestive organs. It is true that sand colic, that scourge of the desert, had almost ceased to trouble the force by the end of the summer of 1917, but the dire effects of the sand were evident in every post-mortem. In a large number of cases the membrane of the stomach and intestines was freely marked with the scars of old ulcers, and in some instances large portions of it had sloughed away. Sand muzzles were almost universally employed up to the commencement of the advance on Beersheba, but it was impossible to prevent sand getting into the forage; indeed quantities of it had been purposely placed there by the dishonest native merchants, in order to increase the weight of bales and sacks.

It is probable that 90 per cent. of the draught horses of the artillery and transport had strained their hearts to some extent during the terrible work in the heavy sands of the desert. The writer carried out, or was present at, upwards of twenty post-mortems on draught horses that died during the advance across Sinai, and, in every case, found an enlargement of the heart greater than could possibly be accounted for by the age of the horse. In one instance, the wall of the heart was ruptured right through. This horse had been led four miles back to camp after first showing signs of extreme distress. On arriving in camp he drank well, ate a bran mash, and lived for six hours afterwards, a wonderful example of endurance.

The experience of the campaign proved that horses cannot be in too 'big' condition at the commencement of operations, provided they have been kept adequately exercised while being conditioned. The really fat, round horses finished both series of operations in better condition than those which had looked harder and more muscular, but not so fat, at the beginning. This was especially the case in the first series, during which the shortage of water was so acute.

Forage.—During both campaigns the forage was of very poor quality and woefully scanty. Up to the commencement of the 1917 operations, the daily issue had consisted of 10 lb. of barley, gram or maize and 10 lb. of tibben (chopped barley straw) and bursȳm (a kind of hay made of a coarse species of lucerne, of good feeding value and much liked by the horses). The food value of the whole daily ration was about 23 per cent. below that of an average horse in England doing the same work. The barley and tibben, being produced in Egypt, were very dusty, and contained a large proportion of earth and small stones. The gram and maize were of fair quality, but the latter was sometimes issued whole, and, when issued crushed, was often very dusty. The daily ration during operations in both campaigns was 9½ lb. of grain per day, and nothing else. So that the horses were called upon to do very much harder work on less than half the amount of food to which they had been accustomed, and only about 36 per cent. of the normal ration for such horses in England.

For the first month of the 1917 campaign this ration was exclusively gram.   As the horses had previously only been accustomed to a small proportion of this grain in their daily feeds, it caused them to scour badly, thus increasing the weakness engendered by hard work and starvation.   It is difficult to understand why gram was decided upon in preference to barley, of which there was plenty available, but, at all events, the lesson was taken to heart, and, for the remainder of the campaign, the marching ration was always barley.

From the 25th September 1918 till the cavalry left the country in November 1919, all forage was bought locally.   It was generally of good quality, and there was a certain amount of grazing available.

Water.—The water difficulties during the 1917 operations have been referred to before.   Prior to this campaign it was generally accepted that cavalry horses could continue to work for a maximum period of about sixty hours without water, after which it would be necessary to give them some days' rest; Arab ponies were thought to be able to last about ten hours longer.   During the Darfur Campaign, Kelly Pasha [1] marched ninety miles in three nights and two days with a mounted infantry regiment equipped with the hardy little mules of Abyssinia. All these estimates were proved to have been erroneous. It has already been pointed out that one battery of the Corps marched and fought for nine consecutive days, during which period its horses were only watered three times,[2] and this was no isolated example.   Even when water was obtainable, the difficulty of raising

---

[1] Brigadier-General P. J. V. Kelly, C.M.G., D.S.O., commanded 5th Mounted Brigade in 1917 operations and 13th Cavalry Brigade in 1918.

[2] See p. 94.

it from very deep wells, and the pressing need for haste, often resulted in many horses being unable to drink their fill.

During the advance across the Sinai desert a number of experiments had been carried out, both by the Royal Army Veterinary Corps and by the commanders of different units, with a view to ascertaining whether horses would do better, under the existing conditions, with two drinks a day or three. The usual plan was to select a large number of horses of the same type and of about equal condition, and put half of these on two waterings and half on three. The result of these experiments was conclusively in favour of the two drinks a day. Not only did the horses on this *régime* improve in condition quicker than those which were watered three times, but it was proved by actual measurement that they drank more water in the day. By the time the force arrived at El Arish, watering twice a day was generally accepted as the standard.

Later on, during the period between the second battle of Gaza and the commencement of General Allenby's operations (May to October 1917 inclusive) many of the horses of the cavalry division in the line had so far to go for water that they could only be watered once a day. It is probable that this resulted in some loss of condition, though, as there were other contributory causes, such as the periodical long reconnaissances, the heat, dust and flies, it is not possible to apportion the blame exactly. During operations, so long as the horses got water once a day, they kept fairly fit, and, given anything in the nature of bulk food, such as might be got in many countries by grazing, there seemed no reason why they should not have been able to continue indefinitely on this regime. During the Beersheba-

Jerusalem operations, however, the average number of waterings per horse in the Corps was only one every thirty-six hours.

During the 1918 campaign there was no lack of water, except for the few days during which the 4th Cavalry Division was advancing on Damascus east of the Jordan. At all other times, water was always available for horses at least once a day.

When marching in waterless country, the writer used to have a large biscuit tin full of water (or, better still, a petrol tin, when it could be ' acquired ') carried on the dash-board of every gun and wagon. At each hourly halt the horses' mouths, nostrils, and eyes used to be wiped with a wet—not merely damp— cloth, and this always seemed to refresh them greatly, and to relieve the symptoms of distress due to thirst. A little water was also mixed with the feeds, and, when the grain was crushed, or there was any bran available, it was found that horses which were off their feed owing to exhaustion would often eat well if fed by hand with small balls made of grain slightly moistened with water. This plan was suggested to the writer by the late Brigadier-General Paul Kenna, V.C., 21st Lancers, who had used it successfully in the Sudan Campaign.

Much has been said and written about the ability of horses to scent water afar off. The experience of this campaign seems to prove that this ability does not extend to water in deep wells, even when the supply is plentiful. There were many instances of horses, which had been without water for a long period, passing quite close to wells, without evincing any signs of knowledge of the proximity of water. That they can, and do, scent water lying in large pools or rivers was made clear on several occasions, but this power was shared by many of the Australian soldiers and by a few Englishmen. Brigadier-General Grant, Commanding the 4th A.L.H. Brigade, a noted ' bushman,' had this useful sense highly developed. The ' sensation ' of water, once experienced, is quite unmistakable, though it is difficult to describe. The sense of smell undoubtedly plays a part, but the sensation is more one of a sudden freshness and sweetness of the atmosphere than a scent. It is noticeable particularly just after sunset, when the presence of water lying in pools may often be detected several miles away. Unfortunately, damp ground, from which water has recently evaporated, produces the same sensation, and frequently deceived horses as well as men.

Remounts.—The last horses shipped to Egypt arrived in May or June 1917, and most of these were issued to units before the commencement of the Beersheba-Gaza operations. From that date till the end of the war, no more horses arrived in the country ; 8000 remounts, which had been bought by the British Government in Australia, could never be moved, owing to the shortage of shipping. When the stock of remounts in Palestine was exhausted, casualties were replaced by horses that had already seen service, and had been sent, sick or wounded, to remount hospitals, and reissued as soon as they were reasonably fit for further work. At the commencement of the advance in September 1918 the remount depots were emptied, and there was scarcely a single fit horse left behind the fighting troops.

Such remounts as reached the country, nearly all from Australia or Canada, were of a good type, sound and reliable. The depots were admirably managed, and the whole remount service was a model of efficiency.

Some 1500 Arab ponies and a considerable number

of mules and camels were captured from the Turks in 1917. They were nearly all in wretched condition and covered with galls, but, after being well fed and looked after for a few weeks, fetched the most astonishing prices. £50 was the average price paid at Jerusalem for a pony, £40 for a small mule, and £35 for a camel. We were able to make use of the camels, and a few of the stouter ponies were issued to the infantry as ' cobs,' but the great majority of ponies and mules were of no use to us. During the 1918 operations about 2000 enemy animals fell into our hands, and these realised even higher prices in northern Syria and the Lebanon.

Horsemastership.—In the early days in Egypt the standard of horsemastership was not high. Among the English troops there was a large proportion in the mounted branches, both of officers and men, who had had little previous experience of horses, and none at all under the severe conditions of active service. The Australian Light Horsemen, though fine riders and thoroughly experienced with horses, were unaccustomed to having to use the same horse day after day, and did not at first realise the necessity of saving their mounts in every possible way, *e.g.* by dismounting at every halt, however short, off-saddling whenever possible, etc. But they have the same, almost instinctive, love of horses as the Irish, and they very soon realised the difference between active service conditions and those in their own country. The Territorials, too, gained valuable experience during the advance across Sinai and in the Western Desert, and, by the time General Allenby arrived in Egypt, the standard of horsemastership in the force had reached a high level. As an indication of this fact, it may be mentioned that, at the end of each series of operations, there was hardly a sore back in the force. A striking contrast to this record was afforded by the French cavalry regiment which took part in the 1918 operations. On arrival at Damascus, nearly every horse in the regiment had a sore back. The Frenchmen carried an astonishing quantity of kit on their saddles, and, though it was all put on in a very neat and soldier-like manner, the weight was undoubtedly far too great. Owing to the difficulty of removing the saddle without taking off all this kit, the horses were scarcely ever off-saddled. The men, too, were far too prone to remain mounted when halted.

Type.—Some remarks on type have already been made in Chapter VIII. The experience of the latter part of the campaign served but to confirm the conclusion as to the superiority of well-bred, fairly lightly-built horses over those of coarser fibre. Well-bred horses will go farther and faster, eat less, and recover condition more quickly than the coarse-bred ones. In this connection, when is the dismal practice of subdividing the horses of a battery into ' Riders ' and ' Draught Horses ' going to be abandoned ? Every gunner wants to have practically nothing but light draught horses, so that every horse in the battery shall be capable of taking its turn in a gun team if necessary. The result of classifying nearly half the horses in a horse artillery battery as ' riders ' too often results in all the weedy, fifteen hand ponies in the remount depots being issued to the gunners. Such horses are even more useless in a battery than they would be in a cavalry regiment. In the latter they might carry a trumpeter; in the former even the trumpeter's horse is expected to be able to take his turn in draught. On more than one occasion in 1917 even officers' chargers were used in the teams.

Diseases.—The horses of the Corps were remarkably free from disease. In the summer of 1918 there were a few sporadic cases of anthrax. The disease is found here and there among the native horses and cattle all over Palestine. The spores are deposited on the ground by the infected animals, with the result that there is always a danger of picking it up. Prompt destruction of all horses affected with the disease, and the removal to a fresh piece of ground of the unit in which the case occurred, leaving the old ground clearly labelled as ' unclean,' prevented any outbreak of the disease. Except for these few cases, there was an almost entire absence of disease throughout the campaign, which may be considered somewhat remarkable, in view of the fact that glanders, anthrax, lymphangitis, and other diseases are rife among the beasts of the native population. Our immunity from these scourges may be attributed to the facts that our horses were seldom camped for long in the same place ; that they were never camped near villages if it could be avoided ; and that no native animals were ever allowed in or near our camps, or to drink where our horses drank.

The 5th Cavalry Division suffered somewhat from laminitis in September 1918, as a result of the rather unnecessarily fast pace the division had set on the morning of the 19th. Thirty or forty horses had to be destroyed on the following day. Neither of the other two divisions, however, had any trouble of this sort.

Equipment.—Leather muzzles proved a necessity in all units whose horses were picketed on ropes stretched between wagon wheels instead of on ground lines. Otherwise the hungry brutes ate the woodwork of the wheels voraciously. It was only necessary to muzzle the two or three horses picketed next to the wheels. The nostril holes of the service pattern muzzle are much too small, and should be enlarged downwards and outwards to an oval shape at least three inches long.

The steel wire picketing ropes issued to the artillery were very much superior in every way to the old pattern hemp ropes, whether 5 feet 9 inch or 66 feet. It is suggested that the 5 feet 9 inch ropes, with loop and toggle, and the heel peg ropes might also in future be made of wire instead of hemp. The wire rope is much stronger and no heavier, and is not so likely to gall horses that get their feet over it. The great objection to it is, of course, its high initial cost, but against this may be set the fact that it is practically indestructible, and lasts indefinitely. Active service head ropes might also be made of wire with a spring hook at each end. A few raw hide head ropes were issued at one time, and these were excellent, except for the fact that the horses ate them wholesale when really hungry.

In the Australian Light Horse regiments neither manes nor tails were ever cut or pulled. During operations there was little time to care for manes and tails, and they looked somewhat untidy, but there is no doubt that in a hot country, it is preferable to let them grow freely. Not only does a mane assist the horse to rid itself of flies, but it appears to give some protection from the fierce rays of the sun, and a long thick tail is unquestionably a very great blessing to a horse in a fly country.

CHAPTER XXVI

TRANSPORT AND AMMUNITION SUPPLY

THE advance to Damascus and Aleppo in September and October 1918 proved with what a small amount of transport cavalry can operate, when local supplies are available. As already explained, during this advance no transport accompanied the divisions, except ammunition wagons and a few motor ambulance cars.

The opportunities for cavalry making a raid such a great distance into enemy country have seldom occurred in the past, and are likely to become even more rare in the future. When they do occur, however, the experience of this campaign points to the conclusion that there can be few countries in which cavalry can operate as such effectively, where they would not be able to dispense almost entirely with transport. The fact that mounted troops can move freely, denotes that the country is not excessively mountainous, and is, therefore (excluding desert land), more or less cultivated, thus providing food for man and horse. It must be remembered that much of the country through which the cavalry passed between the 25th of September and the 28th of October is poorly cultivated, and all of it had been mercilessly laid under requisition by the Turks and Germans for the supply of their armies. Yet it was found possible to secure food and forage for three cavalry divisions, a total of nearly 20,000 men and a similar number of horses, without extreme difficulty, and without in any way depriving the inhabitants of essential food.

If, however, the country through which it is proposed to advance is incapable of supporting the force, sufficient transport must be taken to carry supplies for such a number of days as may be requisite. The pace of the cavalry will then be, to a great extent, limited by the pace of their transport, and for this reason every effort should be made to increase the mobility of cavalry transport vehicles.

Vehicles.—At the beginning of the 1917 operations the cavalry ammunition columns and supply trains were equipped partly with G.S. and partly with limbered G.S. wagons. During the subsequent operations, both at the beginning, when movement took place over a sandy or dusty plain, and later on, when the whole country was a sea of mud, and vast areas were under water, the G.S. wagons were constantly in trouble. The experience of the whole campaign was overwhelmingly in favour of the L.G.S. wagon. The sole advantage of the G.S. wagon lies in its greater capacity for carrying bulky loads. For this reason it is very suitable for use in barracks or standing camps, where such stuff as hay, straw, etc., have to be carried. As regards weight, however, the L.G.S. wagon holds its own against the G.S. on roads, and is superior in roadless or hilly country. That is to say, the L.G.S. wagon, with two men and four horses, can, in such country, carry more than two-thirds of the load possible for the G.S. wagon, with its three drivers and six horses. Further, the lower centre of gravity, four large wheels and much greater lock angle of the former, enables it to cross country over which the latter cannot move at all. One advantage claimed for the G.S. type is that the wagon body is supposed to be capable of being used as a pontoon. The writer has tried it as such, in peace time, and his experience has decided him that he would rather swim.

The above remarks are, of course, to be taken as applying to cavalry transport only.

There is one weakness in the L.G.S. wagon which is commended to the notice of the Royal Ordnance Corps. The bolt which fastens the wagon body on to the carriage passes through the axle. Towards the end of the campaign, after several years' hard and continuous work, a number of these axles began to break, and always at the place where the bolt passed through them. It is suggested that, in future manufacture, the fastening might consist of a steel collar over the axle, instead of a bolt through it.

Horses.—The remarks on type, which have been made with regard to the cavalry riding horse, apply with equal force to the cavalry draught horse. Many of our English draught animals were of far too heavy a type, either for horse artillery or for cavalry transport. It is sometimes argued that a proportion of heavy horses is very useful when wagons begin to get stuck in boggy places. But it is not much use having these equine Samsons at all, if they are not available at the time their services are required. And this is what invariably happens. Nothing in the nature of a cart horse can live with cavalry in a march of forty miles, and, in this campaign, there was one of over ninety miles on end, and marches of forty, fifty and sixty miles were comparatively common. If heavy horses are forced to keep up with cavalry over such distances, they very soon give up the unequal fight and die ; if they are allowed to go their own pace, they are a day's march in rear at the end of twenty-four hours, and the transport thus requires an escort of a size that can ill be spared from the fighting forces.

Another advantage of having a lighter-built, better-bred type of horse for transport, is that they then form a reserve for the cavalry. In the artillery it is the rule for riding and draught horses to change places frequently, thus resting both kinds in turn. This custom might profitably be employed occasionally in the cavalry.

The Australians have an admirable type of cavalry draught horse: 15 to 15.2 hands high, short-backed, well-coupled, and showing a good deal of breeding. The disappearance from our English roads first of the coaches and then of the horse-drawn buses, has deprived us almost entirely of our once fine type of light draught horse, and it seems as if we shall, in the future, have to depend more and more on the Dominions for our supply of such horses. There were a certain number of Canadian horses in the Corps transport. They were hard and sound, but of a coarser type, with heavier shoulders and less handy than those from Australia.

Other transport animals.—At different times, camels, mules, and donkeys were used by the cavalry for transport purposes. The first named are, of course, entirely unsuitable, except for work in the desert, but, as we had some 30,000 of them in our possession in 1917, a legacy from Sinai, and there was a shortage of other transport, they were largely used during the 1917 operations. No attempt was made to keep up, or even near, the cavalry on the march, but the camels worked in a system of convoys along defined routes, forming dumps behind the advancing line of cavalry, from which the divisional trains drew supplies. The uselessness and danger of camels in mountainous country was convincingly demonstrated in the mountains of Judæa and in the two trans-Jordan raids, and, after the second of these, the Imperial Camel Corps Brigade was disbanded, and the cavalry saw no more of the patient but unlovable beasts that had worked for them for more than two years.

Mules were in use in the transport to a certain extent all through the campaign, but the experience of the 1917 operations led to their being replaced by horses in all transport that was required to keep up with the cavalry. Their hardihood, soundness, and remarkable freedom from disease, no less than their patience and docility, render them admirable for infantry transport, and even, possibly, for field artillery, but they suffer from the serious disability, from the cavalry or horse artillery point of view, that they cannot go the pace. Left to themselves, they can march indefinitely, but, if pushed along faster than their natural gait, they rapidly lose condition, and soon become so debilitated as to be well-nigh useless. As this natural pace is slower than that of horses, they must always be pushed when acting with cavalry, and this fact renders them unsuitable for use with mounted troops.

Donkeys were first used in supply convoys in the Judæan Hills in the winter of 1917, some 400 being sent up from Egypt for this purpose. They did most excellent work, supplying the troops in the line at a time when there were no roads available. They are admirably adapted for such special work, being small, hardy, and easily handled, and requiring no attention. For any other purpose they are, of course, not to be seriously considered. Owing to the chronic shortage of horses in the country, those details of regiments who did not usually accompany

their units into action were, in 1917, given donkeys
to ride. There were about half a dozen in each
cavalry regiment or similar unit. Most of these

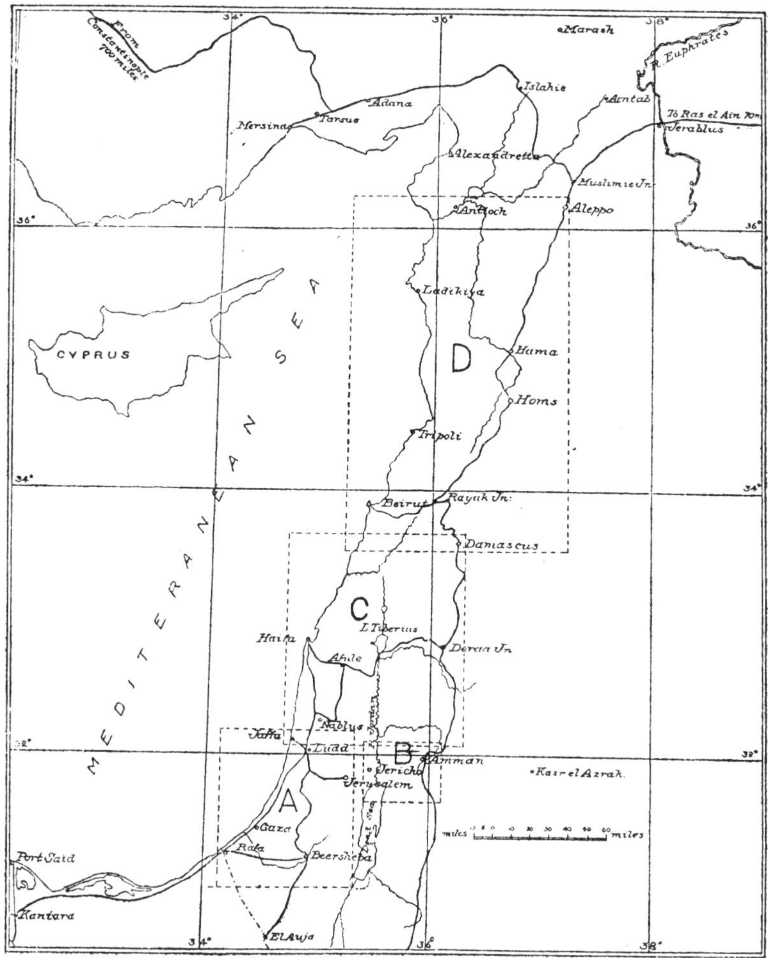

were gradually exchanged for Arab ponies captured
from the enemy, but a few carried on right through
the campaign, up to the capture of Aleppo. How
they kept up through some of the long marches of

1918, carrying a heavy man and all his kit, is a mystery, but they contrived to do so somehow.

Ammunition.—Prior to the commencement of the 1917 operations in Palestine, the amount of small arm ammunition laid down to be carried in a cavalry divisional ammunition column was 250,000 rounds per brigade, or 1,000,000 in the column for the four-brigade divisions of that time. This was a ridiculously over-large amount. On the other hand, the amount of gun ammunition was very small. Indeed the divisional column commander who said that he carried in his column three weeks' supply for the small arms and three hours' for the guns, can scarcely be accused of hyperbole.

After the second battle of Gaza, during which the cavalry were engaged all day long dismounted, in a very heavy fire fight, it was found that, after replenishing the regimental reserves, only about one-sixth of the small arm ammunition in the divisional ammunition columns had been issued. The guns, on the other hand, had expended nearly three times the total quantity of ammunition carried in the column.

As a result of this action, the whole question of ammunition supply was considered afresh, and the columns were reorganised with an establishment of 200 rounds of shell per gun, and 120,000 of small arm ammunition per brigade, calculated as to 84,000 rounds for the machine gun squadron and 12,000 rounds for each regiment. These proportions worked satisfactorily, though the gun ammunition might still be somewhat increased, even at the expense of the small arms. The result of the whole series of operations seems to point to the fact that an establishment of 100,000 rounds of small arm ammunition per brigade, or 300,000 per division, and 250 rounds of gun ammunition per gun, or 4500 for a division, would form the best proportion. This would give a total of 442 rounds of shell per gun, carried in the field, not an unduly large amount for a modern, quick-firing gun, when it is remembered that Napoleon considered that the muzzle-loading, slow-firing field pieces of his day should be supplied with not less than 300 rounds apiece.

Loads.—The weights laid down in the 1914 War Establishments to be carried both in G.S. and L.G.S. wagons were found to be only suitable for transport accompanying infantry along well-metalled roads. After the second battle of Gaza, a new load table was drawn up empirically. A series of experiments, carried out just prior to the commencement of the Beersheba operations, demonstrated that even these reduced loads were far too heavy for G.S. wagons in such country. Unfortunately these experiments were ignored, and the G.S. wagons started the operations with the loads as laid down in the new tables. The result was that, during the march from the Shellal area to Khalasa, the G.S. wagons were strewn over twenty miles of country, and some 200 camels had to be requisitioned at short notice from the supply columns to lighten the wagons.

After the fall of Beersheba, the G.S. wagons of the divisional ammunition column were taken over by the Corps, as already narrated, and they took no further part in the operations until they rejoined their respective divisions on the 19th November.

As a result of the 1917 series of operations, the load question was again reviewed, and the following loads were decided upon.

G.S. wagons, 23 boxes of 13-pounder gun ammunition or 26 boxes of small arm ammunition, a total load behind the 6 horses of about 35 cwt.

L.G.S. wagons, 16 boxes of gun or 18 boxes of

small arm ammunition, a total load behind the 4 horses of about 24 cwt.

These loads were proved by considerable subsequent experience to be the maximum with which wagons could operate efficiently with cavalry in such country. It is to be remarked that practically no sandy country was encountered after the fall of Beersheba, but the unmetalled tracks along which the transport had to march were, in the winters of 1917 and 1918, often almost impassable owing to the mud.

Before leaving the subject of ammunition supply, attention should be drawn to the vital necessity of cavalry regiments replenishing their regimental reserve of small arm ammunition from the ammunition column *every day*. Obvious as this duty may appear, it is one that is frequently neglected, especially during a time of long marches. It frequently happened that, in spite of repeated applications, the ammunition column commanders could not get indents from the regiments for days at a time. Such delays were often followed by sudden demands for the immediate supply of a large quantity of ammunition, which, perhaps, was not all available at the moment. There ensued mutual recriminations, and much extra work for the tired horses of both the columns and the regimental ammunition wagons, all of which might have been avoided by more forethought and attention to detail.

APPENDIX I

(*a*) THE DESERT MOUNTED CORPS

WHEN the Desert Mounted Corps officially came into being, it was constituted as follows :—

Commander : Lieutenant-General Sir Harry Chauvel, K.C.B., K.C.M.G., Australian Imperial Forces.

AUSTRALIAN AND NEW ZEALAND MOUNTED DIVISION (ANZAC).

Commander : Major-General Sir E. W. C. Chaytor, K.C.M.G., C.B., p.s.c., A.D.C., New Zealand Imperial Forces.

1ST AUSTRALIAN LIGHT HORSE BRIGADE.

Commander : Brigadier-General C. F. Cox, C.B., C.M.G., D.S.O., A.I.F.

1st, 2nd, and 3rd Regiments Australian Light Horse.

2ND AUSTRALIAN LIGHT HORSE BRIGADE.

Commander : Brigadier-General G. de L. Ryrie, C.B., C.M.G., A.I.F.

5th, 6th, and 7th Regiments Australian Light Horse.

NEW ZEALAND MOUNTED BRIGADE.

Commander : Brigadier-General W. Meldrum, C.M.G., D.S.O., N.Z.I.F.

Auckland, Canterbury, and Wellington Regiments of Mounted Rifles.

ARTILLERY.

18th Brigade R.H.A. (Inverness, Ayrshire, and Somerset Batteries) and Divisional Ammunition Column.

YEOMANRY DIVISION.

Commander : Major-General Sir G. de S. Barrow, K.C.M.G., C.B., p.s.c., Indian Army.

6TH MOUNTED BRIGADE.

Commander : Brigadier-General C.A.C. Godwin, D.S.O., I.A.
Dorset, Bucks, and Berks Yeomanry Regiments.

8TH MOUNTED BRIGADE.

Commander : Brigadier-General C. S. Rome, D.S.O.
1st City of London and 1st and 3rd County of London Yeomanry Regiments.

22ND MOUNTED BRIGADE.

Commander : Brigadier-General F. A. B. Fryer (relinquished command December 1917).
Brigadier-General P. D. FitzGerald, D.S.O., p.s.c.
Stafford, Lincoln, and East Riding Yeomanry Regiments.

ARTILLERY.

20th Brigade R.H.A. (Berks, Hants, and Leicester Batteries) and Divisional Ammunition Column.

AUSTRALIAN MOUNTED DIVISION.

Commander : Major-General Sir H. W. Hodgson, K.C.M.G., C.V.O., C.B.

3RD AUSTRALIAN LIGHT HORSE BRIGADE.

Commander : Brigadier-General L. C. Wilson, C.M.G., D.S.O., A.I.F.
8th, 9th, and 10th Regiments Australian Light Horse.

4TH AUSTRALIAN LIGHT HORSE BRIGADE.

Commander : Brigadier-General W. Grant, C.M.G., D.S.O., A.I.F.
4th, 11th, and 12th Regiments Australian Light Horse.

5TH MOUNTED BRIGADE.

Commander : Brigadier-General P. D. Fitzgerald, D.S.O.,
p.s.c.(relinquished command November 1917).
Brigadier-General P. J. V. Kelly, C.M.G.,
D.S.O.

ARTILLERY.

19th Brigade R.H.A. (' A ' and ' B ' Batteries Honour-
able Artillery Company, and Notts Battery R.H.A.)
and Divisional Ammunition Column.

CORPS RESERVE.

7TH MOUNTED BRIGADE.

Commander : Brigadier-General J. T. Wigan, C.M.G., D.S.O.,
(relinquished command December 1917).
Brigadier-General G. V. Clarke, D.S.O.

Sherwood Rangers, South Notts and Herts Yeomanry
Regiments, with Essex Battery R.H.A., and Brigade
Ammunition Column.

IMPERIAL CAMEL CORPS BRIGADE.

Commander : Brigadier-General S. Smith, V.C., D.S.O.
Two Australian and one British Camel Battalions,
with the Hongkong and Singapore Mountain Battery
R.G.A.

After the reorganisation consequent on the despatch
of many of the Yeomanry regiments to France, in
April and May 1918, and the arrival of Indian Cavalry
Regiments from Europe, the Corps was expanded
into four divisions as follows :—

4TH CAVALRY DIVISION.

Commander : Major-General Sir G. de S. Barrow,
K.C.M.G., etc.

10TH CAVALRY BRIGADE.

Commander : Brigadier-General W. G. K. Green, D.S.O.,
I.A.

Dorset Yeomanry, 2nd Lancers, 38th Central India
Horse.

11TH CAVALRY BRIGADE.

Commander : Brigadier-General C.L.Gregory, C.B., p.s.c., I.A.

1st County of London Yeomanry, 29th Lancers, 36th Jacob's Horse.

12TH CAVALRY BRIGADE.

Commander : Brigadier-General J. T. Wigan, C.M.G., D.S.O.

Stafford Yeomanry, 6th Cavalry, 19th Lancers.

ARTILLERY.

20th Brigade R.H.A. and Divisional Ammunition Column.

5TH CAVALRY DIVISION.

Commander : Major-General Sir H. J. M. MacAndrew, K.C.M.G., C.B., D.S.O., Indian Army.

13TH CAVALRY BRIGADE.

Commander : Brigadier-General P. J. V. Kelly, C.M.G., D.S.O. (relinquished command September 1918).

Brigadier-General G. A. Weir, D.S.O.

Gloucester Yeomanry, 9th Hodson's Horse, 18th Lancers.

14TH CAVALRY BRIGADE.

Commander : Brigadier-General G. V. Clarke, D.S.O.

Sherwood Rangers Yeomanry, 20th Deccan Horse, 34th Poona Horse.

15TH (IMPERIAL SERVICE) CAVALRY BRIGADE.

Commander : Brigadier-General C. R. Harbord, D.S.O., I.A.

Jodhpur, Mysore and 1st Hyderabad Lancers.[1]

ARTILLERY.

' B ' Battery H.A.C. and Essex Battery R.H.A., with Divisional Ammunition Column.

The Anzac and the Australian Mounted Divisions remained the same, except that the 5th Mounted

---

[1] These regiments were all maintained by the Ruling Princes of their respective States in India.

Brigade was replaced in the latter by the 5th A.L.H. Brigade, which consisted of the 14th and 15th Regiments A.L.H. (composed of men of the Camel Corps Brigade, which had been disbanded after the second trans-Jordan raid), and the French Régiment Mixte de Cavalerie. Swords were issued to the Australian Mounted Division at the beginning of August 1918, and the men had about six weeks' training in the use of them before the operations commenced. The Australian troopers took to their new weapon enthusiastically, and showed, later on, that they knew how to use it.

(b) INFANTRY

During the 1917 operations, the infantry were organised as follows :—

20TH CORPS.

Commander : Lieutenant-General Sir Philip Chetwode, Bart., K.C.B., K.C.M.G., D.S.O.

10TH DIVISION.

Commander : Major-General J. R. Longley, C.B., C.M.G.

53RD Division.

Commander : Major-General S. F. Mott, C.B., p.s.c.

60TH DIVISION.

Commander : Major-General Sir J. S. M. Shea, K.C.M.G., D.S.O., p.s.c., I.A.

74TH DIVISION.

Commander : Major-General E. S. Girdwood, C.B.

21ST CORPS.

Commander : Lieutenant-General Sir Edward Bulfin, K.C.B., C.V.O.

52ND DIVISION.

Commander : Major-General J. Hill, C.B., D.S.O., 𝔄.𝔇.𝔠., I.A.

54TH DIVISION.

Commander : Major-General S. W. Hare, C.B.

75TH DIVISION.

Commander : Major-General P. C. Palin, C.B., C.M.G., I.A.

On the reorganisation of the infantry in the spring of 1918, the 3rd (Lahore) and 7th (Meerut) Divisions replaced the 52nd and 74th Divisions, which were sent to France. The 3rd was commanded by Major-General A. R. Hoskins, C.M.G., D.S.O., p.s.c., and the 7th by Major-General Sir V. B. Fane, K.C.I.E., C.B.

Three-quarters of the British troops in all divisions except the 54th were replaced by Indians.

APPENDIX II

NOTE ON THE ARAB MOVEMENT

A SHERIF (plur. Ashraf) is one who claims descent direct from the Prophet Mohammed, through his daughter Fatima, wife of Ali, the third Khalif. These Ashraf are found all over the Arabic-speaking world, but only those whose pedigrees are inscribed in the Register of Mecca are universally accepted as true descendants of the Prophet. This register has been kept with extraordinary care, and it is probable that it dates back to the time of Mohammed himself. There are in the Hedjaz several families of these true Ashraf, who form the aristocracy of the Arab world, live under a law of their own, and enjoy a number of special privileges.

For the first four centuries after the death of the Prophet, the Ashraf, though regarded with veneration and respect by the Arabs, held no temporal power. At the end of the tenth century, however, a Sherif of Mecca proclaimed himself Emir of the Ashraf, and succeeded in establishing his dynasty as the temporal chiefs (under the Khalif) of the Hedjaz. The ruling prince of the Ashraf of Mecca was known for centuries in Europe as ' The Grand Sherif of Mecca,' and, in former times, when the city was not as jealously guarded as it now is, more than one Christian sovereign sent an embassy to him there.

During the succeeding five hundred years, internecine strife, resulting in frequent changes of dynasty, weakened the temporal power of the Emirs of Mecca, and correspondingly increased the ascendancy of the Turks. In the sixteenth century, however, the Emir Katada, by a series of conquests of rival claimants, possessed himself of the chief power in the Hedjaz, and established his own family as the head of the Ashraf.

Sherif Hussein, a lineal descendant of Katada, succeeded to the Emirate in 1908. A man of powerful will and strong ambitions, Hussein began almost at once to consider the possibility of securing the independence of the Hedjaz, and possibly even of all the Arabs, from Turkish dominion. His task was an exceedingly difficult one. The Sultan of Turkey, as Khalif of Islam, was regarded as the spiritual head of all Moslems, and any open action against him would be likely to meet with strong opposition in all Moslem countries outside Arabia. A Turkish Army Corps, with its headquarters at Sanah, near Aden, garrisoned and controlled the country; and the Emir's own people, split up into innumerable tribes and clans, were torn by bitter inter-tribal feuds, many of which dated back for centuries.

The ease with which the Sultan Abdul Hamid was overthrown by the Committee of Union and Progress at the time of the Turkish Revolution, encouraged the Sherif in his dream of establishing an independent Arab State. He became the representative of the Hedjaz in the Turkish Parliament, and for a time lived in Constantinople. Very soon, however, disgusted with the intrigues and jealousies of the C.U.P., and realising that he had nothing to hope for from this body of needy adventurers, he retired from his position, and went back into the desert, where for the next four or five years he lived the rigorous life of a patriarchal desert Sheikh, preparing his four sons for the struggle to come, and gathering round him a small number of chiefs pledged to the cause of Arabian independence.

The declaration of war by Turkey on Great Britain furnished the Emir with the chance which he had long awaited, and the atrocities committed by the Turks in Syria at the beginning of the war caused the oppressed Arabs to turn to him as their national champion. He at once threw in his lot with the

British, though not openly at first, and set to work, with the fierce energy characteristic of him, to stir up the tribes of the Hedjaz against the Turks.

The outbreak of the rebellion was precipitated by the arrival at Medina in May 1916 of a large Turkish force, charged with the task of re-establishing the waning authority of the Sultan in the Hedjaz. The Emir himself, though as full of energy and determination as ever, was now too old to bear the rigours of a desert campaign, and accordingly placed the command of his Bedouin followers in the hands of his three eldest sons Ali, Abdullah, and Feisal. Of Ali we know little, though he was active in the summer of 1918 and in the early part of 1917. Abdullah, the second son, was of a retiring disposition, a theologian and philosopher, and a deep student of the Koran. Feisal alone inherited his father's energy and power of command, without, however, the old man's ungovernable temper. The youngest son, Zeid, was still only a boy.

A line of Arab pickets was established round Medina, under the command of Feisal, and the railway north of the town was cut in several places. But the Arabs, not being provided at this time with explosives, and being ignorant of modern methods of demolition, did not effect enough before being driven off by relief parties with machine guns, to interrupt seriously the communication of Medina with the north, and the besieging force, short of arms and supplies, and without artillery, could do little more than watch the city from afar. Jiddah, however, the port of Mecca, which was attacked on June 9th, held out barely a week. Cut off from Mecca by the loss of the military blockhouses on the road, and bombarded by British warships and aeroplanes, the Turkish garrison surrendered on the 16th June. The fall of Mecca followed a month later, and an Arab force under Sherif Abdullah then proceeded to blockade the hill town of Taif, where the bulk of the Turkish forces, outside Medina, was established in summer quarters. This place held out till near the end of September, when Ghalib Pasha, the G.O.C., despairing of help, and cut off by the Arabs from all sources of supply, surrendered with the garrison of 2000 men.

By the end of the year all the small Turkish posts scattered throughout the Hedjaz had fallen to the Arabs. Medina still held out, and it was clear that the Arab forces, indifferently armed, and inexperienced in modern siege warfare, could not hope to reduce this city. The Turkish garrison, with the lines of communication troops along the railway to the north, numbered some 15,000 men, well-armed and equipped, and in all respects capable of prolonged resistance.

Acting on the advice of the British officers with them, the Arabs, therefore, abandoned for the time being all attempts on Medina, and concentrated all their efforts on a systematic attack on the Hedjaz Railway north of the town. During the first six months of 1917 a constant succession of raids so interrupted the traffic on the railway that the Turks could with difficulty keep open their communications between Medina and Damascus.

In July 1917 the Emir Feisal seized Akaba, at the north end of the Red Sea, and made this place his base for further raiding operations on the railway as far north as Maan.

In January 1918 he succeeded in destroying the branch line to the Hish Forest, from which the Turkish locomotives were drawing their fuel, and then attacked Maan itself (see p. 153.) Though unable to capture the town, the Arabs established themselves across the railway two miles farther south, and, in the course of the succeeding three months, destroyed seventy miles of the line. Medina was thus finally isolated, and the garrison was faced with the two alternatives of holding out in the town till the end of the war, or of attempting to cut a way out to the north. As the latter alternative meant almost certain destruction, the Turks decided to stay where they were. They remained in Medina till they were compelled to surrender, under the terms of the Armistice of the 31st October 1918.

The strong position taken up by the Turkish IVth Army east of the Jordan during the summer of 1918, prevented the Emir from making any further move northwards. He remained about Maan, collecting his resources for the coming struggle, and carrying on a vigorous propaganda among the surrounding tribes, till the British advance in September caused the IVth Army to retire, and gave the Arabs the opportunity of completing the task to which they had set themselves in 1916.

APPENDIX III

SUMMARY OF TERMS OF THE TURKISH ARMISTICE
WHICH CAME INTO FORCE ON OCTOBER 31, 1918.

Art. 1.—Opening of the Dardanelles and Bosphorus and access to the Black Sea. The Allied occupation of the Dardanelles and Bosphorus forts.

Art. 2.—The position of all minefields, torpedo tubes, and other obstructions in Turkish waters to be indicated, and assistance to be given to sweep or remove them as may be required.

Art 3.—All available information regarding the mines in the Black Sea to be communicated.

Art. 4.—All Allied prisoners and Armenians interned to be collected in Constantinople, and handed over unconditionally to the Allies.

Art. 5.—The immediate demobilisation of the army except troops required for the surveillance of the frontier and maintenance of internal order, their number and disposal to be determined later by the Allies, after consultation with the Turkish Government.

Art. 6.—The surrender of all war vessels in Turkish waters or the waters occupied by Turkey. These ships to be interned at such Turkish port or ports, as may be directed, except such small vessels as are required for police or similar purposes in Turkish territorial waters.

Art. 7.—The Allies to have the right to occupy any strategic points, in the event of any situation arising which threatens the security of the Allies.

Art. 8.—The free use by Allied ships of all ports and anchorages now in Turkish occupation, and the denial of their use to the enemy. Similar conditions to apply to

Turkish mercantile shipping in Turkish waters, for the purposes of trade and the demobilisation of the army.

Art. 9. — The use of all ship-repairing facilities at all Turkish ports and arsenals.

Art. 10.—Allied occupation of the Taurus tunnel system.

Art. 11.—Withdrawal of Turkish troops from north-western Persia. Part of Trans-Caucasia to be evacuated ; the remainder to be evacuated if the Allies require, after they study the situation there.

Art. 12.—Wireless and cable stations to be under Allied control ; Turkish Government messages excepted.

Art. 13.—Prohibition of the destruction of any naval, military, or commercial material by the Turks.

Art. 14.—Facilities to be given for the purchase of coal, oil-fuel, and naval material from Turkish sources, after the requirements of the country have been met. None of the above material to be exported.

Art. 15.—Allied control of all railways, and Allied occupation of Batoum. Turkey not to object to the Allied occupation of Baku.

Art. 16.—The surrender of the garrisons of the Hedjaz, Asir, Yemen, Syria, and Mesopotamia, and the withdrawal of troops from Cilicia, except those maintaining order, as determined under Clause 5. The surrender of all ports in Cilicia.

Art. 17.—The surrender of all Turkish officers in Tripolitania and Cyrenaica to the nearest Italian garrison. Turkey to guarantee to stop supplies to, and communication with, these officers, if they do not obey the order of surrender.

Art. 18.—The surrender of all ports occupied in Tripolitania and Cyrenaica, including Misurata, to the nearest Allied garrison.

Art. 19.—All Germans and Austrians, naval, military, and civilian, to quit Turkey within a month. Those in remote districts to do so as soon as possible thereafter.

Art. 20.—Compliance with the Allies' orders as regards the disposal of arms and the transport of the demobilised, under Clause 5.

Art. 21.—An Allied representative to be attached to the Turkish Ministry of Supplies, to safeguard Allied interests.

Art. 22.—Turkish prisoners to be kept at the disposal of the Allies. The release of Turkish civilian prisoners and prisoners over military age to be considered.

Art. 23.—Turkey to cease all relations with the Central Powers.

Art. 24.—In case of disorder in the six Armenian vilayets the Allies reserve the right to occupy any of them.

INDEX

Edinburgh: Printed by T. and A. CONSTABLE LTD.

A LIST OF BOOKS ON WAR, MILITARY & NAVAL HISTORY

PUBLISHED BY CONSTABLE & CO. LTD. 10 & 12 ORANGE ST. LONDON W.C. 2.

COLONEL REPINGTON'S DIARY : The First World War, 1914–1918.

By Lieut.-Colonel CHARLES à COURT REPINGTON, C.M.G. 10th Impression. 2 vols. 42s. net.

"Here is our Pepys . . . as much at home in the War Office and Whitehall as in Mayfair, who knew everyone worth knowing and heard everything worth hearing. Fortunately he is not one of those who hold that discretion is the better part of revelation.

"Everybody who was anybody flits through these pages. Generals are ungummed and statesmen are stellenbosched, and always the Diarist is watching how the wires are pulled and who pulled them. Thus were set down these pages of secret history, and never was historian more candid."—*The Evening Standard.*

"Colonel Repington is a master of his craft, but he has failed because his pupils would not learn. . . . He gives us through the mouths of the great actors in the drama an extraordinary lively and human story of the most critical period of the world's history. Colonel Repington is a rare diarist, as he is a rare military thinker. In these volumes he has blended the diarist and the thinker with uncommon skill, so that though all the time he is teaching the politician and the public how to make war he never bores."
The Morning Post.

"This book is a remarkable and noteworthy addition to the history of the time. Colonel Repington was in the very thick of affairs, and meeting daily the men and women who influenced them he had unrivalled sources of information. An accomplished soldier and a close student of politics, he was consulted by many who held positions of the highest responsibility. . . . Eminent statesmen and public men are freely criticised, their motives and meannesses exposed and the intrigues by which they sought to oust or overwhelm rivals or opponents laid bare. . . ."—*The Daily Telegraph.*

"Colonel Repington's book is easily the most interesting that has appeared since the war began. He is one of the few great military critics in Europe ; he lives in the Bull's-eye of Society and knows personally the famous personages about whom he writes."
Saturday Review.

"Two volumes of war history which will set the tongues of gossip wagging for many days. These personal experiences are so personal that one is dazed at the thought of 'a certain amount omitted on the recommendation of eminent counsel.' Colonel Repington's diary reveals him as a Cæsar, but fortunately he drops very frequently into the breezy gossip of a Horace Walpole. Records of statesmanship, administrations, and tactics are plentifully peppered by blazing indiscretions of afternoon tea with charming ladies."—*Daily Express.*

AN ENGLISH WIFE IN BERLIN

By EVELYN, PRINCESS BLUCHER. 9th Impression. 19s. net.

"Its absolute fairness and impartiality make it valuable in a peace that knoweth its own bitterness. . . . The book is as entertaining as a novel and a useful contribution to the history of the war."
Manchester Guardian.

"One of the most interesting books written about life in Germany during the war. She writes with ease, sympathy and charm. Princess Blucher has written a book, every word, or almost every word, of which can be read with interest, sympathy and admiration. She is intensely English by nature and education. . . . Passionately sympathetic and unwearyingly active in the interest of British prisoners, yet she feels her international and even her German position too. One would not respect her so much if she did not. . . . As a woman she will not refuse pity even for Casement whom she despised almost as much as he deserved. . . . She several times expresses her admiration of the wonderful patience and self-sacrifice of the German people. . . . Within her limits her book will make for the thing she most desires, a spirit of justice and good feeling. . . . Every reader who honestly wishes that to come about will lay it down with a sense of respect, admiration and gratitude."—*Times Literary Supplement.*

"She gives with intimate knowledge the most wonderful and convincing picture of German life and thought during the war which has yet been published to the world. There are a hundred anecdotes worth quoting, and the last pages describing the final downfall and scenes of revolution are vivid and enthralling."
SIR PHILIP GIBBS in the *Daily Chronicle.*

"Amazingly interesting. 'AN ENGLISH WIFE IN BERLIN' is quite one of the best books about the war for those who cannot read about the actual fighting."—CLEMENT SHORTER in the *Sphere.*

PROBLEMS OF POWER

By W. MORTON FULLERTON. Demy 8vo. 18s. net.
A survey of World's Politics and Economics from 1870 to the outbreak of the Great War. 4th and definitive edition.

"This thoughtful and well packed volume. The author has a remarkably varied and penetrating knowledge of the factors which go to the composition of history. . . . A short review cannot do more than suggest the qualities and appeals of a volume which is free from all loose writing and exceptionally worthy of patient mastication."—*Observer.*

*

THE PEACE NEGOTIATIONS
A Personal Narrative.

By ROBERT LANSING. One volume. 16s. net.

Robert Lansing was Secretary of State to the Wilson Administration throughout the War, and went to the Peace Conference as one of the five American delegates. In February, 1920, he was asked to resign by President Wilson, who wrote in his famous letter that he wished an opportunity to select as Secretary of State "Someone whose mind would more willingly go along with mine." This book has therefore a dual importance. It is the first authoritative and detailed narrative of the Paris Conference by one of the actual Commissioners. It is intimate and dramatic, with the intimacy and drama only clash of personality can give. Lansing, in his clear and impressive pages, puts his case against the President, expounds his view of the task before the Peacemakers at Paris, shows where it conflicted with that of his chief. Which view was the right one?

CONTENTS: Reasons for Writing a Personal Narrative. Mr. Wilson's Presence at the Peace Conference. General Plan for a League of Nations. Substitute Articles Proposed. The Positive Guaranty and Balance of Power. The President's Plan and the Cecil Plan. Self-Determination. A Resolution instead of the Covenant. The Guaranty in the Revised Covenant. International Arbitration. Report of Commission on the League of Nations. The System of Mandates. Differences as to the League Recapitulated. The Proposed Treaty with France. Lack of an American Program. Secret Diplomacy. The Shantung Settlement. The Bullitt Affair. APPENDICES: 1. The President's original Draft of the Covenant of the League of Nations. January 10, 1919. 2. Lord Robert Cecil's League of Nations Plan. 3. The Covenant of the League of Nations, as incorporated in the Treaty of Versailles. 4. The Fourteen Points. 5. Principles declared by President Wilson in his Address of February 11, 1918. 6. The Articles of the Treaty of Versailles relating to Shantung.

THE DIPLOMACY OF THE WAR OF 1914. The Beginnings of the War.

By ELLERY C. STOWELL, Professor of International Law. Med. 8vo. 25s. net.

" A very complete and exhaustive study of the whole of the negotiations preceding the war, equipped with full indices and a large number of illustrative extracts from the Press and other documents. The book is, perhaps, the most complete that has yet appeared, and will be a valuable guide to students."—*The Nation.*

" Professor Stowell's book displays unusual grasp, thoroughness, and industry in research, and the mass of official documents has been skilfully dealt with by selection and condensation."
Times Literary Supplement.

PEACE AND WAR IN EUROPE
By GILBERT SLATER, M.A.   Crown 8vo.   2s. 6d. net.

EXPERIENCES OF A DUGOUT
By Major-General Sir C. E. CALLWELL, K.C.B.   18s. net.

Major-General Sir Charles Callwell held the appointment of Director of Military Operations during the early years of the war, and indeed was in the saddle at the beginning of 1914. In this volume he shows us behind the scenes and enables us to see clearly much that was obscure. His book reveals to us in an intimate way the personality of Lord Kitchener and many others, and introduces us to the War Cabinet.

" Sir Charles Callwell is one of the soundest military writers in the country. . . . His sense of proportion is never at fault."—*Spectator.*

" A mightily interesting and valuable book."—*Outlook.*

" Told keenly and poignantly with a biting humour."—*Times.*

" A vivid and often humorous account of the inner drama of the war years."—*Morning Post.*

THE NEW GERMANY
By GEORGE YOUNG.   8s. net.

This book contains the actual text of the German Republican Constitution.

"An illuminating and lively record of events and experiences which will prove of real value to coming historians. . . . A clear and entertaining survey of German politics between the date of the Armistice and the later months of 1919. . . . At every turn there is much evidence of inside knowledge. . . . *The New Germany* is full of acute observation and is the work of a man who has ideas and insight and can take long and broad views of great questions."
Manchester Guardian.

" An illuminating book which has the merit of combining lively and witty description of outward things with a serious examination of the extraordinarily complicated tendencies of German politics to-day."—*Times.*

" He records what he saw ; he makes his own bold and original comments and reflections ; he gives us the text of the new Constitution with a most valuable chapter of comment and explanation. . . . Those who wish to learn why the New Germany remains unborn should read this book."—LEONARD WOOLF in the *Daily Herald.*

THE HAPSBURG MONARCHY
By H. WICKHAM STEED.   Revised Edition.   8s. 6d. net.

" The most penetrating study of the Dual Monarchy to be found in our language."—*Daily Graphic.*

THE AUSTRIAN PEACE OFFER

Documents edited by G. DE MANTEYER. With three Facsimiles and a Letter Preface by PRINCE SIXTE OF BOURBON. Demy 8vo. 25s. net.

Every one remembers the " Czernin has lied " of M. Clemenceau in the Spring of 1918. Perhaps the greatest diplomatic sensation of the War was the publication, *one year after they had taken place,* of the details of the Austrian offer to conclude a separate peace, on the basis of recognition of "the French just claims regarding Alsace Lorraine." Prince Sixte has now entrusted to M. G. de Manteyer the writing of the full facts of this important and mysterious episode. As he says in the letter preface to this volume : "The narrative of Austria's offer of a separate peace which I have till now refrained from telling can now be told without offence . . . and I turn, for a recorder of this page of history, to M. Manteyer, who was more intimately connected than any other of my friends with my life during the whole war." Contents :— Introduction ; The Emperor's Offer ; Reception of the Offer by France and England ; Baron Sonnino's Veto and the Entente's Reply ; Italy makes Overtures at Berne, and Austria announces her Wish for a Separate Peace ; The Entente ask for Italy's Explanation ; Silence in Rome ; Count Czernin's Plans and the Three Anglo-French Notes of Count Armand ; The Last Offer by Austria, and M. Ribot's definite Refusal ; M. Clemenceau's Ignorance of the Situation : Count Czernin's Downfall ; Victory ; Conclusion ; Appendices.

CHRONOLOGY OF THE WAR

Prepared under the auspices of the Ministry of Information by LORD EDWARD GLEICHEN. Crown 8vo.

Vol. I. 1914–15. 5s. net. Vol. II. 1916–17. 7s. 6d. net. Vol. III. 1918. 16s. net. Atlas. 3s. 6d. net.

The complete set of four volumes, 30s. net.

"This valuable handbook is very welcome. . . . Indispensable to any serious students of the world war. . . . In these two volumes we have found or verified in a few moments dates which would otherwise have required many hours of search."—*Spectator.*

"Will especially appeal to those people who wish to have a comprehensive grasp of events during the war and its use will alleviate endless searching. . . . It will form one of the most valuable reference books on the war."—*Field.*

"This invaluable little handbook. . . . The tables are clear and very full."—*Glasgow Herald.*

THE STORY OF THE HOUSEHOLD CAVALRY, 1661–1902

By Captain SIR GEORGE ARTHUR, BART. Six Coloured Plates, Portraits, and other Illustrations, Maps and Plans. 2 vols. Super Royal 8vo. £3 13s. 6d. net.

A HISTORY OF THE VOLUNTEER FORCES. From the Earliest Times to the year 1860.

By CECIL SEBAG MONTEFIORI. Illustrations. Demy 8vo. 15s. net.

THE STORY OF A SOLDIER'S LIFE

By Field-Marshal VISCOUNT WOLSELEY, G.C.M.G. 2 vols. Portraits and Plans. 32s. net.

THE WAYS OF WAR

By Professor T. M. KETTLE. With a Memoir by Mrs. KETTLE, and a Portrait in Photogravure. Demy 8vo. 7s. 6d net.

TOPOGRAPHY AND STRATEGY IN THE WAR

By DOUGLAS W. JOHNSON. Maps and Illustrations. Demy 8vo. 10s. 6d. net.

ISMAIL KEMAL BEY

The Memoirs of "THE WISE OLD MAN OF ALBANIA" revealing half a century of Near Eastern politics and intrigue. 18s. net.

"Of profound interest and revealing some inner secrets of Near Eastern policy."—*Sunday Times.*

"An invaluable source for the historian of the downfall of the Turkish Empire and adds materially to our knowledge of the intrigues of the great continental powers in Egypt and the Near East."—*Manchester Guardian.*

THE RISE OF NATIONALITY IN THE BALKANS.

By R. W. SETON-WATSON. Maps. 10s. 6d. net.

"This book should be read by all who wish to understand the essence of the Balkan problem."—*Spectator.*

ROUMANIA AND THE GREAT WAR

By R. W. SETON-WATSON. 2s. net.

FROM PERSIAN UPLANDS

By F. HALE. A record in letters of persons and politics in Persia from 1913 to 1919 by a resident of many years' standing. 10s. 6d. net.

"As a sidelight on the intrigues of the Germans in Persian affairs during the war, as a comment on the modes of life and the character of the people, Mr Hale's letters are well worth reading. . . . Those who read the first half of these letters from Persia will undoubtedly read to the end."—*Saturday Westminster.*

"Manners and customs, Government and social life, education and the subjects that would naturally attract the attention of the intelligent foreigner are dealt with. . . . The writer is an admirable correspondent . . . these bright, well-informed and most interesting letters."—*Glasgow Herald.*

GOVERNMENT AND THE WAR
By SPENSER WILKINSON. Crown 8vo. 6s net.

THE NATION'S SERVANTS
Essays on the Education of Officers.
By SPENSER WILKINSON. Crown 8vo. 6d. net.

GERMANY *VERSUS* CIVILIZATION
Notes on the Atrocious War.
By WILLIAM ROSCOE THAYER. Crown 8vo. 4s. 6d. net.

BRITISH WAR FINANCE, 1914–15
By W. L. LAWSON. Crown 8vo. 6s. net.

SUVOROF
By W. LYON BLEASE. With a foreword by Major-General Sir C. E. CALLWELL, K.C.B. 25s. net.

" Sir E. Callwell in his preface pronounces Suvorof to have been, next to Frederick the Great, unquestionably the greatest soldier of the last half of the XVIII Century. . . . We hold that Sir E. Callwell is undoubtedly right. . . . Mr. Blease has done his work uncommonly well. The book is well arranged and well written. . . . Suvorof was a great genius, with a touch of insanity, but cultivated, warm-hearted and humane. He was a very great soldier and a great man."—*Times Literary Supplement.*

BISMARCK
By C. GRANT ROBERTSON, C.V.O. 10s. 6d. net.

MOLTKE
By Lieut.-Colonel F. E. WHITTON.

(These two books are volumes in Constable's " Makers of the XIX Century Series.")

Campaigns and Their Lessons

A Series of Monographs edited by Major-General Sir C. E. CALLWELL, K.C.B., and including *The Dardanelles* (by the Editor), and *The Marne Campaign*, by Lieut.-Colonel Whitton. (See pp. 16 and 12.)

LIAO-YANG

By Major H. ROWAN ROBINSON, R.A. 6s. 6d. net.

BOHEMIA 1866

By Major NEIL MALCOLM, D.S.O. 5s. net.

TIRAH 1897

By Major-General Sir C. E. CALLWELL, K.C.B. 5s. net.

DEDUCTIONS FROM THE WORLD WAR

By Lieut.-General BARON VON FREYTAG-LORING-HOVEN. 2s. 6d. net.

"I have read this morning a little book translated from the German and entitled, 'Deductions from the World War,' and I commend it to the attention of every man in the nation."—Speech by Sir EDWARD CARSON."—*Times*.

A NATION TRAINED IN ARMS OR A MILITIA

By Lieut.-General BARON VON FREYTAG-LORING-HOVEN. 4s. net.

GERMAN IMPERIALISM AND THE INTERNATIONAL LAW

Based on German Authorities and the archives of the French Government. By J. DE DAMPIERRE. 10s. 6d. net.

"This work is one of permanent scientific worth and deserves to be carefully studied by every thinking man."
International Law Notes.

THE GREAT MUNITION FEAT

By GEORGE A. B. DEWAR. Demy 8vo.

CONTENTS: The Task of Titan. Getting to Work. Woolwich. The Armament Firms. Guns and Ammunition. In the Steel Shops. The Tanks. The Aeroplanes. Key Munition Industries; and the Work of Science. Richborough; and the Transport of Munitions. Labour. The Ferment in Factories. Welfare. *Index.*

MEMORIES OF TWO WARS: CUBAN AND PHILIPPINE EXPERIENCES

By F. FUNSTON. Illustrated. 12s. 6d. net.

II.—THE WAR IN FRANCE.

1914

By LORD FRENCH of Ypres. 2nd Edition, with a Preface by MARSHAL FOCH. Maps. 21s. net.

THE MARNE CAMPAIGN

By Lieut.-Col. F. E. WHITTON. 8 Maps. 10s. 6d. net. (A volume in " Campaigns and their Lessons Series." See p. 10.)

" As a full and careful study, more especially of the tactics of the phase of the Western campaign, which reached its climax in the battle of the Marne, this book merits a permanent place in military literature. . . . Many matters obscured by misstatements are cleared up."—*Westminster Gazette.*

FORTY DAYS IN 1914

By Major-General Sir FREDERICK MAURICE, K.C.M.G. 2nd Edition greatly enlarged. 21s. net.

" The book has been thoroughly revised in the light of fresh information, notably from the German side, and in great part rewritten, and is one that no military student can neglect, for it is undoubtedly one of the ablest pieces of military writing . . . and bids fair to remain as the best, most lucid and most valuable account of the Marne campaign."—*Glasgow Herald.*

YPRES, 1914

An official account published by order of the German General Staff. Introduction and Notes by the Historical Section (Military Branch) Committee of Imperial Defence. Crown 8vo. 5s. net.

" The translation will be valued by all students of the war as giving the account of one of the momentous operations in the West as the German General Staff desire it to be understood ; and as a signal witness to the fighting qualities of the old British Army under the French."—*Times Literary Supplement.*

WITH THE INDIANS IN FRANCE

By GENERAL SIR JAMES WILLCOCKS, G.C.M.G., etc. Maps. 24s. net. Also 100 copies on large paper with ten portraits in photogravure. 5 guineas net.

"Sir James Willcocks has compiled an exceedingly interesting and detailed record which tells much that is new. . . . An enthusiastic though discriminating eulogy of the fine qualities of the Indian soldiers and of the British officers who led them."

Times Literary Supplement.

"This finely conceived and well-fashioned book. . . . General Willcocks speaks with insight and authority on many aspects of some of the most difficult and important of imperial problems."

Glasgow Herald.

"A detailed account of the work of the Indian troops in France which shows the difficulties with which the Indian soldiers had to contend, and the courage with which they encountered them. It is extremely interesting to read to-day, and will be a valuable document for the future historian of the Great War."—*Spectator.*

THE ROMANCE OF THE BATTLE LINE IN FRANCE

By J. E. C. BODLEY. Map. 7s. 6d. net.

"Mr. Bodley's brilliant book. . . . Vivid and beautifully written pages."—Sir THEODORE COOK in the *Anglo-French Review.*

"One of the finest short volumes produced by the war."—*Field.*

"This illuminating book by our greatest living authority on French history and letters . . . ."—*Morning Post.*

MONS AND THE RETREAT

By G. S. JORDON. With a Preface by LORD FRENCH. Map. Wrappers. 1s. 6d. net.

"No one desirous of a thorough knowledge of this transcendant feat of the British army at Mons should overlook this little book."

Daily Telegraph.

A HILLTOP ON THE MARNE: June 3rd, 1914—September 8th, 1914.

By MILDRED ALDRICH.   Frontispiece and Map. 6th Impression. 5s. net.

"We do not know any work which tells so forcibly, so unaffectedly the story of the German assault on Paris as does 'A Hilltop on the Marne.'"—*Manchester Courier.*

BY THE SAME AUTHOR:

ON THE EDGE OF THE WAR ZONE
5s. net.

THE PEAK OF THE LOAD
Cr. 8vo. 5s. net.

Sequels to "A Hilltop on the Marne."

R.A.M.C. AND THE GREAT WAR

By Lieut.-Colonel F. E. BRERETON, R.A.M.C. Demy 8vo. Maps. 14s. net.

"Of outstanding interest. . . . Vivid and impressive."
Athenæum.
"A most interesting and clear description."
British Medical Journal.
"A piece of first-rate historical writing . . . . A narrative of breathless interest."—*Manchester Guardian.*

NOTES OF A CAMP FOLLOWER ON THE WESTERN FRONT

By E. W. HORNUNG. Cr. 8vo. 6s. net.

"An admirable picture of the fine work that has been done in the Y.M.C.A. huts, and of the men by whom they were so much appreciated."—*Westminster Gazette.*

WITH THE FRENCH FLYING CORPS

By CARROLL DANA WINSLOW. Crown 8vo. Illustrations. 3s. 6d. net.

SIR STANLEY MAUDE

Authorised memorial biography by Major-General SIR C. E. CALLWELL, K.C.B. Illustrated. 21s. net.

"A good book, written by one who has literary as well as military skill, who knows how to handle a great mass of material with just proportion, and can deal with an attractive subject tersely, sympathetically and judicially. . . . This volume should be put into the hands of every newly-joined subaltern in the army, for no nobler picture of a British officer and a British gentleman could be laid before them."—Hon. JOHN FORTESCUE in *The Observer.*

W. T. Massey's Palestine Trilogy

THE DESERT CAMPAIGNS
Illustrated by JAMES McBEY. Crown 8vo. 6s. net.

HOW JERUSALEM WAS WON
Illustrated. Demy 8vo. 21s. net.

ALLENBY'S FINAL TRIUMPH
Illustrated. Demy 8vo. 21s. net.

These three books are by W. T. Massey, official correspondent of the Associated Press with the E.E.F.

"The army authorities knew Mr. Massey, as his fellow war correspondents knew him, as a model of persistence, endurance, good-temper, modesty and careful accuracy."
H. W. NEVINSON, in *The Nation.*

"Well worthy of a place among the best books that have been written of the many campaigns which the British Army undertook during the War of 1914–1919."—*Daily Telegraph.*

"The record of a man who was the official correspondent of the London newspapers with the Army, a record told so clearly and so effectively that it can be read with equal advantage by the less-informed student of the war, and by the man who desires to understand the more serious side of the events which prepared the way for the final British advance."—*Observer.*

THE DARDANELLES

By Major-General Sir C. E. CALLWELL, K.C.B. Maps. 18s. net. (A volume in "Campaigns and their Lessons Series." See p. 10).

" In this book we really do get at the why, and even more the why not, of this magnificent failure."—*Punch*.

" Sir Charles Callwell's narrative is the most complete and illuminating yet published. From the first page to the last, this book is worthy of its author—that is to say, it is military history of the highest, and therefore of the most instructive class."—*United Service Magazine*.

INNER HISTORY OF THE BALKAN WAR

By Lieut.-Col. REGINALD RANKIN, F.R.G.S. Portrait and Maps. Demy 8vo. 15s. net.

ENGLAND AND PALESTINE

Essays toward the Restoration of the Jewish State.

By HERBERT SIDEBOTHAM. 2 maps. 6s. net.

" Certainly one of the very few pieces of political writing evolved during the war which is likely to have a permanent interest."
Manchester Guardian.

SUVLA BAY

Being the Notes and Sketches of Scenes, Characters and Adventures of the Dardanelles Campaign. By JOHN HARGRAVE. Illustrated by the Author. 5s. net.

" Crisp, graphic and dramatic all through and giving a picture which really grips the attention of trying and hazardous adventure helped by a great number of clever drawings by the author himself."—*Times Literary Supplement*.

THE DESERT MOUNTED CORPS

An account of the Cavalry Operations in Palestine and Syria in 1917–1918. By Lt.-Col. the Hon. R. M. PRESTON, D.S.O. With an Introduction by Lt.-Gen. A. G. CHAUVEL, K.C.B., K.C.M.G. 32 Half-tone Illustrations and various Maps.

SEA POWER IN THE PACIFIC

By HECTOR C. BYWATER. Demy 8vo. Maps and Charts.

Mr. Bywater analyses the comparative sea-power, actual and potential, of Japan and the United States, and studies the future position of Australia as possible participant in a drama of Pacific warfare. This book is a scientific and historical contribution to a vital problem—the new race for naval supremacy between Great Britain, America and Japan.

SEA POWER AND THE HISTORY OF THE BRITISH NAVY

By ARCHIBALD HURD. Crown 8vo. 1s. net.

THE BRITISH FLEET IN THE GREAT WAR

By ARCHIBALD HURD. Demy 8vo. 7s. 6d. net.

" A survey of the policy, service and operations of the Fleet, by one of the most able of the naval writers of the day."
Times Literary Supplement.

SONS OF ADMIRALTY. A short history of the Naval War, 1914–1918.

By ARCHIBALD HURD and H. H. BASHFORD. Crown 8vo. 7s. 6d. net.

"A history by two well-equipped writers admirably suited for popular reading. Mr. Hurd, the well-known naval critic has already written ' The British Fleet in the War.'"
Times Literary Supplement.

THE NAVY EVERYWHERE

By CONRAD CATO. Illustrated. 10s. 6d. net.

" A quite excellent tale . . . told simply and to the point."
Times Literary Supplement.

" This is the book we wanted. . . . Has the true atmosphere of the wardroom."—*Observer.*

THE NAVY IN MESOPOTAMIA, 1914–17.

By CONRAD CATO. 3s. 6d. net.

AIRCRAFT IN WARFARE: The Dawn of the Fourth Arm.

By F. W. LANCHESTER. With an Introduction by Major-General SIR DAVID HENDERSON. Illustrated. 12s. 6d. net.

UNIFORM WITH THIS
LIST MESSRS. CONSTABLE
HAVE CLASSIFIED CATALOGUES OF THEIR PUBLICATIONS UNDER SUCH HEADINGS AS

BIOGRAPHY AND REMINISCENCE.

WAR AND MILITARY HISTORY.

POLITICS, POLITICAL SCIENCE AND SOCIOLOGY.

RELIGION, PHILOSOPHY AND ÆSTHETICS.

LEGAL BOOKS.

ECONOMICS AND COMMERCE.

EDUCATION AND PSYCHOLOGY.

ART AND ILLUSTRATED BOOKS.

HISTORY.

POETRY AND DRAMA.

FICTION.

TRAVEL AND ADVENTURE.

LITERATURE, ESSAYS AND CRITICISM.

THESE LISTS
FREE ON APPLICATION
TO CONSTABLE & COMPANY LTD.
10 & 12 ORANGE STREET LONDON W.C. 2.

The Mayflower Press, Plymouth, England. Wm. Brendon & Son, Ltd.　(Spring 1921